The
Reference Shelf®

Representative American Speeches
2019-2020

The Reference Shelf
Volume 92 • Number 6
H.W. Wilson
A Division of EBSCO Information Services, Inc.

Published by
GREY HOUSE PUBLISHING
Amenia, New York
2020

The Reference Shelf

Cover image: Photo by White House, via Wikimedia.

The books in this series contain reprints of articles, excerpts from books, addresses on current issues, and studies of social trends in the United States and other countries. There are six separately bound numbers in each volume, all of which are usually published in the same calendar year. Numbers one through five are each devoted to a single subject, providing background information and discussion from various points of view and concluding with an index and comprehensive bibliography that lists books, pamphlets, and articles on the subject. The final number of each volume is a collection of recent speeches. Books in the series may be purchased individually or on subscription.

Publisher's Cataloging-In-Publication Data
(Prepared by The Donohue Group, Inc.)

Names: Grey House Publishing, Inc., publisher.
Title: Representative American speeches.
Other Titles: Representative American speeches (2015)
Description: Amenia, N.Y. : Grey House Publishing, 2015- | Series: The reference shelf / H.W. Wilson
Identifiers: ISSN 2639-9016
Subjects: LCSH: Speeches, addresses, etc., American--21st century--Periodicals. | LCGFT: Speeches. | Serial publications.
Classification: LCC PS668 .B3 | DDC 815--dc23

Contents

3

A Year of Social Unrest

4

The Great Divide—The 2020 Election

5

Other Significant Events In 2020

Preface

In a year dominated by the COVID-19 pandemic, Americans also faced protesting in the streets and a bitterly partisan presidential election. A clear picture of a nation divided emerged from the reaction of leaders to the coronavirus crisis, civil unrest over the death of George Floyd and the Black Lives Matter movement, and the political direction of the United States. The high death toll from COVID-19 in the United States drew sharp criticism of President Donald Trump and his lack of leadership. Protests and riots similar to those of the 1960s Civil Rights movement called for systemic change in policing, drawing praise from those frustrated by continuing racial inequities and censure from those who viewed the riots as lawless. The 2020 presidential election was seen as a battle for the essence of America. Republicans talked of personal liberty and the virtues of capitalism over socialism, and Democrats stressed defending the country's democratic institutions from authoritarian encroachment. Although it was easy to lose track of the year's other significant events, this volume covers many of the year's historical moments, including the deaths of Representative John Lewis and Supreme Court Justice Ruth Bader Ginsburg, the first American human space flight launched from the Kennedy Space Center in nine years, the final days of the Trump impeachment trial, the Harvey Weinstein verdict, the signing of the Abraham Accords, and the confirmation of Amy Coney Barrett as a Supreme Court Justice.

Graduating Remotely

This year's commencement speakers acknowledged the unique challenges confronting the class of 2020. The pandemic had a huge impact on the higher education system. School shutdowns, remote learning, and online graduation ceremonies marked students' last year of school, and many had to contend with the loss of campus housing. A precarious economy added to the difficulty of finding employment. While recognizing these added stresses, speakers still focused on the ability of this year's class to change the world into a better place. Entrepreneur Oprah Winfrey and former president Barack Obama encouraged graduates to redefine what's important in life and work toward addressing inequities exposed by the pandemic. Microsoft's Bill and Melinda Gates stressed the importance of creating global ties and uniting with the world to face the suffering and economic destruction created by COVID-19. National Institute of Allergy and Infectious Diseases Director Anthony Fauci welcomed the graduating class of Johns Hopkins University, asking them to use their training to become global leaders in public health and other important areas. Some speakers, like actor and former California governor Arnold Schwarzenegger, concentrated on graduates' strength of character, focusing on the life skills developed by graduating under such extraordinary circumstances, and stressed the importance of having a clear vision. Pakistani activist Malala Yousafzai, herself a member of the 2020 graduating class, urged her fellow students not to be defined by what they lost in this crisis but rather by how they responded to it.

The Story of the Year

From the beginning stages of the COVID-19 pandemic in January to the announcement of a potential vaccine in November, the coronavirus has dominated America's social and political landscape in 2020. Confusion about the virus's impact during its early spread, efforts to prevent public panic, numerous misstatements by President Trump, and outright misinformation all contributed to the United States having the highest fatality rate in the developed world. Americans' characteristic reverence for personal liberty did not improve matters, as some refused to comply with preventative measures like wearing a mask or social distancing. A National Emergency was declared by the Trump administration in March, allowing for increased funding and flexibility in pushing through policy decisions. However, no unified national response strategy was put forward, and differing state policies on interstate travel contributed to the virus's spread. A severe shortage of medical equipment and personal protective equipment (PPE) during the early months of COVID-19 uncovered systemic problems at both the state and federal levels and exposed the nation's medical community and first responders to unnecessary risk. Citizens joined in the effort to make masks, while large corporations reconfigured their manufacturing operations to produce masks and ventilators. Public leaders like Governor Andrew Cuomo of New York—one of the hardest-hit states during the early months of the pandemic—addressed the public to inform and unify people and to praise the efforts of first responders. Cuomo credited government transparency, a reliance on the scientific community, and continuous data updates with turning around the spike in New York's cases. While the Trump administration prioritized mitigating economic fallout, then presidential candidate Joe Biden stressed safely reopening the economy and schools. Biden sharply criticized what he saw as Trump's lack of leadership during the crisis while Trump accused the media of exaggerating the death toll. The devastating effect of the pandemic on the education system brought educational leaders to a hearing at the House of Representatives, where they discussed the future of higher education in the new normal. Campus housing, student food insecurity, systemic inequities, remote learning, the CARES Act, and what educational institutions will need going forward were all topics of discussion. A bright spot was the announcement in November of a possible vaccine for COVID-19, but NIAID director Fauci cautioned the public to remain vigilant in wearing masks and social distancing to continue slowing the spread of the virus.

Civil Unrest and Autonomous Zones

The death of George Floyd at the hands of Minneapolis police in May sparked an ongoing series of police brutality protests and an international response. It's estimated that between 15 million and 26 million Americans have participated in the protests in support of the Black Lives Matter movement, making the protests the largest in U.S. history. At times the protests escalated into riots and looting, and autonomous zones in Capitol Hill and Seattle were created by protestors to mark off police-free areas. There were calls to defund the police, and the Justice in Policing Act was passed by the House of Representatives in June to combat racial bias and excessive force and to increase police accountability. Although there is general agreement that police reform is needed, there is debate on how it should be accomplished. San Francisco Mayor London Breed and Seattle Mayor Jenny Durkan came out in support of the protestors, and Vice President-elect Kamala Harris delivered a scathing rejection of the Senate police reform bill. Portland Police Chief Chuck Lovell emphasized de-escalation as a police response to the Portland riots, but argued that the best way to achieve police reform involved more funding for police departments, not less. President-elect Joe Biden met with the family of Jacob Blake, another victim of racialized police brutality, in Kenosha, Wisconsin, and pledged to make police reform and racial equality priorities. On the other side of the debate, Donald Trump criticized the Democratic Party for supporting violence and came out in support of law enforcement.

The 2020 Election

This year's election has been one of the most divisive in recent history. Both major parties framed the election as a battleground for America and everything it stands for. While Donald Trump ran on a platform of "America First" and denounced Democrats for constantly "blaming" America, Joe Biden described his campaign as a return to normalcy and morality, rejecting the authoritarian tendencies of the Trump administration. Biden stressed international cooperation and science as the best hope for defeating the COVID-19 pandemic, and supported sweeping changes to address racial inequities and police reform as well as economic inequality, immigration, and health insurance for all. Trump questioned the workability of Biden's proposals and claimed that these radical changes would change the very nature of America's free enterprise system, turning America into a socialist nation. Biden sharply criticized Trump's response to the pandemic, while Trump focused on the economic repercussions of extended shutdowns. The stark contrast and hostility between both candidates was obvious during their final debate. At the Democratic National Convention, Biden supporters Barack Obama and Michigan Governor Gretchen Whitmer stressed the importance of a Biden win to protect America's democratic institutions and to defeat the pandemic by relying on science. Vice President Mike Pence and former United Nations ambassador Nikki Haley, at the Republican National Convention, came out in support of Donald Trump and of preserving the character of America by refusing the radical agenda of the Democratic Party.

The nomination of Kamala Harris for vice president was indeed a significant event in 2020. Harris is the first woman, the first Black person, and the first Asian American to hold this position in the United States, and she credited the sacrifices of many who came before her in her nomination acceptance speech. Shortly after the polls closed, Senate Majority Leader Mitch McConnell posited that Trump was well within his rights to contest the election, while Biden and Harris promised a healing period for America in their joint acceptance speech. Although the election was closer than many expected in its early stages, Biden was the clear victor, winning 306 electoral votes and 51.1 percent of the vote, versus Trump's 232 electoral votes and 47.1 percent of the vote. Trump took legal action and demanded recounts in several states, and as of December 2020 had still not conceded the election. In late November, however, he did agree to begin the transition to a Biden administration and Biden/Harris announced several key picks for their cabinet.

The Rest of the Year

Although the pandemic, the riots, and the election riveted the attention of Americans in 2020, many other significant events occurred during 2020. The beginning of the year saw the final days of the impeachment trial of Donald Trump, in which Kamala Harris lambasted the Senate trial as a miscarriage of justice while Senator Lamar Alexander insisted that the evidence did not warrant impeachment. Manhattan District Attorney Cyrus Vance discussed Harvey Weinstein's guilty verdict and how it would forever change the discussion of sexual assault in the United States. In February, Justice Ruth Bader Ginsburg spoke on the centennial anniversary of the Nineteenth Amendment and of her personal engagement with it and in September, Chief Justice John Roberts delivered her eulogy, extolling her extraordinary career and personality. Later in the year, Amy Coney Barrett honored Justice Ginsberg in her acceptance speech as a Supreme Court Justice nominee. In May, members of the SpaceX crew reflected on the first American human space flight in almost a decade, noting space travel's ability to unite people around the world. In July, Civil Rights giant and U.S. Representative John Lewis passed away, and was honored by all members of Congress at a moving service at the Capitol. And in September, Middle Eastern leaders spoke at the signing ceremony for the Abraham Accords, which normalized foreign relations between Israel and the United Arab Emirates.

1
Virtual Commencement Inspiration

As part of the "Dear Class of 2020" virtual commencement event, Barack Obama urged graduates to create a more fair world, one with opportunity for everyone.

Remarks to the Graduating Class of 2020

By Oprah Winfrey

Actor and entrepreneur Oprah Winfrey urged graduates to redefine success and evalu-ate what is genuinely meaningful, and to work toward addressing the inequities exposed by the pandemic. She encouraged graduates to take all that they know to be true, and use it to create more equity, more justice, and more joy in the world—to be the class that commenced a new way forward.

Thank you, Cheryl. Hello everyone. I know you may not feel like it but you are in-deed the chosen class for such a time as this—the class of 2020. You're also a united class, the pandemic class, that has the entire world striving to graduate with you. Of course, this is not the graduation ceremony you envisioned. You've been dreaming about that walk across the stage, of family and friends cheering you on, the caps flung joyously in the air. But even though there may not be pomp because of our circumstances, never has a graduating class been called to step into the future with more purpose, vision, passion, and energy and hope.

Your graduation ceremony is taking place with so many luminaries celebrating you on the world's Facebook stage, and I'm just honored to join them and salute you. You know the word graduate comes from the Latin *graduātus*, meaning a step toward something. And in the early 15th century, graduation was a term used in alchemy to mean a tempering or refining. Every one of us is now being called to graduate, to step toward something even though we don't know what. Every one of us is likewise now being called to temper the parts of ourselves that must fall away, to refine who we are, how we define success, and what is genuinely meaningful.

And you, the real graduates on this day, you will lead us. I wish I could tell you I know the path forward: I don't. There is so much uncertainty. In truth there always has been. What I do know is that the same guts and imagination that got you to this moment, all those things are the very things that are going to sustain you through whatever is coming.

It's vital that you learn, and we all learn, to be at peace with the discomfort of stepping into the unknown. It's really okay to not have all the answers. The answers will come for sure if you can accept not knowing long enough to get still and stay still long enough for new thoughts to take root in your more quiet, deeper, truer self. The noise of the world drowns out the sound of you. You have to get still to listen so you can use this disorder that COVID-19 has wrought. Can you treat it as an uninvited guest that's come into our myths to reorder our way of being? Can you,

Delivered on May 15, 2020, for Facebook's #Graduation2020 Event.

the class of 2020, show us not how to put the pieces back together again but how to create a new and more evolved normal? A world more just, kind, tender, luminous, creative, whole.

We need you to do this, because the pandemic has illuminated the vast systemic inequities that have defined life for too many for too long. For poor communities without adequate access to health care, inequality is a pre-existing condition. For immigrant communities forced to hide in the shadows, inequality is a pre-existing condition. For incarcerated people with no ability to social distance, inequality is a pre-existing condition. For every person burdened by bias and bigotry, for every black man and woman living in their American skin fearful to even go for a jog, inequality is a pre-existing condition.

You have the power to stand for, to fight for, and vote for healthier conditions that will create a healthier society. This moment is your invitation to use your education to begin to heal our afflictions by applying the best of what you've learned in your head and felt in your heart. This moment has shown us what Dr. King tried to tell us decades ago. He understood that we are caught in an inescapable network, . . . mutuality tied into a single garment of destiny. That's what he said. Whatever affects one directly affects all indirectly. If humanity is a global body, every soul is a cell in that body, and we are being challenged as never before to keep the global body healthy by keeping ourselves healthy in mind and body and spirit. As all the traditions affirm, the deepest . . . care is at once caring for the human family, and we see this so clearly with essential workers.

Look who turns out to be essential. Teachers, health care workers, of course, the people stocking grocery shelves, the cashiers, the truck drivers, food providers, those who are caring for your grandparents, those who clean the places where we work and shop and carry out our daily lives. We are all here because they—at great and profound risk—are still providing their essential service.

What will your essential service be? What really matters to you? The fact that you're alive means you've been given a reprieve to think deeply about that question. How will you use what matters in service to yourself, your community, and the world? For me it's always been talking and sharing stories. For you, well, that's for you to discover, and my hope is that you will harness your education, your creativity, and your valor, your voice, your vote, reflecting on all that you've witnessed and hungered for, all that you know to be true, and use it to create more equity, more justice, and more joy in the world—to be the class that commenced a new way forward, the class of 2020. Bravo. Bravo. Bravo.

Print Citations

CMS: Winfrey, Oprah. "Remarks to the Graduating Class of 2020." Commencement address for Facebook's #Graduation 2020 Event, May 15, 2020. In *The Reference Shelf: Representative American Speeches, 2019-2020,* edited by Annette Calzone, 3-5. Amenia, NY: Grey House Publishing, 2020.

MLA: Winfrey, Oprah. "Remarks to the Graduating Class of 2020." Facebook's #Graduation 2020 Event, 15 May 2020. Commencement address. *The Reference Shelf: Representative American Speeches, 2019-2020,* edited by Annette Calzone, Grey House Publishing, 2020, pp. 3-5.

APA: Winfrey, O. (2020, May 15). Remarks to the graduating class of 2020. Facebook's #Graduation 2020 event. In Annette Calzone (Ed.), *The reference shelf: Representative American speeches, 2019-2020* (pp. 3-5). Amenia, NY: Grey House Publishing.

This Year's Graduates Can Help Build a Healthier, More Equal World

By Bill and Melinda Gates

Referencing the chaos after World War II, Microsoft's Bill and Melinda Gates stressed to the graduating class of 2020 the ties of the global community, and how the world must pull together to rebuild after the devastating suffering and economic destruction brought about by COVID-19. Regardless of the career path chosen, the Gates' encouraged graduates to contribute in ways big and small, wherever they live and whoever they are, in making the world better for everyone.

Most commencement addresses do not change the course of history. On a sunny afternoon in 1947, then-Secretary of State George C. Marshall gave one that did. Speaking at Harvard University, the former general reminded his audience that a few thousand miles away from where they gathered that day, the aftermath of World War II had plunged Europe into poverty, hunger and despair. The American people, he explained, had a responsibility to come to Europe's aid despite being themselves so "distant from the troubled areas of the earth." Even if you've never heard that speech, you are probably familiar with the policy agenda it proposed: the Marshall Plan, which helped speed Western Europe's recovery and usher in a new era of peace and prosperity.

Today, as then, the world faces mass suffering and economic devastation. Again, nations will need to pull together to rebuild. But this time, you, the graduating class of 2020, don't need a commencement speaker to paint a picture of the "troubled areas of the earth." The Covid-19 crisis we confront today is not a localized experience but a truly global one.

The inextricable ties between the people of the world are something that your generation understands better than perhaps any that has come before it. Many of you have been logging onto the Internet since you could read. You've grown up with access to pop culture, news and perspectives from societies thousands of miles from your home. And the major challenges looming over your future—disease outbreaks, climate change, gender inequality, poverty—are also being confronted by your peers in every part of the globe.

So, what does all of this mean for the next chapter of your lives? As a member of our global community, your actions can have a global impact. Whatever your

Delivered on May 5, 2020, to *The Wall Street Journal*.

professional goals, wherever you live, whoever you are, there are ways, big and small, that you can participate in making the world better for everyone

If this crisis has inspired you to pursue a career in public service, that's fantastic   but it's not the only way to contribute. You can always use your voice and your vote to advance change. You can insist on policies that create a healthier, better future for everyone, everywhere—whether they live down the street or on the other side of the planet.

It's true that you are entering this new phase of your life at a daunting time. For many of you, the path you'd envisioned after graduation may suddenly be much steeper. With so many things to worry about—from your health to your family to what the job market means for your ability to pay off your loans—it is understandable that you may need to put on hold the bigger questions about your role in improving the world.

But there is no question that you have a role to play, whether that's now or in the future. You inherit a world that has already proven that progress is possible—a world that has rebuilt after war, vanquished smallpox, fed a growing population, and enabled more than a billion people to climb out of extreme poverty.

That progress didn't happen by accident or fate. It was the result of people just like you who made a commitment that whatever else they did with their lives and careers, they would contribute to this shared mission of propelling us all forward. Class of 2020, these are not easy times. But we will get through them. And with your leadership, the world will be stronger than before.

Print Citations

CMS: Gates, Bill, and Melinda Gates. "This Year's Graduates Can Help Build a Healthier, More Equal World." Commencement address in *The Wall Street Journal*, May 5, 2020. In *The Reference Shelf: Representative American Speeches, 2019-2020,* edited by Annette Calzone, 6-7. Amenia, NY: Grey House Publishing, 2020.

MLA: Gates, Bill, and Melinda Gates. "This Year's Graduates Can Help Build a Healthier, More Equal World." *The Wall Street Journal*, 5 May 2020. Commencement address. *The Reference Shelf: Representative American Speeches, 2019-2020,* edited by Annette Calzone, Grey House Publishing, 2020, pp. 6-7.

APA: Gates, B., & Gates, M. (2020, May 5). Commencement address on this year's graduates can help build a healthier, more equal world. *The Wall Street Journal*. In Annette Calzone (Ed.), *The reference shelf: Representative American speeches, 2019-2020* (pp. 6-7). Amenia, NY: Grey House Publishing.

Build Bridges between People Instead of Dividing Them

By Barack Obama

Former president Barack Obama acknowledged the unique uncertainty faced by the graduating class of 2020 while encouraging members to be proud of their achievements and use their talents to create online cultures and communities that respect differences of opinion and freedom of speech and that foster debate based in fact. He also urged graduates to have faith in our democracy and not to fall for easy cynicism.

Congratulations to the Class of 2020. Some of you have graduated already. Some of you still have finals. All of you should be very proud. Graduation is a big achievement under any circumstances. Yours comes as the world is turned upside down. By a pandemic, and by a country that's been swept up by protest. I can barely imagine how head-spinning these last few months have been for you. Just as winter was thawing and you were thinking about spring break, those of you who are away at college were either whisked home or stayed behind on a shuttered campus. Most of you had to finish semesters online, which had its ups and downs. You didn't have to worry about what you wore to class, but watching your teachers and professors try to work Zoom wasn't always pretty either. Either way, none of this is how any of you imagined finishing your final spring at school.

Even if we can't all gather in person, I want you to remember that a graduation ceremony doesn't celebrate just a moment in time. It's the culmination of all your years of learning about the world and about yourself. The friends and family who supported you every step of the way, they aren't celebrating a piece of paper, they're celebrating you. How you've grown, the challenges you've overcome, and the experiences you've shared. You can see that love in all the amazing ways that families have come up with their own at-home graduations, from drive-by parades to hand-made yard signs. The point is, don't let the lack of a big crowded ceremony take anything away from what your graduation signifies. Go ahead and bask in the glory of your achievement. And wherever you are, take lots of photos. Although, when I look at my graduation pictures, the main thing I realize is that I should have gotten a haircut more often.

Now, as was true for generations before you, graduation marks your final passage into adulthood. The time when you're expected to fully take charge of your life's direction. It's when you get to decide what's important to you. The career you want

---

Delivered on June 7, 2020, on YouTube.

to pursue, the values you want to live by, who you want to build a family with. That can be intimidating even under normal circumstances. And given the current state of things, let's face it, it can be downright scary. It's fair to say that your generation is graduating into a world that faces more profound challenges than any generation in decades. It can feel like everything's up for grabs right now. A lot of this uncertainty is the direct result of COVID-19. The 100,000 lives it's taken from us. The economic disruption it's caused. No one can say for sure how much longer the crisis will last. A lot of that will depend on the choices we make as a country. But, you know, it will eventually end. Vaccines and treatments will emerge, the economy will begin to heal, and life will start returning to normal, and you'll still have your whole life ahead of you. The thing is, Class of 2020, what these past few weeks have also shown us is that, the challenges we face go well beyond a virus, and that the old normal wasn't good enough. It wasn't working that well. In a lot of ways, the pandemic just brought into focus problems that have been growing for a very long time, whether it's widening economic inequality, the lack of basic healthcare for millions of people, the continuing scourge of bigotry and sexism. Or the divisions and dysfunction that plague our political system.

Similarly, the protests in response to the killing of George Floyd and Breonna Taylor, and Ahmaud Arbery, and Nina Pop, aren't simply a reaction to those particular tragedies, as heartbreaking as they are. They speak to decades worth of anguish and frustration over unequal treatment and a failure to reform police practices and the broader criminal justice system. These shocks to the system that we are seeing right now, just as you prepare to go out into the world, they remind us that we can't take things for granted. We have to work to make things better. They remind us that our individual well-being depend on the well-being of the community that we live in.

That it doesn't matter how much money you make, if everyone around you is hungry and sick. It reminds you that our country and our democracy only function when we think not just about ourselves, but also about each other. So, as scary and uncertain as these times may be, they are also a wake-up call, and they're an incredible opportunity for your generation. Because you don't have to accept what was considered normal before. You don't have to accept the world as it is. You can make it into the world as it should be and could be. You can create a new normal. One that is fairer, and gives everybody opportunity, and treats everyone equally, and builds bridges between people instead of dividing them. Just as America overcame slavery and Civil War, recessions and Depression, Pearl Harbor and 9/11, and all kinds of social upheaval, we can emerge from our current circumstances stronger than before, better than before. But, as has always been true at key moments in history, it's gonna depend on young people like you to go out there and rewrite what is possible.

I'll admit that it's a little unfair to lay such a heavy burden on you, I wish that my generation had done more to solve some of our country's big problems, so you didn't have to. But the good news is that I know you're up to the challenge. You are the best educated generation in history, and a whole lot more technologically-savvy. You've been exposed to more knowledge and perspectives than my generation ever was.

You're more tolerant and empathetic, entrepreneurial, environmentally conscious. Even before graduation, many of you have already started to make your mark, feeding the hungry, mentoring kids, fighting racial injustice, helping veterans, battling climate change. And now, to see so many of you participating in peaceful protests, to see so many of you of every race and background raise up your voices on behalf of justice for all... Well, it's been unbelievably inspiring. You make me optimistic about our future. So, as you prepare for the next stage of what I know will be a remarkable journey, I'll leave you with a few quick pieces of advice, for what they're worth. First. Do what you think is right, not just what' convenient or what' expected or what's easy. While you have this time, think about the values that matter to you the most.

Too many graduates who feel the pressure to immediately start running that race for success, skip the step of asking themselves, "What's really important?" And too often they end up as adults who... only do what's good for them and say, "To heck with everybody else," and they end up not having a lot of meaningful relationships or not really feeling as if they made a serious contribution to the world. I hope that, instead, you decide to moor yourself in values that last, like responsibility, fairness, generosity, and respect for others. That will make you part of the solution, instead of part of the problem.

And if experience is any guide, it actually makes for a happier life. Second, listen to each other. Respect each other. And use all that critical thinking you've developed from your education to help promote the truth. You are the Internet generation and the social media generation. It's not just how you shop or listen to music or watch videos. It's part of your social lives. It's the new town square, where you all come together and meet. In many ways, it's been an amazing tool. In your pockets, you have access to more information than any group of people in history. It's allowed movements of like-minded people to mobilize on behalf of worthy causes. But what's become clear is that social media can also be a tool to spread conflict, division and falsehoods. To bully people and promote hate. Too often, it shuts us off from each other instead of bringing us together, partly because it gives us the ability to select our own realities, independent of facts or science or logic or common sense. We start reading only news and opinions that reinforce our own biases. We start cancelling everything else out. We let opinion masquerade as fact, and we treat even the wildest conspiracy theories as worthy of consideration. And the irony is that, usually the people who are peddling falsehoods on the Internet or social media, are doing so for their own purposes. Either to sell you something, or distract you from the real issues that matter.

You can change that. If a friend tells you COVID-19 is a hoax, politely correct them. If an older relative sights some video to promote a racist stereotype, show him or her why that video is a sham. As a generation that understands social media and technology a lot better than anyone, it's gonna be up to you to create online cultures and communities that respect differences of opinion and freedom of speech. And also, restore the kind of honest, informed, fact-based debate that is the starting point for tackling the challenges we face. Finally, even if it all seems broken...

Have faith in our democracy. Participate and vote. Don't fall for the easy cynicism that says, "Nothing can change." Or that there's only one way to bring about change. In the midst of recent protests, I've noticed that there've been some debates among young people about how useful voting is compared to direct action and civil disobedience, in ending discrimination in our society. The fact is, we don't have to choose. We need both.

Peaceful protests and demonstrations are patriotic. They shine a light on injustice. They raise public awareness. They make the folks in-charge uncomfortable, in a way that's healthy. After all, we're a nation that was founded on protest.

Eventually though, your aspirations have to be translated in to specific laws and institutional practices. And that only happens when we elect good people at every level, who are responsive to our demands. And that includes local offices like the office of mayor or the office of district attorney. They don't get as much attention as a presidential race, but have the most direct impact on issues, like how communities are policed. In fact, you don't even have to be an activist to make a contribution to our democracy. If you've always dreamed of starting your own business, go build a company that is a model for paying its workers a fair wage.

If you've dreamed always of being a doctor, think about working in a community that's short on doctors. There are so many ways to serve. The important thing is to recognize that this nation needs your talents, your passions, your voice to make it better. You know, it's not always pretty, this democracy of ours. Trust me, I know. It can be loud and messy and sometimes depressing. But because citizens took seriously the mandate that this is a government of and by and for the people, well, bit by bit, generation by generation, we've made progress, from cleaning up our air and water to creating programs that lifted millions of seniors out of poverty, to winning the right to vote, and to marry who you love. None of these changes happened overnight. Or without sustained effort. But they did happen. Usually because young people marched and organized and voted and formed alliances and just led good lives and looked after their community, their families, their neighborhoods, and slowly changed hearts and minds. America changed, has always changed because young people dared to hope. Democracy isn't about relying on some charismatic leader to make changes from on high. It's about finding hope in ourselves and creating it in others, especially in a time like this.

You don't always need hope when everything's going fine. It's when things seem darkest. That's when you need it the most. Now, someone once said, "Hope is not a lottery ticket, it's a hammer for us to use in a national emergency, to break the glass, sound the alarm, and sprint into action." That's what hope is. It's not the blind faith that things will get better, it's the conviction that with effort and perseverance and courage and a concern for others, things can get better. That remains the truest part of our American story. And if your generation sprints into action, it will still be true of America's future. Congratulations, Class of 2020. Make it mean something. And keep making us proud.

Print Citations

CMS: Obama, Barack. "Build Bridges between People Instead of Dividing Them." Commencement address on YouTube, June 7, 2020. In *The Reference Shelf: Representative American Speeches, 2019-2020,* edited by Annette Calzone, 8-12. Amenia, NY: Grey House Publishing, 2020.

MLA: Obama, Barack. "Build Bridges between People Instead of Dividing Them." YouTube, 7 June 2020. Commencement address. *The Reference Shelf: Representative American Speeches, 2019-2020,* edited by Annette Calzone, Grey House Publishing, 2020, pp. 8-12.

APA: Obama, B. (7 June 2020). Commencement address on build bridges between people instead of dividing them. YouTube. In Annette Calzone (Ed.), *The reference shelf: Representative American speeches, 2019-2020* (pp. 8-12). Amenia, NY: Grey House Publishing.

Dear Class of 2020

By Malala Yousafzai

<hr>

In this brief but engaging talk to the graduating class of 2020, Pakistani activist Malala Yousafzai shared her fears and hopes as a fellow graduate and urged members of the class not to be defined by what they lose during this crisis but rather by how they respond to it. Malala's congratulations and best wishes were delivered via "Dear Class of 2020," a virtual commencement celebration bringing together inspirational leaders and artists to celebrate graduates, their families, and their communities.

Dear Class of 2020, like all of you, I'm also missing my graduation ceremony this year. When I pictured my last few months at Oxford, I saw myself studying in the library, working day and night, revising, and then in the end, celebrating our achievements with my friends. But right now, I'm stuck in the house, in my room, trying to study while my brothers interrupt me and annoy me. To the extent that I have put a sign outside my door that says, "Studying, do not enter." While this is not the ending that we imagined, our education will outlast any party or any ceremony. Don't be defined by what you lose in this crisis, but by how you respond to it. You have gained your education, now it's time that you go out and use it for the betterment of the world. Congratulations to the Class of 2020. I wish you all the best.

Print Citations

CMS: Yousafzai, Malala. "Dear Class of 2020." Commencement address at Oxford University Oxford, UK, June 10, 2020. In *The Reference Shelf: Representative American Speeches, 2019-2020,* edited by Annette Calzone, 13. Amenia, NY: Grey House Publishing, 2020.

MLA: Yousafzai, Malala. "Dear Class of 2020." Oxford University, 10 June 2020. Commencement address. *The Reference Shelf: Representative American Speeches, 2019-2020,* edited by Annette Calzone, Grey House Publishing, 2020, pp. 13.

APA: Yousafzai, M. (2020, June 10). Commencement address to dear class of 2020. Oxford University, Oxford, UK. In Annette Calzone (Ed.), *The reference shelf: Representative American speeches, 2019-2020* (pp. 13). Amenia, NY: Grey House Publishing.

Delivered on June 10, 2020 at Oxford University, Oxford, UK.

Remarks to the Johns Hopkins University Class of 2020

By Anthony Fauci

NIAID director Dr. Anthony Fauci welcomed the graduating class of Johns Hopkins University to use their talents to help solve the challenges of the global pandemic, noting the university's reputation for fostering global leaders in public health and other important areas. Fauci acknowledged the disappointments faced by this year's graduates but focused on their talents, resolve, and character in adapting to this extraordinary situation.

Warm greetings to you all. My name is Tony Fauci, director of the National Institute of Allergy and Infectious Diseases at the National Institutes of Health and a member of the White House Coronavirus Task Force. I'm really delighted to address the outstanding graduates in the Johns Hopkins University Class of 2020.

We are currently confronting an unprecedented global pandemic, and I am profoundly aware that celebrating your graduation virtually is extremely disappointing at best. However, we must adapt to this extraordinary situation, as you have done so well, and unite in overcoming the challenges we face because of COVID-19. We need your talent, your energy, your resolve, and your character to get through this difficult time. In the next phase of your lives, whatever professional path you choose, all of you directly or indirectly will be doing your part, together with the rest of us, to come out from under the shadow of this pandemic.

Hopkins has a rich tradition of nurturing scholars who excel in their fields of study, and, by extension, enhance the global society in which we live. I have no doubt you will become leaders in your respective fields and help respond to the many public health and other challenges to come. So congratulations on your graduation, keep well, and I wish you all the best in your future endeavors.

Print Citations

CMS: Fauci, Anthony. "Remarks to the Johns Hopkins University Class of 2020." Commencement address at Johns Hopkins University, Baltimore, MD, May 21, 2020. In *The Reference Shelf: Representative American Speeches, 2019-2020*, edited by Annette Calzone, 14-15. Amenia, NY: Grey House Publishing, 2020.

Delivered on May 21, 2020, at Johns Hopkins University, Baltimore, MD.

MLA: Fauci, Anthony. "Remarks to the Johns Hopkins University Class of 2020." Johns Hopkins University, 21 May 2020, Baltimore, MD. Commencement address. *The Reference Shelf: Representative American Speeches, 2019-2020,* edited by Annette Calzone, Grey House Publishing, 2020, pp. 14-15.

APA: Fauci, A. (2020, May 21). Remarks to the Johns Hopkins University class of 2020. Johns Hopkins University, Baltimore, MD. In Annette Calzone (Ed.), *The reference shelf: Representative American speeches, 2019-2020* (pp. 14-15). Amenia, NY: Grey House Publishing.

This Virus Won't Be the Last Obstacle You Face, but It Can Help You Prepare for the Next One

By Arnold Schwarzenegger

Actor and former California governor Arnold Schwarzenegger focused on the inner strength and life skills that come from overcoming obstacles while acknowledging the extraordinary challenges the class of 2020 is facing. He stressed the importance of having a clear vision so that every setback builds character and becomes a stepping stone toward a goal.

Congratulations to the Class of 2020. But I'm not going to stand here and bull**** you about this being a fantastic time to graduate. I mean, just recently, I participated in my son Christopher's graduation from the University of Michigan over Zoom. I know that virtual graduations aren't the celebration that you envisioned, but the world is in a crisis. This coronavirus is unbelievable. But no matter how much damage this coronavirus does around the globe, let me be clear. Coronavirus can't erase your success. No way. But life is messier than an Instagram feed. That's clear. I can promise you that this virus won't be the last obstacle that you face, but it can help you prepare for the next one.

That's what life is all about is overcoming obstacles. You see, throughout your whole life, you will see obstacles being thrown in front of you like that. I mean, let me just tell you a brief story about the biggest obstacle that I faced just two years ago, literally four months before shooting *Terminator 6: Dark Fate*. I got a physical. I went to the doctor and he checked me up. That's what you always do before you start a movie. The doctor said, "You're in great health, but I would recommend that you go and replace your valve, your heart valve. It's leaking blood." So I said, "Well, I'm not going to have open heart surgery now, four months before shooting *Terminator*. Are you crazy?" I was just in the middle of working out really with heavy weights and everything, getting ready, doing my standard training and everything. I'm not going to go now and have open heart surgery.

And he says, "No, no. The technology has changed. This is not anymore open heart surgery. This is a noninvasive surgery that it goes through your artery in the bottom, go up to your heart, replace the valve, and the next day you go home. And then a week later you can continue with your regular training." And then I remembered that a friend of mine, a 90-year-old producer, had the procedure done just

Delivered on May 28, 2020, on Snapchat.

recently. Two days after the procedure, he was there at a meeting in the studio in Hollywood, and he looked fantastic. So I said, "Okay, I'll do it." So after I woke up from the surgery, I woke up 16 hours later instead of four hours. And there was a tube sticking out of my mouth. And then the doctor moved forward and he took the tube and ripped it out of my throat.

And I was coughing violently. And he says, "Just keep coughing." He says, "And then let us tell you what happened." So then he told me that they had to do an emergency surgery, that something went wrong during this kind of noninvasive procedure. And then it became very invasive. They said that they broke through the heart wall and there was internal bleeding and I could have died if they didn't open up my sternum and then do open heart surgery. So imagine. A day before I was in the hospital, I was training really hard for *Terminator 6*, and now all of a sudden, he's telling me that they were saving my life. Then he goes on and he says, "You're not out of the woods yet. There's another danger. There are still patients in our heart unit here that, after heart surgery, pass away, die, because, not because of the heart surgery, but because of the lung. They get pneumonia. So we are really worried about you getting pneumonia."

He says, "The only way you can really protect yourself is to do breathing exercises. Here's a plastic tube. Breathe into that all the time, throughout the whole day. And then start walking. Get up and walk around with a walker." Now, all of a sudden, I had to go and make myself get out of the bed and start walking with the walker. I did the first 10 steps like an old man. It was unbelievable, but I'll tell you one thing. My usual principles worked, because I was visualizing right away that I'm going to be on the date, August 1st, I will be on the set, and I will be shooting *Terminator*. And I will be doing my fight scenes and everything that it requires. That's what I was shooting for.

So I started declaring little victories. After I did the first 500 steps with the walker, I declared victory. After I had an appetite again to eat normal, I declared victory. Then I was discharged to go home, out of the hospital finally. And finally, I could train again with the light weights. Then I could train with heavier weights. But you know something? I always had a very clear vision of me being on that set of Terminator on August 1st, exactly the day when I was supposed to be there. A very clear vision. And I concentrated on that vision in everything that I did, my walking and my breathing exercises, the weight lifting and everything like this was going towards that vision, to make that a reality.

Sure enough, comes August 1st, I am there in Budapest on the set of *Terminator 6* and battling it out with the new *Terminator*, the more sophisticated *Terminator*, the Rev-9. You had the fight scene, kicking each other, and punching each other, and rolling around and falling down the steps and on and on and on. It was the most wild kind of a fight scene that you can imagine. We did this for two days. The director, Tim Miller, came up to me after these two days and said to me, he says, "Arnold, you're a . . . machine." I said, "No. I'm just back." The reason why I'm telling you all this is because no matter how successful you are, life will throw obstacles in your path like it was with my heart surgery or like with your graduation now. But if you have a very clear vision, like I talked about earlier, of exactly what you want to do and who do you want to be, you can go and find a way around all of these obstacles.

And because I had a very clear vision, I was able to find a way around and to get right there and do my movie. The reason why I'm talking about the vision is because one time I gave a graduation speech, and I remember it very clearly, the next day I was celebrating with the students and I was asking them, I said, "What do you want to do now? You have this degree. What do you want to do with this degree?" And they said to me, "Well, if I'm lucky, I'll maybe get a job." And they were all over the place with what they said, but they didn't have a very clear vision. As a matter of fact, one guy looked at me like a deer in a headlight. Like, "Uh, uh, uh." Didn't even know what to say when I asked him about his vision, where he wanted to go.

I'm concerned that young people, that they don't have a clear vision. And that's a real problem, because you see in America, we do the poll, and 70% of the people were not happy with their job, what they were doing during the day or at night. Think about that, 70% of the people are not happy with their work. Every day they go to work, they're not happy. That is a terrible statistic. I don't want you to be part of that statistic. This is why it is so important to have a vision. If you know your vision, your working will be fun. When you have a vision, then it's not a grind anymore to go towards your vision in the work that you're doing.

This is why people ask me all the time, they say, "Arnold, we saw you in *Pumping Iron* and we saw you smiling all the time and being happy and the other guys all had serious faces and looked very intense." And I said to them, "That was because I was happy to work out. I smiled because I was looking forward to every 500-pound squat, every 700-pound deadlift, every crunch, every chin-up, every curl, every squat, everything because every rep brought me closer to my vision. Every weight that I lifted brought me one step closer to that vision of becoming Mr. Universe, the greatest bodybuilder of all time."

If you only remember one thing today, it is you must have a very clear vision. You must develop that very clear vision. Ask yourself, who do you want to be? Not "what." But "who?" You see, a disaster can change what you are. It can steal jobs and force your inside. But it is who you are that rises in the face of adversity. Marcus Aurelius, who was the great emperor in the *Gladiator* movie, and who was one of the greatest minds among the Roman emperors, he said, "What stands in the way becomes the way."

Now, what does that mean? That means that a life will be always about obstacles in front of you. And it is the way to overcome those obstacles is nothing unusual. That's the way it is. So when you know your vision, every setback, every stepping stone, every struggle, all resistance builds your inner strength, builds your character, makes you stronger as a person. You see, your mind is no different than your body. I could be doing curls like this with no weights all day long, nothing would happen to my arm. But as soon as I put a weight into my hand and there is a resistance, now the bicep will respond, and it will grow. It will get bigger. It will pump up, and the arms will get stronger. The same is true with the mind. Embrace the climb towards your vision, and not just the selfie you take at the top. Because the climb is what made you grow and build who you want to be.

You can ask any mountain climber that has climbed Mount Everest. They would tell you that it was the climb up to the top, to the peak that was the learning experience, that was the thing that they will remember. Not just standing up there on top of that peak and doing the selfie, take the photograph, and then have to turn around again right away so they make it down before it gets dark. It's the climb.

And think back over the last four years. Te struggle that you went through to get this degree now, the all-nighters before the test, the essays that required two pots of coffee, the study groups that you put together. You came together to study together and struggle together. Those are the things that you'll remember. Not just this degree. You are celebrating that journey today. Not just a piece of paper that you hang on the wall. This is nothing. We all have these pieces of papers, but let's be honest. This celebration, by the way, is not the end. Yes, it is the end of this particular chapter, but it is the beginning of your next climb. It is time to celebrate now. Be in the moment. Enjoy, go all out. Yes, of course. But tomorrow, when this is all over, it is time to start developing your vision, and it's time to start climbing towards that vision. Thank you very much all of you for listening. God bless America. And God bless all of you around the globe. Hasta la vista.

Print Citations

CMS: Schwarzenegger, Arnold. "This Virus Won't Be the Last Obstacle You Face, but It Can Help You Prepare for the Next." Commence address on Snapchat, May 28, 2020. In *The Reference Shelf: Representative American Speeches, 2019-2020,* edited by Annette Calzone, 16-19. Amenia, NY: Grey House Publishing, 2020.

MLA: Schwarzenegger, Arnold. "This Virus Won't Be the Last Obstacle You Face, but It Can Help You Prepare for the Next." Snapchat, 28 May 2020. Commencement address. *The Reference Shelf: Representative American Speeches, 2019-2020,* edited by Annette Calzone, Grey House Publishing, 2020, pp. 16-19.

APA: Schwarzenegger, A. (2020, May 28). Commencement address on this virus won't be the last obstacle you face, but it can help you prepare for the next. Snapchat. In Annette Calzone (Ed.), *The reference shelf: Representative American speeches, 2019-2020* (pp. 16-19). Amenia, NY: Grey House Publishing.

2
The Pandemic

After New York experienced a crisis in the early months of COVID-19, Governor Andrew Cuomo praised first responders and citizens for their cooperation in reversing the progress of the disease.

Declaration of Coronavirus Emergency

By Donald Trump

In March of 2020, President Donald Trump declared a National Emergency in response to the COVID-19 crisis, releasing funding and other types of aid to states and other municipalities to help in the fight against the spread of the disease. The declaration also enabled the Department of Health and Human Services to waive revisions of regulations to give doctors and hospitals maximum flexibility to respond to the virus and care for patients.

To unleash the full power of the federal government in this effort today, I am officially declaring a National Emergency. Two very big words. The action I am taking will open up access to up to 50 billion dollars of very important and a large amount of money for states and territories and localities in our shared fight against this disease.

In furtherance of the order, I'm urging every state to set up emergency operation centers effective immediately. You're going to be hearing from some of the largest companies and greatest retailers and medical companies in the world. They're standing right behind me and the side of me. I'm also asking every hospital in this country to activate its emergency preparedness plan so that they can meet the needs of Americans everywhere. The hospitals are very engaged. New York and various other places are also various engaged. I just spoke with governor Cuomo. We had a very good conversation and we're working very strongly with the many states including New York.

The urgency orders I'm issuing today will also confer broad new authority to the Secretary of Health and Human Services. The Secretary of HHS will be able to immediately waive revisions of applicable laws and regulations to give doctors, hospital all hospitals and healthcare providers, maximum flexibility to respond to the virus and care for patients. This includes the following critical authorities, the ability to waive laws to enable telehealth, a fairly new and incredible thing that's happened in the not so distant past. I tell you what they've done with telehealth has incredible. It gives remote doctors visits and hospital check-ins the power to waive certain federal license requirements so that doctors from other states can provide services in states with the greatest need.

Number two, the ability to waive requirements that critical access hospitals limit the number of beds to 25 and the length of stay to 96 hours. The ability to waive the requirements of a three-day hospital stay prior to admission to a nursing home;

Delivered on March 13, 2020, at the White House, Washington, DC.

big thing. The authority to waive rules to hinder hospital's ability to bring additional physicians on board or obtain needed office space. They can do as they want. They can do what they have to do. They know what they have to do. Now they don't have any problem getting it done.

The authority to waive rules that severely restrict where hospitals can care for patients within the hospital itself. Ensuring that the emergency capacity can be quickly established. We'll remove or eliminate every obstacle necessary to deliver our people the care that they need and that they're entitled to. No resource will be spared. Nothing whatsoever. 10 days ago, I brought together the CEOs of commercial labs at the White House and directed them to immediately begin working on the solution to dramatically increase the availability of tests.

Other countries have called us and worked with us and they're doing similar things or will be doing similar things as a result of that action. Today we are announcing a new partnership with private sector to vastly increase and accelerate our capacity to test for the Coronavirus. We want to make sure that those who need a test can get a test very safely, quickly and conveniently but we don't want people to take a test if we feel that they shouldn't be doing it and we don't want everyone running out and taking; only if you have certain symptoms.

Using federal emergency authorities, the FDA approved a new test for the virus. We did this within hours after receiving the application from Roche, a process that would normally take weeks. We therefore expect up to a half a million additional tests will be available early next week. We'll be announcing locations probably on Sunday night. I want to thank Roche, great company for their incredible work. I'd also like to thank Thermo Fisher. The FDA's goal is to hopefully authorize your application within 24 hours. It'll go very quickly. It's going very quickly. Which will bring additionally 1.4 million tests on board next week and five million within a month. I doubt we'll need anywhere near that.

At the same time, we've been in discussions with pharmacies and retailers to make drive-through tests available in the critical locations identified by public health professionals. The goal is for individuals to be able to drive up and be swabbed without having to leave your car. I want to thank Google. Google is helping to develop a website. It's going to be very quickly done, unlike websites of the past, to determine whether a test is warranted and to facilitate testing at a nearby convenient location. And we have many, many locations behind us, by the way. We cover this country and large parts of the world, by the way. We're not going to be talking about the world right now. But we cover very, very strongly our country.

Stores in virtually every location. Google has 1,700 engineers working on this right now. They've made tremendous progress. Our overriding goal is to stop the spread of the virus and to help all Americans who have been impacted by this. Again, we don't want everybody taking this test. It's totally unnecessary. And this will pass. This will pass through and we're going to be even stronger for it. We've learned a lot, a tremendous amount has been learned. I want to thank Deborah Birx and I want to ask her maybe to come up and say a few words as to what's happening. Dr. Birx is a highly respected person. I've gotten to know her very well over the last six days and what we've done is we built something that was very old, very old fashioned, somewhat obsolete, certainly obsolete when it comes to the kind of numbers that we're talking about. Dr. Birx, please. Thank you, Deborah.

[Coronavirus Response Coordinator, White House Coronavirus Task Force, Dr.] Deborah Birx: Thank you, Mr. President. It's a pleasure to be here with all of you. I think you know at the beginning of this epidemic, HHS through CDC proactively developed an assay, built on the existing flu surveillance system. That surveillance system was then converted to diagnostic system. But last Tuesday, seeing the spread of the virus around the globe, the President realized that our current approach to testing was inadequate to meet the needs of the American public. He asked for an entire overhaul of the testing approach. He immediately called the private sector laboratories to the White House, as noted, and charged them with developing a high throughput quality platform that can meet the needs of the American public.

We are grateful to LabCorp and Quest for taking up the charge immediately after the meeting and within 72 hours, bringing additional testing access, particularly to the outbreak areas of Washington State and California and now across the country. We are also very grateful to the universities and large hospital systems that took up the charge to develop their own quality tests made available by new FDA guidance. This has resolved and expanded testing across New York, California, Washington, Colorado, and you see sometimes those drive-through options that have been made available through these high throughput options.

Following the meeting last week, major commercial laboratory equipment and diagnostic companies took immediate action to adopt and develop new testing systems. Last night, the initial company, Roche, received FDA approval, moving from request, to development, to approval in record time. This innovative approach centered fully on unleashing the power of the private sector, focusing on providing convenient testing to hundreds of thousands of Americans within short turnaround times. In less than two weeks together, we have developed a solution that we believe will meet the future testing needs of Americans. I understand how difficult this has been. I was part of the HIV/AIDS response in the 80s.

We knew from first finding cases in 1981, it took us to almost 1985 to have a test. It took us another 11 years to have effective therapy. It is because of the lessons learned from that, that we were able to mobilize and bring those individuals that were key to the HIV response to this response. I understand that a lot of this behind the scenes action over the last couple of weeks was invisible to the press and the American people, but this intense effort has not only resulted in innovative solutions, but an automated high throughput system bringing the availability of these quality corona-viral testing to the American people at unprecedented speed.

Finally, I want you to know in South Korea, they did have a large number of tests available over the last several weeks. Their positivity rate is between three and 4%. With LabCorp and Quest expanded testing, their positivity rate is between one and 2%. So we want to also announce this new approach to testing, which we'll start in this screening website up here facilitated by Google, where clients and patients and people of interest can go, fill out a screening questionnaire, move down for symptoms or risk factors. Yes, they would move down this and be told where the drive-through options would be for them to receive this test. The labs will then move to the high throughput automated machines to be able to provide results in 24 to 36 hours. That is the intent of this approach. We have seen it work just in our own United States and we want to bring this across the continent. Thank you very much.

Donald Trump: Thank you very much. I'd like to maybe have, Tony, do you want to come up? You've become a … I think everybody out here knows you pretty well, but Tony has been doing a tremendous job working long, long hours and you've seen a lot happen, but this has been … It's been a great experience and working with you has been terrific. Tony, please.

[National Institute of Allergy and Infectious Diseases Director] Anthony Fauci: Thank you very much, Mr. President. This is an example of another example of what I've been referring to in my discussions with many of you in the audience as a proactive leaning forward, aggressive, trying to stay ahead of the curve. And what you've seen now with this order is that we're going to be able to remove the constraints so that people at the state, the local level, the individual physician, all the way up through the federal government will have as many constraints as possible, removed for them to do everything they possibly can so that we can implement the things that we've been talking about.

The containment, the mitigation, so that as I've said, many times, that curve that I refer to that goes up. We don't want to have that curve. We want to suppress it down to that small mound and I think what we've done today is something that is going to be a very important element in having us be successful in doing that. We still have a long way to go. There will be many more cases, but we'll take care of that. And ultimately, as the President said, this will end, but what's going on here today is going to help it to end sooner than it would have. Thank you. . . .

Mike Pence: Thank you, Mr. President. This day should be an inspiration to every American, because thanks to your leadership from early on, not only are we bringing a whole of government approach to confronting the coronavirus, we're bringing an all of America approach. Mr. President, from early on you took decisive action. You suspended all travel from China, you created travel advisories to South Korea and Italy. We screened all travelers from all airports in both of those countries. And on the unanimous recommendation of your health experts, you at midnight tonight will effectively suspend all travel from Europe and Americans that were returning will be screened and asked to voluntarily participate in a 14-day quarantine.

Throughout this process, Mr. President, you've put the health of America first, but you brought the best of America to address it. And it's not just at the federal level. As you said, Mr. President, we've been working with states across the country. We issued broad guidelines from the CDC for every American. But this week at your direction, we tailored specific recommendations from CDC for New York, Washington State, California, Massachusetts and Florida. And we've been in continuous contact, as you said, with governors around the country. Mr. President, you have forged a seamless partnership with every state and every territory in this country to put the health of our nation first.

But today, I trust that people around the country that are looking on at this extraordinary public and private partnership to address the issue of testing with particular inspiration. After you tapped me to lead the White House Corona Taskforce, Mr. President, you said this is all hands on deck and you directed us to immediately reach out to the American business sector, commercial labs to meet what we knew then would be the need for testing across the spectrum. And today, with this historic public- private partnership, we have laid the foundation to meet that need. For Americans looking on, by this Sunday evening, we'll be able to give specific guidance on when the website will be available.

You can go to the website, as the President said. You'll type in your symptoms and be given direction whether or not a test is indicated. And then at the same website you'll be directed to one of these incredible companies that are going to give a little bit of their parking lot so that people can come by and do a drive by test. Mr. President, I want to join you in thanking Walmart, and CVS, and Target, and Walgreens. These are companies that are synonymous with communities, large and small, where people come together and now they're going to come together to meet the needs of the American public. These commercial laboratories, LabCorp, and Quest, and Roche have just done an incredible job stepping forward and they're going to literally make, literally make hundreds and thousands of tests available and being processed with results to patients in the very near future.

But it's all a result of you tasking us with bringing together not just government resources, which all state labs can now test across the country. CDC is testing. But you said, Mr. President, that we wanted to bring all the resources of the country together and that's what this partnership really means. Truth is that we have coronavirus cases now in 46 American states and while the risk of serious illness of the coronavirus remains low, we want to encourage every American to practice common sense, practice good hygiene, go to the CDC's website to see what the guidance is for your community, or for the American people broadly. And as the President has said, it's especially important now that we look after senior citizens with chronic underlying health conditions.

Last week the President directed the Center for Medicaid and Medicare Services to raise the standards in our nursing homes, increase inspections at our nursing homes. And today, we're offering very specific guidance, which Seema Verma will articulate about visitations at nursing homes. It's important to remember that they were there for us when we were growing up, Mr. President. They helped us with our homework. They tucked us in at night, they cheered us on as we pursued educations, cheered us on in our careers. Now it's time for us to be there for them and to recognize that seniors with chronic health conditions are the most vulnerable and Americans can make a difference. So wash your hands. Use common sense. Look after the most vulnerable. And Mr. President, I know I join you in saying that every American should be proud of this incredible public private partnership that's going to be speeding access of testing to millions of Americans in the weeks ahead. And together, as you've said many times, together we'll get through this, together we'll put the health of America first.

Donald Trump: Thank you.

Print Citations

CMS: Trump, Donald. "Declaration of Coronavirus National Emergency." Speech at the White White, Washington, DC, March 13, 2020. In *The Reference Shelf: Representative American Speeches, 2019-2020,* edited by Annette Calzone, 23-28. Amenia, NY: Grey House Publishing, 2020.

MLA: Trump, Donald. "Declaration of Coronavirus National Emergency." The White House, 13 March 2020, Washington, DC. Speech. *The Reference Shelf: Representative American Speeches, 2019-2020,* edited by Annette Calzone, Grey House Publishing, 2020, pp. 23-28.

APA: Trump, D. (2020, March 13). Speech on the declaration of coronavirus national emergency. The White House, Washington, DC. In Annette Calzone (Ed.), *The reference shelf: Representative American speeches, 2019-2020* (pp. 23-28). Amenia, NY: Grey House Publishing.

A Briefing on the Coronavirus Outbreak

By Andrew Cuomo

New York Governor Andrew Cuomo lauded the state's first responders, health care workers, and citizens in a March briefing for their dedication in reversing one of the nation's highest death tolls from COVID-19 in the early months of the pandemic. Cuomo commented on the importance of keeping the public informed with real facts and avoiding partisan misinformation, which in turn elicits an intelligent response from the citizenry.

Let us give you the facts and some of the new thinking that we are doing here in New York. Number of total hospitalizations in the state is down again. That is good news. The net change in hospitalizations, three-day rolling average, a little more accurate. That's down. The intubation rate is down. The closedown and—lives lost, 195. Yesterday is the most devastating number that we have to deal with every day. It's actually up a little bit from the day before. But overall, the trend is down. And if you look at the number of lives lost, again, we're just about where we were when we started before we saw the onslaught of the virus. And then dealt with it and changed the trajectory of the virus. Never forget what we did here. What New Yorkers did by their actions and their sacrifice. They saved lives. They saved hundreds of thousands of lives. Because that projection of what the virus was supposed to do was much, much worse than what it wound up doing.

We are making real progress, no doubt. But there's also no doubt there is no time to get cocky, arrogant. This virus has deceived us every step of the way. We have been behind this virus from the very beginning. And it still surprises us. We thought initially that it didn't affect children. We're now dealing with an issue that is very disturbing. We have about 100 cases of an inflammatory disease in young children that seems to be created by the COVID virus. And this is something that is just starting, and New York is leading the investigation of this situation. The symptoms of the children are analyzed to the Kawasaki disease or toxic-shock-like syndrome. It is an inflammation of the blood vessels and can affect the heart. We lost three children, a 5-year-old boy, 7-year-old boy and an 18-year-old girl. The symptoms are all across the board as you can see: less than 1-year-old; predominantly 5 to 14. But we lost a young lady at 18 years old. And we have some cases up to 21 years old. So this is a truly disturbing situation. And I know parents around the state and around the country are very concerned about this, and they should be. If we had this issue in New York, it's probably in other states and probably hasn't been diagnosed yet in

Briefing on May 12, 2020, on YouTube.

other states. Because, again, these children don't present the usual COVID symptoms. They're not respiratory symptoms. And I think that's one of the reasons why people haven't found it yet. But they know what the symptoms are. If your child has the symptoms that they are saying or are symptoms that should cause an alert, we need parents to be advised. We have the state department of health that is telling hospitals and medical providers to prioritize testing for the COVID virus for any children that are demonstrating these symptoms.

At the same time, while we're not cocky or arrogant, we are talking about getting back to work. We talk about New York being tough, but that also means smart. We have been smart all through this. Look at where we are today, the curve in New York, New York is on the decline. You take New York out of the numbers for the rest of the nation, the nation is still on the incline in the number of cases. So we have been smart. We got hit worst because the virus was coming through Europe. And nobody even told us. Nobody even knew. But we took the worst and we turned the curve and we are—We have a better curve now than you see in many other states and certainly the United States as a whole. So reopening, yes. But it still means we have to be smart. What does smart mean? It means following the CDC guidelines, to begin with. Follow the data, follow the science. We said that from day one. Don't fall subject to emotion and politics. Stay with the science and the data. Listen to Dr. Fauci. Even this morning he said if you don't follow the CDC guidelines, you run a real risk of triggering an outbreak that can get out of control. What is out of control? Out of control is when the number of people infected going into your hospital system [is] overwhelming your hospital system. That is what happened in Italy. That was our great fear here in New York. But that is a very real situation that people have to watch from. Smart means learning from the mistakes of others. We're not the first ones down this path. Study what China did and South Korea did and Germany did. Look what's happening in the other states and inform your actions by what happened in other places that went through the same process. And you'll see many of the other places rushed reopening and actually had to backtrack and then close again. That's the last thing that we would want here in New York. Smart means regional management, local government, managed and engaged and citizen participation because this all turns on what people do.

This is not about government. Government can offer advice and suggestions and guidance. But it's about what people do. Why did we turn the curve in New York? Because people acted responsibly and intelligently. And we also have to do it in a way that is totally transparent. I want every New Yorker to know all the facts. Because it's up to New Yorkers. It's up to the people and how they respond, then give them the information and trust their judgment. Trust their judgment. What did we learn in here? That when people are informed of facts that they actually believe, which is saying something, but if you give them the real facts, that they believe the real facts and not political facts, not partisan facts, not spin, not hype, not some rhetoric from a politician who is trying to get something for themselves, if you give them the real facts, they will respond intelligently. But you have to give them the real facts. And that's transparency. That's what smart means. And that's what we're doing here in New York. All the facts are on the website. All the facts for your region are on the website. You know exactly what I know. I don't know anything more than I am telling the people of the state of New York. And you can see the changes in your region, capital district in New York changed overnight. You can see the changes in the direction in your region.

Then what are we doing? We have our hand on the reopening valve. And we're turning the reopening valve and we're starting to reopen. But we're calibrating it and we're monitoring it. Right? The first monitoring device is the diagnostic testing. Positive or negative. People need to go. People need to be tested. We have more tests than ever. We are testing more than any other state in the United States. We have come up to speed faster than any other state. People have to take the [test]. We have it available in drive-throughs and in pharmacies. And you watch that testing rate day-to-day to see if the testing rate is going up. More people testing positive. Then, once you test, then comes your tracing. Then comes your isolation operation, et cetera. Second monitoring device is you: are doing antibody testing? The antibody testing tells you how many people have had the virus and have recovered from the virus. There's a little lag in the antibody testing because it's really telling you who was infected two weeks ago or two and a half weeks ago. But if you see that number going up, you know more people have gotten infected. You then have the hospitalization rate, which is very important. You know every day now, because of the system we put in place, how many people walked into a hospital with COVID. Watch that hospitalization rate. If you see that hospitalization rate going up, you have a problem. And watch the hospitalization rate in terms of the capacity of the hospitals. That's what we have been dealing with for the past two months. We've said you have to have a 30% buffer in the capacity of hospitals. So if that infection spikes you have a 30% buffer in terms of capacity. But watch that hospitalization rate. And they will then give you the infection rate. The rt. They will tell you— those gauges will tell you the rate of transmission one person to another person. And if one person is infecting more than one other person, 1.1. That's the outbreak that Dr. Fauci was talking about. And you can compute these rates. You can monitor exactly what you're doing.

There is a science to this. And there's a methodology to this that erases all the theories, right? Everybody has a theory. I think this. I think that. I think warm weather is going to make a difference. I think God is going to do something. Everybody has a theory. Tell me the facts. Tell me the numbers. And that's what I want to tell the people of the state. And respond to the facts. Local region then manages the system. They monitor those numbers we're talking about. They control that valve. They make sure businesses are complying with the safety precautions when the businesses go back. Every business will say don't worry, don't worry, I will have safety precautions, I will socially distance. I'll give equipment. Are we actually doing that? Are we staying away from large gatherings? Are we making sure? That's up to the local government. And then built in is a circuit breaker that when those gauges hit red, turn off the valve. Hopefully you don't get to that point because you have been monitoring and you calibrate and you adjust the valve a little Bit at a time. But worst-case scenario, you turn off the valve. That's what other countries have had to do when they open that reopening too quickly. More of the states had this accurate or transparent a monitoring mechanism.

But I want people to know exactly what is going on in your community day-to-day. Because you are the ones who are determining what happens in your community. Nobody else. No governor. No senator. No elected official. It's what people do. It's what our neighbors do. The regional control group are the top elected officials, academic officials, top health care professionals in that region, in that community. And they're the ones who are going to have to make it work. But this will be online every Morning or every day. And everyone can see exactly what is happening literally day-to-day.

No other state has this system. No other state is as transparent. No other state is gathering local data so it can present data statewide every day. We're doing it because the secret of our success has been exactly this. The secret of our success, the one thing I did right was communicate to people and trust people that with the right information they will make the right decisions. This is the most advanced way in the nation to give people, to give citizens the information They need to lead their lives correctly. And that will be online in the next couple of days.

But Friday is May 15th, the opening date. And this will be online—smartly, right. We all have heard Washington say—many, many times—the governors are in charge of reopening. Thank you very much. So the governors are in charge of reopening. But that doesn't mean the states are on their own, the governors are on their own. We need federal help. We need federal assistance. They're talking about passing a piece of legislation in Washington this week. It has to be a smart piece of legislation this time. What does that mean? No handouts to greedy corporations. No political pork. And no partisanship. Sometimes—there has to be a time in history when the federal government is willing to stop playing partisan politics. And if it's not through this experience, through this crisis, it will never be. That's the first definition of smart for the federal government. The bill has to fund state and local governments. It has to fund working families. It has to fund state testing and tracing. Everybody talks about testing and tracing. It's up to testing and tracing. It is. No one has done it before. No state has this testing capacity. No state has this tracing capacity. We have to build it. We can do it, but it's a heck of a logistical endeavor. And we need funding to do it. And we need a real economical stimulus.

This economy has been damaged through no fault of anyone but the coronavirus. But to get this economy back up and running we are going to need an intelligent stimulus bill from Washington. When I say no pork barrel, what does that mean? When they pass a piece of legislation in Washington, every Senator sees it as their opportunity to bring home bacon to their state. This is supposed to be out the COVID virus and repairing damage from the COVID virus. Keep it about the COVID virus. Last bill when they did it, they were talking about providing money to states that didn't have a major COVID problem. They were talking about building a new state capitol in some states because they didn't have enough COVID cases to justify the federal allocation, so they were looking for ways to spend the money.

How ludicrous is that, right? This is somebody's money. This is the taxpayers' money. They worked hard. They're willing to help solve the problem of COVID, but keep it about the COVID virus. . . .

This doesn't have to be a giveaway to the rich millionaires who are doing just fine anyway. And it doesn't have to be a giveaway to big business. It shouldn't be that, another episode in history where somehow the rich figure out a way to get more assistance when it is supposed to be about helping average Americans. And that's the people who really need help here, are the working families, the families that go paycheck to paycheck. They're the ones who are struggling. And the essential workers who have been so great for so long. Police officers, firefighters, nurses, school teachers, the people who literally need food. I have people literally saying I need food to feed my family. We have unprecedented demand at food banks. Those are the people who really need help. And those are the people who the state government funds. New York State, we know what happened to our economy. We know what our budget looks like. We need $61 billion in federal support or we will wind up aggravating the situation. Because when you don't fund the state, who does the state fund? The state funds schools, local governments, and hospitals. You really want New York State to turn around and have to cut schools and cut local governments? You know who local governments are? That's police, firefighters. You want me to get hospitals? Hospitals are the nurses and the doctors who just got us through this, and everyone celebrates as heroes. If you don't fund the state, that's who you're cutting in terms of finances.

Now, this is not a red issue, blue issue. Yes, I'm a Democrat. But this is not about politics. I have Democrats and I have Republicans in my state. I have Independents, short people, tall people. New York, we have everything. If you're going to be an effective statewide leader, forget red and blue. It does not work. And every state, red states, blue states, they all need funding. You put the governors in charge, the states are heading the reopening. They need funds to do it.

Print Citations

CMS: Cuomo, Andrew. "A Briefing on the Coronavirus Outbreak." Briefing on YouTube, May 12, 2020. In *The Reference Shelf: Representative American Speeches, 2019-2020,* edited by Annette Calzone, 29-33. Amenia, NY: Grey House Publishing, 2020.

MLA: Cuomo, Andrew. "A Briefing on the Coronavirus Outbreak." YouTube, 12 March 2020. Briefing. *The Reference Shelf: Representative American Speeches, 2019-2020,* edited by Annette Calzone, Grey House Publishing, 2020, pp. 29-33.

APA: Cuomo, A. (2020, March 12). A briefing on the coronavirus outbreak. YouTube. In Annette Calzone (Ed.), *The reference shelf: Representative American speeches, 2019-2020* (pp. 29-33). Amenia, NY: Grey House Publishing.

Reopening the Country Amid COVID-19

By Joe Biden

In a June 2020 address, Joe Biden spoke of the need for safely reopening businesses and schools in the face of the pandemic, calling for access to testing, more resources dedicated to health care, and transparency about the virus from government officials. Biden stressed the need to stay vigilant and criticized Donald Trump's lack of leadership.

We thank the local officials for joining today. I know they've got a lot to do and they've really been very, very busy. Before I begin my remarks, I want to acknowledge that it was five years ago today when a white supremacist walked into Mother Emanuel Church in Charleston, South Carolina and slaughtered a friend of mine, Clementa Pinckney, and eight other parishioners. It was hate unbridled, and it was poisonous, a poisonous expression of white supremacy that still infects our nation and many of our institutions and of the dangers we face as a society if we don't root out this corrosive and deadly ideology.

When I reflect back on the amazing grace and compassion and forgiveness of the Mother Emanuel community, I see the very best in what we see in America as Americans, but we know that grace alone is not enough. We have to put it to work, that grace, and we're seeing the best of America in that as well. In the weeks of peaceful protest, civil action is taking place in cities and towns of every size, in this state and every other state across the country. People are keeping their eyes focused on how danger it is, how much danger it is to live a life of a black or a brown-skinned person in this country, and Americans are out there marching, notwithstanding the fact that we're in the middle of a pandemic. That's how critical they think it is.

On Monday, Donald Trump said, "If we stopped testing right now for COVID-19, we'd have very few cases if any." If we stopped testing, we'd have very few cases if any. It's a statement that's not only absurd, it's absolutely tragic. Yesterday, the head of the White House task force on coronavirus, the vice president, claimed success in the fight because deaths are "down to fewer than 750 a day." 750 fathers and mothers, sisters and brothers, uncles, aunts, husbands, wives, children dying every day. More than 20,000 a month. That's greater than World War II level casualties each month, that's more than five 9/11s each month, and this administration is engaging in self-congratulations? Maybe good enough for Donald Trump, but it will never, ever be acceptable if I'm your president. Researchers have shown that tens of thousands of Americans have died needlessly because Donald Trump was slow to respond to the crisis and then when he did he bungled the response.

Delivered on June 17, 2020, in Darby, PA.

For weeks in January and February, I but I wasn't alone, I was raising my concerns about how we need to take this virus seriously, all while Trump was ignoring the reporting from his own intelligence community in his daily briefings, and the warnings of his closest advisors, all the while praising the Chinese government for being transparent in handling this virus instead of demanding access for the CDC that Beijing was refusing to give in Wuhan. The American people have sacrificed so much to fight this virus. We've lost lives, we've lost businesses, we've lost paychecks, and now thanks to Donald Trump's bungling, we may lose some of the progress we begun to make. All because he's lost interest. He's once again ignoring the facts. The public health response is still woefully, woefully lacking from this administration. More than 117,000 people have died in the United States of America, with an average daily number of cases still climbing in 21 states.

We still don't have what we need when it comes to rapid results testing, contact tracing capacity, widely available personnel protective equipment for them, or clear nationwide guidance. Instead, President Trump pushes dangerous disproven drugs, stands in the way of the CDC issuing guidelines on reopening. They had them, wanted to issue them and he wouldn't let them. He refuses to wear a mask, failing even the most basic test of leadership. He scaled back meetings of the COVID-19 task force. I guess there's not much to do in spite of experts saying that testing and tracing is necessary for reopening, he sent his testing czar home. The money provided to the Pentagon for essential medical supplies, only 15%, only 15% has made it out the door.

Donald Trump wants to style himself as a wartime president against this invisible enemy, the coronavirus. Unlike any other war, any other wartime leader, he takes no responsibility, he exercises no leadership, and now he's just flat surrendering the fight. Instead of leading the charge to defeat the virus, he just basically waved a white flag and has retreated to get back on his campaign, to his campaign rallies that he'll put people at risk as everyone's pointed out, in violation of the CDC Guidelines that still warn against large gatherings as long as he's going to allow this to happen, but he's ready to do it as long as, notwithstanding CDC guidance, as long as the people showing up sign a waiver promising they'll not hold the campaign liable.

Donald Trump's failure to fight the coronavirus with the same energy and focus that he uses to troll his enemies on Twitter has cost us lives and is putting hope for an economic recovery at risk. Job numbers and retail sales were better than expected in May, and that's great news for the country, but now Donald Trump's desire to declare victory and be done with it is only going to imperil the continued progress we have to make. Our economy is still sputtering, with more than 20 million people unemployed and no clear guidance from the federal government for what businesses need to do to reopen safely, efficiently, and generate a strong recovery.

This isn't a debate about whether to reopen. It's about how we make reopening work for everyone. The employees at the White House, they get daily COVID-19 tests. They know they're safe before they go to work and they know their co-workers are safe. They have the confidence to resume their lives. Workers across the country aren't asking for daily testing. They're just asking for regular, reliable access to tests. Don't they deserve that?

So it's not that Donald Trump doesn't recognize the importance of testing, it's that he's not up to the task or doesn't care and now he's seemingly decided he doesn't even want to try, but just like he couldn't wish COVID-19 away in March, just like he couldn't tweet it away in April, he can't ignore it away in June. So I have some basic questions for President Donald Trump. What are you going to do to make sure every worker has access to regular testing so they have the same confidence to go into a store or go back to work that White House staffers have? Why are you leaving schools and child care centers to navigate the uncertainty all on their own without an effective guidance and resources that they need to protect the kids and their communities? Why don't you enforce the OSHA standards for worker protection during this global pandemic? Why is it the Main Street Lending Program created more than two months ago by the Congress to help struggling small businesses only opened for registration to lenders two days ago, and still hasn't distributed a single penny. Why don't you disclose the names, Mr. President, of the businesses that received a total of $500 billion in taxpayer's funding? Why are they being hidden?

How many cronies got bailouts? How many donors? How many big businesses that didn't need it? What business had to shut down because they were denied funding in April? What businesses didn't get special approval that others got by a nod from the top? Why did you get rid of the watchdog, Mr. President? Why did you get rid of the watchdog, appointed to oversee every dollar distributed, an inspector general? Why did you get rid of that person the Congress passed? What are you trying to hide? It's bad management on top of bad planning on top of neglect and it's totally unacceptable for a great nation like ours.

Folks, here's the truth. The pandemic is still here. It's going to be here for the foreseeable future until we get it under control or until we have safe and proven widely available vaccine. COVID-19 is a fact of nature. We have to deal with this virus and everything that comes with it. We have to deal with it head on, honestly, tell the people the truth. To paraphrase Franklin Roosevelt in the Depression, the American people can handle anything, just tell them the truth. We can't deal with it the way you're doing it. The only way to deal with it, Mr. President, if we put in the work, investing and building a dynamic, resilient economy and health system capable of getting and then staying ahead of new outbreaks. We have the capacity and the resources to do that. I have laid out baseline steps of what needs to be done from make it work checklists for a successful accountable recovery that I put out back in early April to the steps for a strong reopening that I released last week. It's not rocket science. Granted I have incredible scientists advising me on almost a daily basis on how to proceed, but it's not rocket science, it's common sense.

It's straightforward, and that's why this is perhaps the greatest indictment of Donald Trump's complete, compelling lack of leadership. He wasted months and months and months passing the buck, blaming everyone else, refusing to act when he should have been preparing our country for a long-term response and building our resiliency to respond to future flareups. Yet we still don't have a comprehensive system for collecting COVID-19 case data. These are the basics. He should have been preparing us to weather the valleys and peaks of this virus. He should have been working to shore up the vulnerabilities in our healthcare system that have been laid bare in this crisis that he's trying to eliminate in court. He should have been working to bridge the inequities and strengthen the cracks in the foundation of our economic system that are exposed for everyone to see. He hasn't done any of it. Because of the depth of Donald Trump's failures, this pandemic will continue to be worse for all Americans and much worse for black and brown Americans who are getting hit the hardest.

Folks in communities like . . ., Donald Trump thinks if he puts his head in the sand, the American people will too, but it doesn't work that way. Not when hundreds of people are still dying every day and millions are unemployed wondering how in God's name are they going to keep the lights on and food on the table. Not when workers are weighed down with worries about their safety or what happens if they get sick. There are the steps that we need to be taking now to steer us steadily and strongly in the right direction, see us through this time, to make a more resilient future. They're all available.

First, we have to do everything we can to avoid deadly spikes in the infections as people begin to back out into the world. We're not that much better prepared today for the run of cases that overfills our intensive care units than we were three months ago. Second, we have to help give people the assurance and precautions that are necessary to restart the economy with confidence. If Americans lose what faith they have left, what little faith they have left in the government's ability to manage this pandemic, we'll see much deeper and longer lasting economic impacts than we even, and with even greater repercussions for people's well-being.

Mr. President, don't leave the American people to face this threat on their own with no guidance, resources, or leadership from the federal government. Don't let support from the CARES Act expire next month while people are still hurting. Don't leave our frontline workers exposed without the resources they need and don't waste any more of our time, Mr. President. The American people need confidence and clear guidance grounded in science that's going to allow them to resume their daily lives. American businesses need the support of the federal government to continue to backstop them through these phases of reopening and workers need assurances that their health is your first concern. Americans need a president who will put the American people first, not his or her own ego. America needs a president who will do the work. I'm ready on Day One, after more than three years in office, why isn't Donald Trump ready? Mr. President, wake up. Get to work. There is so much more to be done. Thank you.

Print Citations

CMS: Biden, Joe. "Reopening the Country Amid COVID-19." Speech in Darby, PA, June 17, 2020. In *The Reference Shelf: Representative American Speeches, 2019-2020,* edited by Annette Calzone, 34-38. Amenia, NY: Grey House Publishing, 2020.

MLA: Biden, Joe. "Reopening the Country Amid COVID-1917." 17 June 2020, Darby, PA. Speech. *The Reference Shelf: Representative American Speeches, 2019-2020,* edited by Annette Calzone, Grey House Publishing, 2020, pp. 34-38.

APA: Biden, J. (2020, June 17). Speech on reopening the country amid COVID-19. Darby, PA. In Annette Calzone (Ed.), *The reference shelf: Representative American speeches, 2019-2020* (pp. 34-38). Amenia, NY: Grey House Publishing.

Hearing on COVID-19's Impact on the Future of Higher Education

By Susan Davis, Lloyd K. Smucker, Sharon Pierce, Timothy White,
Scott Pulsipher, and Shaun Harper

In July, members of Congress and higher-education leaders met to discuss COVID-19's devastating impact on the education system and on students. Many students, especially minorities, have experienced a loss of housing and food insecurity in addition to the challenges of taking classes online. The CARES Act, passed in March, provided emergency relief funding for higher education and froze student loan payments, although payments were delayed by eligibility requirements. Moving forward, leaders asked for equal access to necessary technology and for support services for students whether they were on campus or working remotely. They also called for investment in facilities upgrades like contactless hardware, additional cleaning supplies, and personal protective equipment.

Chairwoman [Susan] Davis [D-San Diego]: Thank you very much. . . . Today, as we know, we are examining how the COVID-19 pandemic is straining our higher education system and discussing what Congress must do to support students and institutions through this difficult time. Across the country, the rush to suspend on-campus activities and switch to online learning has exacerbated preexisting systemic inequities in higher education. For example, the on-campus resources that many students from low SES backgrounds normally rely on, like computer labs and reliable internet, are now unavailable to those students. The suspension of on-campus activities is also threatening many students' access to basic essentials like food and housing. And for these students, going to school had been their primary way of meeting these needs. The survey from earlier this year found students of color are disproportionately suffering high rates of food and housing insecurity due to the closure of campuses. Research also indicates how most students do not perform as well in online classes. Now, imagine how students who are already started off with fewer resources are more likely to struggle . . . under these new educational conditions.

To address these disparities, Congress secured 14 billion in emergency relief funding for higher education in the bipartisan CARES Act, and half of this funding was allocated specifically for direct student emergency aid. Additionally, Congress provided immediate relief to student loan borrowers by suspending student loan

Hearing on July 7, 2020, at the U.S. House of Representatives, Washington, DC.

payments and freezing interest on all Direct and federally held student loans. Unfortunately, instead of quickly dispersing these urgent relief funds to students, however, according to the law that we had passed in March, Secretary DeVos created an arbitrary eligibility requirement for students trying to access the support. These restrictions not only prevent relief funding from quickly reaching students, but they exclude several underserved groups of students who cannot apply for Title IV aid, such as undocumented students and veterans.

In response, the state of Washington and the California Community College System, which includes the San Diego Community College District, sued Secretary DeVos. Thankfully, these lawsuits have temporarily stopped the department from denying California community college students and students across Washington access to the emergency student aid that Congress secured. But setting aside the delays and the unnecessary restrictions created by the department, we must also address how the CARES Act simply did not go far enough to prepare our institutions for this looming economic recession. Due to the pandemic, institutions are facing unprecedented state and local budget shortfalls that will trigger drastic funding cuts for higher education, and they are facing massive revenue losses due to decreased enrollment and suspended activities. . . . These cuts and revenue loss … end programs that many vulnerable students need to complete their degree and find fulfilling careers. We know that the worst of these consequences are going to fall on historically black colleges and universities, private colleges and universities, minority-serving institutions and community colleges, which have the fewest resources despite serving most of our country's low-income students and students of color. Impending budget shortfalls are also putting many institutions under pressure to permanently reopen their campuses, even at the risk of exposing students, educators and communities to COVID-19. The evidence is overwhelmingly clear: Congress must do more to support our students and our institutions.

The HEROES Act would take a critical step in the right direction. It provides nearly one trillion to help state and local governments avert massive budget shortfalls and cuts to education. It also provides over 35 billion in relief funds for public institutions and other institutions that have suffered financially, including almost two billion for HBCUs, TCUs and MSIs. Beyond extra funds, however, Congress must also protect students from predatory for-profit schools. These institutions have a record of using taxpayer dollars to target vulnerable students during economic downturns, often leaving them with worthless degrees and debt that they cannot repay.

Simply put, the COVID-19 pandemic is testing not only our students and our institutions, but Congress's commitment to ensuring all students have access to safe, affordable and quality education. Today, with the help of our witnesses, and we appreciate their being here, we will discuss whether we can live up to that commitment. I now yield to the ranking member, Mr. Smucker for an opening statement.

[Representative Lloyd] Smucker [Rep-Lancaster]: Thank you, Chairwoman Davis. It's great to see you.

Chairwoman Davis: Thank you.

Mr. Smucker: Before I discuss the topic of today's hearing, I'd just like to mention the importance of doing our work in person. I and several other members . . . All right. Again, before I discuss the topic of today's hearing, I just did want to talk about the importance of doing our work in person. I and several other members are here in the hearing room. Leader McCarthy had recently written in a letter to Speaker Pelosi that our Congress, which is literally a coming together of people and ideas, works best when it happens in person, face to face. And while I know that we've all learned how to Zoom and WebEx and all of this, I really do think that we could be operating here in person. And so I will make the same requests that ranking member Foxx made at the start of our last hearing, which is let's return to Congressional precedent and hold our hearings here in person.

Turning to the topic of today's hearing, COVID-19 certainly has disrupted nearly every aspect of American society, including our higher education. And it was back in early March, University of Washington became the first school to cancel in-person classes. Today, over 1,000 colleges and universities have switched to online-only instruction. From abrupt school closures to remote online learning, students and educators have faced overwhelming challenges during this pandemic, and that's why Congress and the Department of Education took several steps to ease the burden for states, for institutions and for students. The bipartisan CARES Act, which was passed in March, included provisions to help students, schools and state governments cope with the changes wrought by the pandemic.

In addition to regulatory relief measures for students and institutions, the CARES Act provided borrowers with temporary respite from their repayment obligations. Specifically, the legislation requires the secretary to suspend all interest accumulation and monthly payments on federally held student loans through September 30th of this year. Most critically, the CARES Act created and funded the Higher Ed Emergency Relief Fund, which provided billions in direct aid to students in post-secondary education institutions, including the HBCUs and MSIs. But of course, that's not to say our work is done. On the contrary, the pandemic has exposed serious underlying deficiencies in our education system.

Government overreach and unnecessary intervention has contributed to a bloated post-secondary education sector at the expense of students. Tuition and fees have far outpaced inflation for decades. Federal requirements stifle interaction between businesses and college campuses. And unfortunately, rather than innovating, the Democrat's partisan HEROES Act really doubles down on what have been failed policies. This legislation forgives $10,000 of federal and private student loan debt for some borrowers, which really does nothing to combat COVID-19 or lower college costs. I really do recognize that we want to help people struggling to make ends meet, but we have data from the Urban Institute to prove that across-the-board loan forgiveness disproportionally helps high-earning, highly educated individuals.

Many Americans facing the greatest financial strain as a result of the pandemic do not have student loans at all. The bill also launches a socialist takeover of the private student-loan market by forcing private student-loan companies to offer income-driven repayment terms and conditions that are dictated by the federal government. In contrast, Committee Republicans continue to support reforms that strengthen innovation and completion, modernize federal student aid and promote student opportunities. By giving students the tools needed to complete an affordable post-secondary education, we can prepare them to enter the workforce with the skills they need for lifelong success, regardless of their background. However, these reforms won't matter if we don't reopen our nation's schools and businesses safely and responsibly.

We have a duty to lead this country back to the pre-pandemic economic prosperity that benefited millions of hardworking Americans. Congress can help further unleash our nation's economic potential by increasing pathways for Americans to succeed in the 21st century workforce. Specifically, this means permitting colleges and universities to leverage employer expertise, encouraging short-term and stackable credentials, and creating a regulatory framework for new methods of learning like competency-based education. These types of forward-looking reforms have been championed by the Trump administration. Just a few weeks ago, President Trump issued an executive order to prioritize skills-based hiring within the federal government to help strengthen and diversify our workforce.

This action will take our nation's workers and students in a positive direction as we recover from COVID-19, and Congress should follow the administration's lead on this issue. I look forward to hearing from our witnesses today about how we can improve our education system to better meet the needs of students, families and workers. Thank you, Madame Chair.

Chairwoman Davis: Thank you. Thank you, ranking member Smucker. . . It's now my pleasure to introduce our witnesses. First is Dr. Sharon Pierce, PhD, president of Minneapolis Community and Technical College since 2016. Dr. Sharon Pierce has been leading the effort at Minneapolis College to provide transformative student experiences. Dr. Pierce has dedicated her career to advancing the role of community and technical colleges in reducing disparities and providing underrepresented students with an opportunity to achieve academic success. Prior to her higher education career, Dr. Pierce worked as a clinical nurse for 12 years and was appointed by Maryland's governor to serve on the state's Board of Nursing. She earned her Bachelor's and Master's degree from the University of Maryland and her doctorate degree in urban education from Morgan State University.

Our next witness is Dr. Timothy White, PhD, chancellor of California State University. Since 2013, Dr. White has been leading the California State University, the CSU system, a system comprised of 23 campuses and 481,000 students and 53,000 faculty and staff. Dr. White is a champion of inclusive excellence and student success, and a proponent of bringing individualized education to scale through the expansion of proven best practices. Prior to becoming CSU chancellor, Dr. White served as chancellor and professor of biology and biomedical sciences at the University of California Riverside for five years, and as president of the University of Idaho for four years. Dr. White pursued his higher education from Diablo Valley Community College, Fresno State, CSU East Bay, and the University of California Berkeley.

Next is Scott Pulsipher. I hope I have that right, sir. President of Western Governors University. Since 2016, Scott Pulsipher has served as president of Western Governors University, the nation's first and largest competency-based university. Under his leadership at WGU, WGU has expanded access to online competency-based degree programs that serve students across the country. Prior to joining WGU, Pulsipher gained extensive leadership and experience in technology-based customer-focused businesses including Amazon, Sterling Commerce, which is now part of IBM, and two successful startups. Pulsipher holds a Bachelor's degree from Brigham Young University and a Master's degree from Harvard University.

And last is Dr. Shaun Harper, recognizing [him] as a PhD as well, president of the American Educational Research Association and a provost professor in the Rossier School of Education and Marshall School of Business at the University of Southern California at USC. Dr. Harper is also the Clifford and Betty Allen Chair in Urban Leadership, founder and executive director of the USC Race and Equity Center, and a past president of the Association for the Study of Higher Education. For two decades, Harper has studied racial and gender equity in K-12 schools, colleges and university, and corporate context. He has been recognized in Education Week as one of the 10 most influential education professors in the United States. Dr. Harper earned his Bachelor's degree from Albany State University and a Master's and Doctor's degree from Indiana University.

We greatly appreciate the witnesses for participating today and look forward to your testimony. . . . It's now my pleasure to first recognize Dr. Pierce for five minutes. Dr. Pierce.

Dr. Sharon Pierce: Thank you. Chairwoman Davis, ranking members, sub-committee members, thank you for the opportunity to testify today. I'm Sharon Pierce, president of Minneapolis College. My testimony will describe the impact of the global pandemic on community and technical colleges and our students, and the need for Congress to provide additional aid. Our college, located in an urban setting, is the only comprehensive community and technical college in Minneapolis. We serve students who are unlikely to succeed elsewhere, provide an opportunity to complete a credential and elevate their socioeconomic status and ability to contribute to the economy.

Our students face multiple barriers to academic success. COVID-19 put many students out of work, leaving them unable to support family or access transportation or social services, and elevated mental health concerns. Now, they must learn to navigate courses through an online platform, often using a smartphone without reliable internet access, creating difficulty connecting to instructors, classmates, tutors, the library and support services. Our college received 2.3 million in CARES funding for direct student aid. The guidance for this funding was difficult to unravel, and distribution plans needed frequent revising, resulting in more than two weeks delay in disbursement. Ongoing eligibility rulemaking by the Department of Education created uncertainty and limited our ability to direct aid to the most at-risk students.

In response to COVID-19, we transitioned over 900 classes to alternative re-mote delivery. Moving forward, technology investments need to be at the forefront of decision-making. Students need hardware or software, network access, training and more. Faculty, especially in career and technical programs, need training to advance their pedagogy using alternative delivery in synchronous and asynchronous format. Equitable access to education can only be achieved by ensuring students have the technology tools they need within their academics and receive support services whether they are on campus or working remotely. To provide a safer campus, we need to invest in facilities upgrades, including contactless hardware, additional cleaning supplies, personal protective equipment, and to engineer facilities to allow for physical distancing. We will continue to reallocate and reduce expenditures as part of our effort to survive potentially significant revenue losses.

Moving forward, students who already face significant barriers must navigate and new economic reality. Additional funding from the federal government providing direct aid to students impacted by COVID-19 will support their continuous enrollment and aid the economic recovery of our nation. In addition, the importance of ongoing federal stabilization . . . [to] operating costs of institutions like ours during this trying time cannot be overstated. While the CARES Act provided badly needed stabilization funding, more assistance is vital for us to continue to effectively serve our students, provide remote learning and prepare to safely reopen our campus. According to recent estimates, community colleges could face a collective revenue reduction of $10 billion over the next year. We want to stress the importance of using a student head count based formula to allocate future federal stabilization funding to institutions of higher education. This will allow us to account for the needs of all of our students, including those who attend part-time. Thank you for replacing the CARES Act formula with a head-based formula in the recently passed HEROES Act.

We appreciate your recognition that part-time students need access to the same resources as their full-time peers. We are committed to providing access to the transformative power of education, regardless of socioeconomic status. As the nation strives to recover from COVID-19, higher education will be a critical component of rebuilding the economy. Your unprecedented level of commitment to education is needed now, as your decisions will directly influence students' ability to achieve their academic goals and support the viability of communities. Thank you.

Chairwoman Davis: Thank you, Dr. Pierce. Now, Dr. White, I look forward to hearing from you.

Dr. Timothy White: Okay. Great. Chair Davis, ranking member Smucker and members of the subcommittee, thank you for providing me the opportunity to address you today. For those who may be unfamiliar with the California State University, we are the nation's largest and most diverse four-year university system: 23 campuses, more than 480,000 students and approximately 53,000 faculty and staff. One out of every 20 Americans with a college degree is a graduate of the California State University. Over half of our students are students of color, and one in three are the first in their family to attend college. 54% of our enrolled students, 230,000 of them, are Pell Grant recipients, and just last year alone, 63,000 of those Pell recipients earned their Bachelor's degree. This dynamic diversity, together with our sheer size, and the quality of our academic programs makes us one of America's most powerful drivers of socioeconomic ascent.

Our response to the COVID-19 pandemic has been guided by twin North stars: safeguarding the health and wellbeing of our students, faculty, staff, and the communities we serve; and maintaining our students' progress to degree. In March, the CSU made the massive pivot to virtual instruction, transitioning over 70,000 classes, together with academic and student support services, to virtual modalities. We've taken great care to mitigate the pandemic's impacts to our students, especially our most vulnerable. Measures include maintaining on campus housing and essential services for students who had nowhere else to call home, distributing thousands of laptops and tablets and offering safe WI-Fi hotspots to help address the digital divide, continuing to meet our students' basic needs with no contact food distribution and emergency housing services for students who are food and housing insecure. Campus counseling services are offered virtually, serving students presenting with a variety of mental health issues during the crisis, and providing necessary flexibility around academic policies for current students and adjusting admission policies to mitigate hardships to perspective students and their families.

We're extremely grateful for the more than $563 million in financial relief provided to our students and campuses through the CARES Act. Because Education Department guidance limited eligibility for CARES Act emergency grants, we have augmented those funds with campus resources so that all of our students in need due to COVID-19, including DACA students and international students, could receive much needed financial emergency support. Informed by the guidance of scientific and medical experts, along with public health officials, we are planning for a primarily virtual fall with exceptions for critical in-person experiences that can be conducted within rigorous standards of health and safety.

As we plan for the fall and beyond, the CSU confronts a grim new fiscal reality. Our campus has faced soaring costs and mounting revenue losses associated with the pandemic, putting our students' wellbeing and success at significant risk. The recently passed California budget cuts our appropriation by $299 million, 4.2% of our operating budget, unless additional federal relief funds are forthcoming. So I ask for additional support and investment during this historic public health crisis, I believe so on behalf of the nation's largest and most diverse student body. Keeping these students, students from all walks of life enrolled and graduating with a high quality degree not only benefits them, their families and communities, it is also a vital public good for the nation.

Supporting higher education at this critical moment, stimulates employment for hundreds of thousands of Americans now and into the future, spurring tax revenue while reducing reliance on social services. America, for the economic recovery, will require an increasingly nimble educated workforce. We need culturally competent problem-solvers, comfortable and capable in the sciences and technology, climate literate, and inspired to lead the world to a sustainable future. We need them to ensure a vigorous American economy in the changing world of work, and we need them for a vibrant and more equitable society. We stand ready to be a resource as you continue to explore ways to support higher education. Thank you again for the opportunity to address you today, and I'm happy to answer any questions that you might have.

Chairwoman Davis: Thank you. Thank you, Dr. White. Now I recognize Mr. Pulsipher for five minutes. Thank you for being with us, sir.

Mr. Scott Pulsipher: Chairwoman Davis, ranking member Smucker and members of the subcommittee, thank you for this opportunity to share my views on the impact of COVID-19 on the future of higher education. At WGU, we are compelled by our belief in the inherent worth and ability of every individual and in the transformative power of education. We believe that the pathways to opportunities should be open to everyone. WGU is a private nonprofit self-sustaining institution founded in 1997 by a bipartisan group of 19 governors who saw the opportunity to use technology and competency-based education to expand access to higher education and better align with workforce needs. Today, we serve over 120,000 full-time students in all 50 States, over 70% of whom would be classified in one or more underserved categories. We deliver affordable, relevant, high quality programs combined with a student-centered instructional model entirely online, and that propels students towards completion, great jobs and opportunity.

Recent months have seen life upended for every American, and particularly for the nearly 20 million students enrolled in higher education. There are immediate and persistent challenges, students have acute needs for material support to stay on their path to opportunity, and we need to ensure access to the online world in which learning now takes place. Over 21 million Americans, disproportionately people of color, do not have sufficient bandwidth to stream this hearing, take part in our civic life, access education or participate in the digital workforce. There are also many anxious questions about the fall semester. But students also need us to look well beyond the fall and address strategic questions facing American higher education.

Higher education entered the pandemic with preexisting conditions: rapidly escalating costs, widening disconnect with workforce needs, crushing student debts, unacceptable racial disparities and outcomes, and low completion rates. Now the sector is in the throes of technology-driven disruption, irreversibly accelerated by COVID-19. Near-term issues are certainly pressing, whether safely reopening campuses, enabling institutions' online shift, or the protection of displaced students due to potential closures. We must reestablish the purpose and mission of post-secondary education and modernize the way we invest in it. We must embrace the technology-first approach to teaching and supporting students. We must move swiftly and radically to not only get the 20 million currently enrolled students back on their path to completion, but also upskill many of the 40-plus million Americans who have been displaced during the pandemic and the tens of millions more whose work is being reshaped by technology. That simply, we need to reimagine post-secondary education as a true lifelong model, providing high quality relevant pathways to both an individual's first and next opportunities. Even short-term support and accommodation should be designed and prioritized with the long term in mind.

The written testimony I've submitted includes various policy ideas that I believe address many of the challenges our country and its students faced as a result of COVID-accelerated shifts. Its policy ideas are based on a few simple guiding principles. First, students should be prioritized over institutions. Second, student outcomes matter more than institutional inputs and learning or mastery rather than time should be the critical denominator of education.

In the 1930s, our nation responded to a great economic crisis by passing the New Deal. In the 1940s, facing an unprecedented need for education as young soldiers returned from war hungry for opportunity, Congress opened the door to direct federal investment in higher education by passing the GI Bill. In the 1960s, facing widespread protests and social unrest and response to structural racism, we saw a wave of legislation around civil rights. Today we find ourselves at the intersection of several similar, great forces. We face a significant economic challenge, have an unprecedented need for education in threatening the future workforce, and sadly continue to grapple with inequities which have been both exposed and widened by the pandemic.

We're living in unprecedented times, times that demand our best thinking, new frameworks, and smart investment. Congress can renew the pathway to opportunity for every American. We need landmark legislation on education and work, a new approach that can meet the challenges of this moment and the future that follows it, that is designed for the digital and information age, and that can fundamentally modernize our approach to investing in and unlocking the potential of every individual. Thank you for the opportunity to be here today and to be of assistance as you take on the critical question facing America's higher education system.

Chairwoman Davis: Thank you very much. Appreciate it. Now recognize Dr. Harper for five minutes.

Dr. Harper: Thank you for including me in this important hearing. It is imperative that we devote serious attention to the numerous racial equity consequences of reopening campuses. I present 10 considerations in the written version of my testimony. I will talk only about nine of them here as the one pertaining to student visas and travel bans is outside the purview of this subcommittee.

Here are nine critical racial equity considerations. One, disproportionately placing essential workers at risk. Custodians, food service professionals, and maintenance workers will inevitably be deemed essential workers when campuses reopen. Professionals of color are disproportionately performing these roles. Being required to come to campus and interact with other workers and students, places employees of color and the family members with whom they live at greater risk of exposure to COVID-19. Campus reopening plans must consider the health implications of employees of color and lower-income essential workers. Federal aid specifically earmarked for the safety of employees who are deemed as central workers would help institutions provide PPE cleaning supplies, contact tracing, and testing.

Two, the racialization of layoffs and terminations. Financial effects of the pandemic will force higher education leaders to make tough workforce reduction decisions. Inattention to the race of the persons being terminated and laid off will inevitably yield pronounced negative effects on employees of color given the low-level service positions they disproportionately occupy. Hence, campus reopening plans must specify ways to avoid even more significant racialized employment inequities. Federal investments would help minimize the necessity workforce reductions at higher education institutions.

Three, risk of violence for Asian American and Asian international students and employees. Recent studies documented horrifying acts of discrimination and physical violence toward Asian Americans and Asian immigrants in the US throughout the pandemic. Thus, reopening plans must include ways to protect these students and employees as they return to campuses so our trauma and grief support for persons disproportionately experiencing loss. COVID-19 deaths are disproportionately affecting communities of color. Because of this, students of color and employees of color from these groups are likelier than their white counterparts to have lost a family member, friend, or someone in their community. Reopening plans must include ways to ensure these persons have more than adequate mental and emotional support resources.

Four, trauma and great support for persons disproportionately experiencing loss. COVID-19 deaths are disproportionately affecting communities of color. Because of this communities of color and employees of color are more likely than their white counterparts to have lost a family member, friend, or someone in their community. The reopening plan must include ways to ensure these persons have more than adequate mental and emotional support.

Five, sending infected students home to vulnerable families and communities. Many institutions plan conclude on campus living and learning by Thanksgiving in anticipation of a possible second wave of the coronavirus. Given the disproportionately higher numbers of COVID-19 infections and deaths among people of color, it is plausible that students of color returning home from college could pose an especially big risk to communities that have already been disproportionately devastated by COVID-19.

Six, placing black football and men's basketball players at disproportionately higher risk. In 2018, black men were 2.4% of undergraduates enrolled at universities that make up the five most financially lucrative intercollegiate sports conferences, yet they comprise 55% of football teams and 56% of men's basketball teams on those campuses. Thus, participation in these two contact sports places black undergraduate men at disproportionate risk of COVID-19 infection.

Seven, financial support for chronically underfunded minority-serving institutions. Investing significant federal COVID-19 recovery funds specifically into historically black colleges and universities, tribal colleges, and community colleges would help them better serve the low income Americans they disproportionately educate, most of whom were students of color.

Eight, addressing racialized digital access inequities. As we have seen throughout the pandemic, low income students lack access to reliable high speed internet. Many of them are students of color. As institutions consider reopening in phases with the fraction of courses meeting on campus and others online, plans must include strategies and investments in closing digital access gaps for students of color who continue to access courses from their homes in lower income communities.

And ninth, upskilling faculty members in teaching students of color online. Faculty development activities included in campus reopening cannot focus just on creating teaching tricks to keep all students . . . . They must also pay attention to ensuring that students of color are not experiencing the same racism in virtual classrooms that they experienced in on campus learning environments long before the pandemic. Thank you.

Chairwoman Davis: Thank you, Dr. Harper. We appreciate all of you.

Print Citations

CMS: Davis, Susan, Floyd K. Smucker, Sharon Pierce, Timothy White, Scott Pulsipher, and Shaun Harper. "Hearing on COVID-19's Impact on the Future of Higher Education." Hearing at the U.S. House of Representatives, Washington, DC, July 7, 2020. In *The Reference Shelf: Representative American Speeches, 2019-2020,* edited by Annette Calzone, 39-49. Amenia, NY: Grey House Publishing, 2020.

MLA: Davis, Susan, Floyd K. Smucker, Sharon Pierce, Timothy White, Scott Pulsipher, and Shaun Harper. "Hearing on COVID-19's Impact on the Future of Higher Education." U.S. House of Representatives, Washington, DC, 7 July 2020, Washington, DC. Hearing. *The Reference Shelf: Representative American Speeches, 2019-2020,* edited by Annette Calzone, Grey House Publishing, 2020, pp. 39-49.

APA: Davis, S., Smucker, F. K., Pierce, S., White, T., Pulsipher, S., & Harper, S. (2020, July 7). Hearing on COVID-19's impact on the future of higher education. U.S. House of Representatives, Washington, DC. In Annette Calzone (Ed.), *The reference shelf: Representative American speeches, 2019-2020* (pp. 39-49). Amenia, NY: Grey House Publishing.

TikTok, Dr. Fauci, and COVID-19 Relief

By Donald Trump

Donald Trump delivered a speech in August touching on many major topics, including a TikTok ban, the efficacy of hydroxychloroquine as a treatment for COVID-19, the progress of the pandemic, and the Democratic Party's involvement in the holdup of the second stimulus package, once again insisting that the mainstream media was misreporting on his administration.

Donald Trump: It [TikTok] can't be controlled for security reasons by China, too big, too invasive, and it can't be. Here's the deal. I don't mind whether it's Microsoft or somebody else, a big company, a secure company, a very American company buy it. It's probably easier to buy the whole thing than to buy 30% of it. Because I say, how do you do 30%, who's going to get the name? The name is hot. The brand is hot. Who's going to get the name? How do you do that if it's owned by two different companies? So my personal opinion was, you're probably better off buying the whole thing rather than buying 30% of it. I think buying 30% is complicated.

I suggested that he can go ahead. He can try. We set a date. I set a date of around September 15th, at which point it's going to be out of business in the United States. But if somebody, and whether it's Microsoft or somebody else buys it, that'll be interesting. I did say that if you buy it, whatever the price is, that goes to whoever owns it, because I guess it's China essentially, but more than anything else. I said a very substantial portion of that price is going to have to come into the Treasury of the United States because we're making it possible for this deal to happen. Right now, they don't have any rights unless we give it to them. So if we're going to give them the rights, then it has to come into this country.

It's a little bit like the landlord-tenant. Without a lease, the tenant has nothing. They pay what's called key money or they pay something. But the United States should be reimbursed or should be paid a substantial amount of money. Because without the United States, they don't have anything, at least having to do with the 30%. So I told him that.

Maybe a deal is going to be made. It's a great asset. It's a great asset, but it's not a great asset in the United States unless they have the approval of the United States. So it'll close down on September 15th unless Microsoft or somebody else is able to buy it and work out a deal, an appropriate deal. Really, the Treasury, I guess you would say, of the United States gets a lot of money, a lot of money. Okay?

Delivered on August 3, 2020, at the White House, Washington, DC.

Speaker 2: Mr. President,

Speaker 3: Mr. President!

Speaker 2: … can you explain why so many of the public health experts on the Coronavirus Task Force are contradicting you on things like why the virus has been widespread in this country, on the efficacy of hydroxychloroquine? Why are so many of these people on your task force contradicting you?

Donald Trump: Well, I think we're doing a great job. I think we're doing great on vaccines. We're doing great on therapeutics. You'll be seeing that very soon. When you look at a map, this is a map of the … I've sort of shown that around a little bit. The red is the area of most concern. It's a pretty recent map of the country. There's a lot of people in a lot of areas that have gotten better very fast.

Hydroxy has tremendous support; but politically, it's toxic because I supported it. If I would have said, "Do not use hydroxychloroquine under any circumstances," they would have come out and they would have said, "It's a great thing." Many doctors have come out strongly in favor of it. They want it very badly. It's a great malaria drug. . . .

Donald Trump: Let me finish my answer. It's, I guess, 60 years it's been a malaria drug. Very successful, as you know. It's been also a drug for lupus. It's caused no trouble, virtually nothing in terms of causing people to get sick or having problems with anything. You add the zinc and you add the azithromycin, the Z-Pak as they call it, and it's been very … I happen to take it myself, the threesome. I took it myself for a period of two weeks. I had no problem. I had no problem whatsoever. Importantly, I didn't test positive. That's very nice. I'm very happy about that negative. That's the story. It's very highly thought of.

Interestingly, a great doctor, from what I understand, a great doctor from Yale feels very strongly about hydroxychloroquine. The Ford Clinic in Michigan came out with a very, very powerful paper saying it's very good. In France, as you know, they came out with a very positive statement. Many individual doctors have come out with very positive statements. I will tell you that if I was surrounded by people, as I was at the time, the reason I took it, we had some people that were relatively near me that tested positive. I took it for that reason just because I've heard good things.

Speaker 2: But Fauci says it doesn't work. Dr. Weil says it doesn't work.

Donald Trump: Well, I don't agree with Fauci on everything.

Speaker 2: Your own task force . . .

Donald Trump: I don't agree with Fauci. I like him. I get along with him actually great. But he didn't want to ban people from China from coming into the country, and I overrode him and I did the right thing. He was saying face masks are no good a short while ago. It doesn't mean he's a bad person, because he's not. He's a good person. I like him. But we disagree on things. We disagree on things.

Now I will say this, we've done an amazing job with ventilators. We're supplying the world with ventilators. Ventilators are very hard, very expensive, very hard to make, very complex, very complicated machines. Very, very expensive.

Speaker 2: Well, why does the—

Donald Trump: Hold it, hold it.

Speaker 2: Well, why does the US have so many deaths?

Donald Trump: Hold it.

Speaker 2: The US has so many deaths compared to so—

Donald Trump: Hold it.

Speaker 2: … many countries around the world.

Donald Trump: Fake news, CNN. Hold it. We have done a great job in this country. Not me. I'm not talking about me. Vice President and the task force have not been given the kind of credit. If you look, countries all over the world are exploding right now. People that you said were doing a wonderful job, so wonderful; but right now, take a look at the countries that are exploding. You have Italy back, you have Spain back, you have France back, you have Germany back. You have a lot of countries, and that's not to knock them. It is a very delicate, very contagious disease.

It was released by China. It should never have been allowed to release. There was the source where you could have stopped it, and they did stop it from going into China. Although now, they say that China is having a lot of problems. Moscow in Russia is having tremendous problems. What China unleashed was a very, very sad situation.

With all of that being understood, the United States has done an amazing job, a great job. You're going to see that because we have vaccines and we have therapeutics coming very soon.

Yeah, go ahead.

Speaker 4: Mr. President, why are you not involved directly in negotiations with Capitol Hill?

Donald Trump: I am. . . Why? The fact that I'm not over there with Crazy Nancy? No, I'm totally involved. . . . I'm totally involved. We're going to be doing some things that are very good because we don't think that she … Look, what Chuck Schumer wants more than anybody, and I would say Nancy Pelosi would be second, they want to bail out cities and states that have done a bad job over a long period of time. Nothing to do with coronavirus or China virus or whatever you want to call it. They want to bail out cities and states. They want bailout money. They want a trillion dollars in bailout money. A lot of people don't want to do that because we don't think it's right. The Democrats have run some very bad states and some very, very bad cities, and a lot of people don't want to give them a trillion dollars to reward them for doing a bad job.

If you look at some of the states, I won't insult anybody by naming those states, but you know what they are. They want bailout money. They're not interested in the people. They're not interested in unemployment. They're not interested in evictions, which is a big deal. The evictions, they want to evict. A lot of people are going to be evicted. But I'm going to stop it because I'll do it myself if I have to. I have a lot of powers with respect to executive orders. We're looking at that very seriously right now.

But what the Democrats want, they're slow rolling it. All they're really interested in is bailout money to bail out radical left governors and radical left mayors, like in Portland and places that are so badly run. Chicago, New York City. You see what's going on over there? Bail out cities and states who have been poorly run and spent a fortune doing it. They want a trillion dollars, and we're really not interested in that. Okay, thank you very much, everybody. Thank you. Thank you very much.

Speaker 5: Let's go, guys. Let's go. Let's go.

Donald Trump: Thank you very much.

Speaker 5: Come on, gentlemen.

Donald Trump: Thank you, Jim, very much.

Donald Trump: Thank you.

Speaker 5: Thank you.

Donald Trump: Thank you very much. You're doing a great job. Even Sarah's afraid of you.

Speaker 5: All right, come on guys.

Donald Trump: Sarah's afraid of you. Sarah's afraid of nobody.

Print Citations

CMS: Trump, Donald. "Tik Tok, Dr. Fauci, and COVID-19 Relief." Speech at the White House, Washington, DC, August 3, 2020. In *The Reference Shelf: Representative American Speeches, 2019-2020,* edited by Annette Calzone, 50-53. Amenia, NY: Grey House Publishing, 2020.

MLA: Trump, Donald. "Tik Tok, Dr. Fauci, and COVID-19 Relief." The White House, 3 August 2020, Washington, DC. Speech. *The Reference Shelf: Representative American Speeches, 2019-2020,* edited by Annette Calzone, Grey House Publishing, 2020, pp. 50-53.

APA: Trump, D. (2020, August 3). Tik Tok, Dr. Fauci, and COVID-19. The White House, Washington, DC. In Annette Calzone (Ed.), *The reference shelf: Representative American speeches, 2019-2020* (pp. 50-53). Amenia, NY: Grey House Publishing.

COVID-19 Response

By Anthony Fauci

National Institute of Allergy and Infectious Diseases Director Dr. Anthony Fauci participated in a discussion at Washington National Cathedral on the fall spike in COVID cases, the overall coronavirus response and the promise of a vaccine by the end of the year. Fauci discussed the politicization of science and the need to continue to reach out to people to convince them to vaccinate while at the same time keeping up other public health measures like wearing a mask and social distancing. Fauci also talked about strengthening the Global Health Security Network to help in managing global pandemics.

Dr. Anthony Fauci: My job as the director of the NAH Institute and as a public health official is to focus entirely on what my mission and goal is, to use science and health to preserve the health, safety, and welfare of the American people regardless of what the administration is. You know, and many people know, that I have had the privilege of serving six presidents since I became director of the NIAID in 1984. That is what we focus on as scientists. I know we are living in a charged political environment, but that is not primary for us. We continue to do our job to foster public health, but also to do the science that leads to the things like the vaccine. . . . That is what I focus on. When you hear those things in the newspapers, many people think I get shook back and forth by that. To be honest with you, I don't.

[The politicization of science] is what we have seen a lot in the United States, but not just restricted to the United States, because we are also seeing it with my colleagues in the U.K. and in Europe and in other regions of the world. I don't think there is a simple explanation for it, but I think there has been an anti-authority component to this. We had anti-vax, people don't like to be told to be vaccinated. Scientists are often perceived as authoritarian. And sometimes they made that perception themselves by the way they act also. I think we can improve on that. But right now it has been just lumped into the politics of what is going on. We live in a divisive society, and even if we didn't have a pandemic, it would be a divisive society. And the fact that we do have a pandemic, and a pandemic is a public health issue and public health is intimately related to science, . . . all of a sudden science gets caught in a lot of this divisiveness. That is unfortunate. What we as the scientists hope . . . that when we get past this, science will resume its rightful place in being something that is for everyone without divisions. . . .

Delivered on November 12, 2020, at the Washington National Cathedral, Washington, DC.

When we get out of the charged nature of the stress and strain put upon us by an outbreak, people will realize the importance of science. Data speaks for itself. We are in a very difficult situation. It is quite problematic. I have said that many times not to scare people, but to bring a reality check to where we are. If you look at it, we have 10 million infections in the United States, almost 250,000 deaths. We have had 60,000 hospitalizations. Now last count we had 143,000 infections in a single day. When I testified—143,000 infections in a single day. When I testified before Congress, people thought I was being hyperbolic. Now look what is happening. That is the bad news. I think . . . the encouraging news that people need to understand, public health measures—not knocked out of the country, but public health measures that are simple and easy to understand, the universal [mask] wearing, physical distancing, avoiding crowded places, outdoors better than indoors, washing hands, it sounds simple in the context of this ominous outbreak, but it can turn it around, and that is what we need to do.

I wouldn't say [the country's response] is horribly wrong. I think what we have not done, and it is not just the United States—if you look at what is going on in Europe and the U.K. now, they are, in many respects, in the same boat as we are with major surges. But when you look at what happened in our own country, we did not act in a unified way. I always say one of the wonderful things about our country, that I love so much, is that we are the United States of America. And we are a federalist country, and we have states that are independent, and . . . in some respects [it is] important that they are that way. However, when you are dealing with an infectious disease, the infectious disease does not know the difference of the border between Mississippi and Louisiana, or between Florida and Georgia and South Carolina. An infectious disease means the entire country. We did not approach it that way. We had too much individual approaches towards how we are going to handle the outbreak. Our baseline never came down to the local level that we wanted it to be, so when community spread came in as we tried to open the country, it just soared right out. It is a self-propagating issue because the more community spread we get, the more difficult it is to contain it by identification, isolation, and contact tracing, because there is so much of it going on that it becomes very difficult. That is the problem we are in right now. We have an enormous amount of community spread.

Models are as good as the assumption we put into the model. I have been one to challenge models—not challenge the validity of the modeling process, but to challenge the assumptions that are put into it. If we all literally pushed together as a group and did it in a uniform way, we do not necessarily need to see the 1,000 to 1,300 desperate day. We don't need to see the 140,000 infections per day. We can turn it around. If we stay the way we are, you do the civil math. 1,000 deaths a day and 140,000 cases a day. You multiply it by 31 days in December, two weeks left in November. By the time you get to January 1, we have a really bad situation. So what I am saying as a public health official, and as my colleagues say, we don't need to accept that. I want to make one point that is important. . . . One of the things about a vaccine which is really important, not only in and of itself as being a tool that is essential to end this outbreak. When people know that help is on the way—and what I mean by help is on the way is we will start giving vaccines in December, and then as we get into January, February, March, we get the prioritization of the people who need it the most—that there is light at the end of the tunnel, I hope we can get over what we call COVID fatigue, where people are so exhausted with the public health measures that they really feel like they want to either give up and say let's do what you want to do, which is not the time to do that now. Now we need to double down on the public health measures as we are waiting for the vaccine to come and help us out.

I think it is pretty clear when you see congregate settings where people are gathered indoors without a mask, there is no doubt that—we have seen that with the Sturgis Rally, [a] number of other situations. We have seen it in clear-cut examples of people getting together in a congregate away, particularly indoors, where you trace after that, there is clear outbreaks.

If you look at infectious diseases in general, what you need to get society protected, you need a certain number of people who are protected because they are immune to the virus. There are a couple of ways to do that. One way is very painful, that everybody gets infected. That leads to a lot of deaths. That is an unacceptable way to get this fire under control. The other way is to have a highly effective vaccine that the vast majority of the population takes. So in other words, if you have a 50%, 60% effective vaccine, even if the majority take it, there is a large segment of the population that is not immune. But we are fortunate, because the first one out of the gate is more than 90%, probably close to 95% effective. What we are hoping is that those who have vaccine hesitancy, who are skeptical about a vaccine, will see that the efficacy of this is so high that they may change their mind about wanting to get vaccinated. The other part of the good news is that there are other vaccines, some that are almost identical, such as the Moderna product, which will be evaluated in the next week to a few days, that we anticipate, though you never want to get ahead of yourself, that it will be as good or close to that. That is the case, we have two of them. We have the capability—what science has done in an unprecedented way—if this were 15 or 20 years ago, it would have taken a few years to get to where we are now. The idea that you went from a recognition of the virus on July 9 with the sequence to a phase-one trial literally 60-some-odd days later to a phase-three trial a few months later to a vaccine that will be getting to people next month is extraordinary. I have been doing this for 40 years, and this is really extraordinary. But as extraordinary as it is, what we don't want people to do is to say, "Oh, we have a vaccine out, we are done." We are not done. We still need to implement public health measures in a very intense way.

The standard thing that happens when you have a vaccine that is not readily available to everyone at once is . . . prioritization. That is the responsibility of the Centers for Disease Control and Prevention, the CDC. They rely heavily on an Advisory Committee on Immunization Practices, ACIP. The CDC makes the ultimate—this year we complemented that by asking the National Academy of Medicine to also weigh in. I'm not going to get ahead of their decision, but likely it will be frontline workers like health-care workers who are taking care of individuals, people who have underlying conditions that make them susceptible to a severe outcome were they to get infected, people in nursing homes, people with underlying conditions, . . . then children in schools, adults, teachers in schools, fundamental people who are responsible for making society run in an orderly way. That is the kind of prioritization you get. We hope by the time we get into the second quarter of 2021, we will have enough vaccine that we will progressively vaccinate people so that when we get to April, May, June, we will get people in the general population starting to get vaccines.

You have to continually outreach . . . and do what we call community engagement. There will be a core of people who will not take a vaccine [no] matter what you do. I don't think you should give up on them, but I don't think you should necessarily expect. But there was a larger group of people who probably just have misinformation and don't understand the process. And what we have been trying to do—myself, Dr. [Francis] Collins, and others—we have been trying to explain clearly what the process is of making a decision that a vaccine is safe and effective. It is an orderly process, it is done by independent groups that have no allegiance to an administration or a company or to anyone. They make that decision. They look at the data and determine, is it safe and effective. Then there are letters of advisory committees, the career scientists at the FDA that I trust, the scientists like myself and Dr. Collins who will be looking at the data. There will be a very transparent process. I don't think people who are anti-vax fully appreciate how transparent the process is. They think there is something hidden and people are trying to put something over on them. We need to reach out to them and make them realize that is not the case, and it is to their benefit and the benefit of society to get vaccinated.

I think that would be quite problematic, and it would not be good for the country in general, because if you really want to essentially crush, that word they use, an outbreak, to get the level of transmission so low that it is no longer a public health problem, if you have 50% of the people who don't get vaccinated, there is a lot of infection that is going to be going around the community. If you get a 90, 95% effective vaccine, and 80% of the population get vaccinated, you have an umbrella of protection already that the virus has no place to go. It would be looking for vulnerable people and not finding it. That is when it goes way down and it is no longer a threat. If 50% of the people don't want to get vaccinated, it is going to take quite a while to get to that point.

There is a lot we don't know, and we have to be humble that we have learned an extraordinary amount in the last 10 months, but there is a lot we do not know. That is the reason why the study, the cohorts, the research we are doing is going to be going on for quite a while even after we have the outbreak under control.

At this point in time we don't know the durability of infection. If you get infected and recover, it is likely that for a finite period of time you are protected. You have seen that is the case for what we have seen [in] specific instances of reinfection—people who got infected, recovered, and got infected with another SARS COV-2. We don't know how extensive that is going to be. Even though antibodies are in a lot of people who recover, . . . we don't know what is related to production and how long that lasts. We don't want to scare people to think, "Oh my god, I got infected and I will get infected again." Unlikely. But what we have a lot to learn is what the durability of protection is. The one thing I can say as an infectious disease person is it is very unlikely it will be like measles. I got infected by measles as a child. I'm sure you did also. The fact is you are protected essentially for life. It likely is not of that magnitude, because what we know about the common cold coronavirus is, that keeps reinfecting people. We feel like that it is measured in several months to a year or more, but it doesn't look like it is going to be 20, 30 years. Which means people need to get vaccinated even if they have been infected before, which we think is going to happen, and it is conceivable but not absolute that you may need to boost people every once in a while after the vaccine, which is fine. . . .

Pandemic outbreaks over history have occurred before even recorded history, before understanding what a pathogen is. They have occurred in our own lifetime. Within the memory of some people, 1918 was a disaster for the world with the flu pandemic. You have seen outbreaks, some of which have been trivial, some of which have had a major impact. Right now this is the most serious outbreak that we have had on this planet in 102 years. Will it happen again? Yes. Will it happen 10, 15, 20 years from now? We don't know. The thing about outbreaks are they are unpredictable. As scientists . . . you likely cannot prevent the emergence of a new microbe, but you can prevent that emergence from becoming a catastrophic pandemic. That is what we mean by pandemic preparedness, to prevent the inevitable emergence of microbes. As long as we have an interface with the animal world, 75% of all the new pathogens that emerged have jumped from an animal species to a human—they were zoonotic and they jumped to a human. That will continue to happen. The question and the challenge for us is, are we prepared enough so it doesn't become a catastrophic outbreak. . . .

There are a number of things we can do. We have got to think globally. Pandemics are global, so we have to pull together globally. There is a thing called the Global Health Security Network or agenda that was established several years ago. We need to strengthen that. We need to strengthen our international collaborations. We need to have people speaking to each other. It has got to be open and transparent. When you do that, you can detect it early and respond early. Scientific approaches, technologies, are going to allow us to do what we did with this outbreak and rapidly make a vaccine. We can do even better than that, but you can't do science alone. It has got to be public health and classic science. . . .

Right now it seems like every country is suffering. We are often compared with countries that are not comparable to us. We are not a little island of 5 million people that we can shut off. We are not a country that would accept if a ruler tells us "You must do this." I was talking with our U.K. colleagues just today who were saying the U.K. is similar to where we are now in outbreak because each of our countries have an independent spirit, we don't want to be told what to do. Well, I understand that, but now is the time to do what you are told. [laughter] . . .

I believe you have to be sensitive to distress and restraint of lockdowns. The economic and psychological consequences. I do not believe at this point that we do need to lock down. We have to leave that on the table. We are not going to just push it off the table. I don't think we need to do it, because my experience is that when you as a group, as a nation, implement the public health measures I mentioned to you, we can turn this around without locking the country down. . . .

No, [herd immunity is not a viable strategy]. . . . It just is not. I don't want to disrespect any of those who feel that way from that is their opinion, but it is just not the case. If you look now, 25% will say some of the people of this country [that] got hit badly in New York are immune. 10% of the country as a whole. The CDC did a very good study and said 10% of the people in the country have gotten infected and are therefore protected. We have 245,000 to 250,000 deaths and 10 million infections. You were not going to get to herd immunity until you get to 70 or so percent. Now, if you want to go from 10 to 70, multiply that by seven and look at the number of people who will have to have died to get to natural herd immunity. It is not feasible and it is not acceptable.

Print Citations

CMS: Fauci, Anthony. "COVID-19 Response." Speech at the Washington National Cathedral, Washington, DC, November 12, 2020. In *The Reference Shelf: Representative American Speeches, 2019-2020,* edited by Annette Calzone, 54-59. Amenia, NY: Grey House Publishing, 2020.

MLA: Fauci, Anthony. "COVID-19 Response." The Washington National Cathedral, 12 November 2020, Washington, DC. Speech. *The Reference Shelf: Representative American Speeches, 2019-2020,* edited by Annette Calzone, Grey House Publishing, 2020, pp. 54-59.

APA: Fauci, A. (2020, November 12). COVID-19 Response. The Washington National Cathedral, Washington, DC. In Annette Calzone (Ed.), *The reference shelf: Representative American speeches, 2019-2020* (pp. 54-59). Amenia, NY: Grey House Publishing.

3
A Year of Social Unrest

Photo by harris.senate.gov/news

Vice President-elect Kamala Harris announced a stronger version of the Justice in Policing Act in November 2020 and has made police reform one of her top priorities.

The George Floyd and Black Lives Matter Protests

By London Breed

San Francisco Mayor London Breed expressed her grief over the death of George Floyd and her support for the Black Lives Matter movement, calling for an end to deadly force by police against black individuals. She also rebuked people who were trying to latch on to the BLM movement to incite violence or for their own purposes, insisting that the movement was born out of a need to fight racism in all its forms.

London Breed: First of all, I want to thank everybody that came out today to honor George Floyd's memory. My heart has been heavy. Yes, I'm the mayor, but I'm a black woman first. I'm a black woman first. I grew up in this city. I grew up not too far from here, in public housing. I never thought I'd be mayor, I never thought I'd be in any situation to push for change. But it's been a blessing, and let me tell you why. I grew up at a time where there was a lot of poverty, still is, a lot of violence, still is, a lot of hopelessness and frustration. I still can't believe that I'm mayor. Because the reason why I got involved in public office in the first place, had everything to do with wanting to make sure that I'm the norm and not the exception.

In 2006, sadly, my cousin was killed by the San Francisco Police Department. And at that time there was a lot of anger and hurt. This was my cousin who I grew up with, who I played with, who I kicked it with, who I loved. And when his mom showed up, wanting to know what happened, she was treated like a criminal. There was no independent investigation, and I didn't understand why. I get it, nobody's perfect, but my cousin didn't deserve to die.

And let me tell you, I'm so proud when I served on the board of supervisors that any time in San Francisco, there's an officer involved shooting, there is an automatic investigation. I get it. What I'm seeing is the hurt, and the pain, and the frustration on everybody's face right now. And for African Americans, we've been feeling that hurt and that pain, and that frustration for far too long. We are glad to see other people understanding our hurt, and our pain, and our frustration. And I want to be very clear, I'm in charge of this city, and as a mayor, who's in charge of this city, I will do everything I can to push for the right policies for our law enforcement here in the city, to make sure that what we know has been happening sadly all over this country, doesn't happen in our city. There is nothing more important to me than to do that.

And let me also say another thing. The hate, the frustration born out of this

---

Delivered on June 1, 2020, in San Francisco, California.

movement at this time, think about it. Racism, what's happening in this country is pure and simple, it's racism. What happened to George Floyd is because he was black, what happened to my cousin, because he was black, what happened to the CNN reporter who was arrested, because he was black. And let me tell you, I appreciate all of you for being here, I appreciate those who care and are genuinely concerned. But I want to say one thing. I want to say one thing, Black Lives Matter is nobody's joke. I'm tired of people treating it that way, I'm tired of people masking their racism in Black Lives Matter. It is not a joke, it is not a joke. It is born out of pain, it is born out of racism that we are going to fight against, it is born out of our struggle, our blood, sweat, and tears, for all that we have struggled through in this country. Don't get it twisted, it is not a joke.

So, for those of you who are genuine in this struggle, who are genuine in this struggle, we thank you and we welcome you. But for those of you who are using this movement as a way to push violence, to go after other black people, to tear us down, we will not tolerate that. Don't get it twisted. I am the mayor, but I'm a black woman first. I am angry, I am hurt, I am frustrated, I am sick and tired of being sick and tired. I don't want to see one more black man die at the hands of law enforcement. That's what this movement is about. Not one more, not one more. Not one more, not one more.

And I want to again, appreciate the fact that, yes, we have had a number of challenges around protests, but I understand the spirit of what the protest represents. We got to make sure people understand that we don't want to see this happen again, and we won't sit quietly by, and let it happen again. I understand that. So I know you already did a kneel in, and I want to tell, we got Jamie Foxx in the house, and Reverend Brown is going to introduce him in just a minute. But Jamie, I want to ask you to come out here because it's time to do another kneel in in solidarity. It's time to do another kneel in in solidarity. So everybody, please join me. Let's do it. . . Yes, thank you, thank you, thank you, thank you, thank you. Not one more, not one more, not one more, not one more, not one more, not one more, not one more…

Print Citations

CMS: Breed, London. "The George Floyd and Black Lives Matter Protests." Speech in San Francisco, CA, June 1, 2020. In *The Reference Shelf: Representative American Speeches, 2019-2020*, edited by Annette Calzone, 63-64. Amenia, NY: Grey House Publishing, 2020.

MLA: Breed, London. "The George Floyd and Black Lives Matter Protests." 1 June 2020, San Francisco, CA. Speech. *The Reference Shelf: Representative American Speeches, 2019-2020*, edited by Annette Calzone, Grey House Publishing, 2020, pp. 63-64.

APA: Breed, L. (2020, June 1). Speech on the George Floyd and Black Lives Matter protests. San Francisco, CA. In Annette Calzone (Ed.), *The reference shelf: Representative American speeches, 2019-2020* (pp. 63-64). Amenia, NY: Grey House Publishing.

Congressional Democrats Unveil Police Reform Bill in Press Conference

By Karen Bass, Nancy Pelosi, Chuck Schumer, Steny Hoyer, Cory Booker, and Kamala Harris

Congressional Democrats in June announced the release of a sweeping police reform bill, The Justice in Policing Act, in response to the protests for the killing of George Floyd. The bill would make it easier for victims of abuses to recover damages, create a national registry of police misconduct, ban chokeholds, ban no-knock warrants in drug cases, and more.

Karen Bass: The Justice and Policing Act establishes a bold, transformative vision of policing in America. Never again should the world be subjected to witnessing what we saw on the streets in Minneapolis, the slow murder of an individual by a uniformed police officer. The world is witnessing the birth of a new movement in our country. This movement has now spread to many nations around the world, with thousands marching to register their horror and hearing the cry, "I can't breathe." People marching to demand not just change, but transformative change that ends police brutality, that ends racial profiling, and ends the practice of denying Americans the right to have the ability to sue when they have been injured by an officer, that denies local jurisdictions the power to fire or prosecute offending officers.

Black communities have sadly been marching for over 100 years against police abuse, but for the police to protect and serve our communities like they do elsewhere. In the 1950s, news cameras exposed the brutal horror of legalized racism in the form of segregation. The news cameras of the 1950s exposed the brutal treatment of people who dared to challenge the system. News cameras exposed to the world that black people did not have the same constitutional protections, that freedom of speech, the right to assemble, and protest were not rights extended to African-Americans. 70 years later, it is the cell phone camera that has exposed the continuation of violence directed at African-Americans by the police, and exposed the reality that the right to life, liberty, and the pursuit of happiness is not guaranteed to all African-Americans at all times. Now the movement for police accountability has become a rainbow movement, reflecting the wonderful diversity of our nation in the world. The power of this movement will help move Congress to act, to pass legislation that not only holds police accountable and increases transparency, but assists police departments to change the culture.

Press Conference on June 8, 2020, at the U.S. House of Representatives, Washington, DC.

Now, I know that change is difficult, but I am certain that police officers, professionals who risk their lives every day, are deeply concerned about their profession and do not want to work in an environment that requires their silence when they know a fellow officer's abusing the public. I am certain police officers would like to be free to intervene and stop an officer from using deadly force when it is not necessary. And I am certain that police officers want to make sure they are trained in the best practices in policing. A profession where you have the power to kill should be a profession that requires highly trained officers who are accountable to the public. Embarking on a journey toward a new vision for policing in America is only possible because of the incredible leadership in the House of Representatives. We now have over 200 co-sponsors in the House and the Senate. Speaker Pelosi has said she wants to see a bold transformative effort. And that is exactly what Justice and Policing will do. Join me in welcoming the most powerful woman in Congress and the nation, Madam Speaker Pelosi.

Nancy Pelosi: Thank you very much. Thank you very much, Karen Bass, for your tremendous leadership. Under the leadership of Karen Bass, many of us had the privilege last year of going to Ghana to observe the 400th anniversary of the first slaves going across the Atlantic, America really, there was no United States, but going across the Atlantic. It was a horrible … The kidnapping, the purchase of those slaves, the dungeons in which they were kept. And if they survived that, to be on a slave ship. And if they survived that, to be sold into slavery. And then everything that came from that. When we were in Selma only just in March, we saw at Bryan Stevenson's, one of his museums, a beautiful display, heartbreaking display. But children, little children saying, "Mama? Mama? Has anyone seen our mother?" These children separated from their mothers, the cruelty of that. And that's why when George Floyd called out for his mother when he was subjected to that knee in the neck, it was just a continuation of some horror that has existed in our country for a very long time.

This is Mr. Clyburn, Mr. Hoyer, distinguished leader. Mr. Clyburn, our whip, joined Karen Bass, Leader Schumer, the two senators, leaders on this issue. Congresswoman Harris, Congressman, Senator, did I say Senator? Senator Harris, Senator Booker in the Emancipation Hall, aptly named for those who built the capital of the United States in their honor. We were there for eight minutes and 46 seconds on our knees. My members will attest, it's a very long time. It's a very long time. And I graciously led them in falling over when it was over so that they could do the same thing. But here we are. The martyrdom of George Floyd gave American experience a moment of national anguish as we grieve for the black Americans killed by police brutality. Today, this moment of national anguish is being transformed into a movement of national action as Americans from across the country peacefully protest to demand an end to injustice. Today, with the Justice and Policing Act, the Congress is standing with those fighting for justice and taking action.

Let us, my colleagues, just go over some of those names of martyrdom. George Floyd, Jackson Davis, Oscar Grant. So sad. Breonna Taylor, Ahmoud Arbery, Botham Jean, Terence Crutcher, Philando Castile, Freddie Gray, Walter Scott, Tamir

Rice, Michael Brown, Eric Garner, Trayvon Martin. My colleagues, any other names you want to add?

Speaker 2: Sean Bell.

Nancy Pelosi: Thank you. We cannot settle for anything less than transformative structural change, which is why the Justice and Policing Act will remove barriers of prosecuting police misconduct and covering damages by addressing the quality immunity doctrine. It will demilitarize the police by limiting the transfer of military weaponry to state and local police departments. It will combat police brutality by requiring body and dashboard cameras, banning choke holds, no knock warrants in drug cases, and end racial profiling. We'll finally make lynching, Mr. Hoyer, a federal hate crime. And I support Chairwoman Bass and Representative Bobby Smith and our two distinguished Senators, Harris and Booker, and others for their work in helping to pass H.R.35 this year.

Police brutality is heartbreaking reflection of an entrenched system of racial injustice in America. True justice can only be achieved with full comprehensive action. That's what we are doing today. This is a first step. There is more to come. In the coming weeks, the bill, the House will hold hearings, mark up the bill. Once the House passes it, the Justice and Policing Act, Leader McConnell will, hopefully, he must swiftly take it up. Leader in the Congress, the President must not stand in the way of justice. The Congress in the country will not relent until this legislation is made into law.

My colleague, Mr. Clyburn, is always getting awards for liberty and justice for all. That's what this is about. That's what our distinguished Leader, Mr. Schumer, talked about in Emancipation Hall, and pleased to yield to the distinguished leader in the United States Senate, Democratic Leader, Mr. Schumer. Mr. Schumer.

Chuck Schumer: Thank you. Well, thank you, Speaker Pelosi. And I'm so proud to be joined by so many of my colleagues, Leader Hoyer, Senators Booker and Harris, Representatives Bass, Clyburn, Nadler, and Jeffries for joining us in speaking this morning, and all the support that we have from so many wonderful people behind us. Over the past week, hundreds of thousands of Americans have engaged in peaceful demonstrations against police violence and systemic racism. This large diverse group, so many of them young, gives us hope that Americans are prepared to march and fight to make this a more perfect union once and for all. And so today, we are taking the first of many steps, many necessary steps, to respond to this national pain with bold action.

As my colleagues will explain, the Justice and Policing Act proposes crucial reforms to combat racial violence and excessive force by law enforcement through strong accountability measures, increased data and transparency, and important modifications to police training and practices. This has never been done before at the federal level. In the Senate, Democrats are going to fight like hell to make this a reality. Americans who took to the streets this week have demanded change. With this legislation, Democrats are heeding their calls. Now we must collectively, all Americans, raise our voices and call on Leader McConnell to put this reform bill on the floor of the Senate before July to be debated and voted on.

Now, some Senate Republicans have acknowledged the egregious wrongs, but few have expressed a need for floor action. Too many have remained silent. Maybe they're hoping the issue goes away. I promise them it will not. Democrats will not let this go away and we will not rest until we achieve real reforms. Leader McConnell, let's have the debate, not just on TV and Twitter, but on the floor of the United States Senate. A divided nation cannot wait for healing, for solutions. The poison of racism affects more than our criminal justice system. It runs much deeper than that. There are racial disparities in housing and healthcare, education, the economy, jobs, income, wealth. And COVID has only placed a magnifying glass on them.

It is our job, our job as Representatives of an imperfect union to right those wrongs, bring the reality and promise of America into closer alignment. Equal justice under law is one such promise. That's what this morning and the Justice and Policing Act is all about, the centuries long struggle to make those words actually true for black Americans and every American. Senator Hoyer, or Congressman Hoyer.

Nancy Pelosi: Leader.

Chuck Schumer: Leader Hoyer.

Steny Hoyer: These are serious times. I've walked across the Edmund Pettus Bridge 15 times hand in hand with my brother, John Lewis. My grandchildren have been there. My daughters have been there. In Selma in 2015, President Obama asked us this. What greater form of patriotism is there-

What greater form of patriotism is there than the belief that America is not yet finished, that we are strong enough to be self critical, that each successive generation can look upon our imperfections and decide that is in our power to remake this nation to more closely align with our highest ideals. That is what the Boston Tea Party was about. A demonstration. Some Britain's would say a violation of law to redress rights. We remain a nation of imperfections, calling out to us to be addressed with the seriousness and determination to make good on the promise that all are created equal, all entitled to life, liberty, and the pursuit of happiness, and the right to breathe. . . .

The right to have their lives matter. We've heard our people cry out, "I can't breathe." We've heard our people speak out, "Black lives matter." Black lives matter. The protests we've seen in recent days are an expression of rage born of despair. Today, democrats in the House and Senate are saying, "We see you. We hear you. We are acting." Thank you, Karen Bass. Thank you, Congressional Black Caucus. Thank you, Leader Pelosi and Leader Schumer. The killing must stop. The carnage must end. That begins with transparency and accountability. Among other provisions, this bill will increase transparency and accountability of law enforcement nationwide by one, requiring state and local law enforcement agencies to collect and report data. Secondly, incentivizing the creation of independent investigation structures for police involved in deaths and creating best practice recommendations based on the Obama administration's 21st century policing task force.

This legislation makes it clear that police department are serving and are answerable to all the residents in their communities, including African-Americans. I want to thank my colleagues who have been leading this effort in the House, Chairwoman

Bass, Chairman Nadler, Chairman Jeffries, and Whip Clyburn, and Senator Harris. We keep in our minds today the word of our dear departed colleague, Elijah Cummings, "We are better than this." And now it's my privilege to introduce a former mayor of a great city in our country, a representative the state of New Jersey, and a leader in this effort, Senator Cory Booker. We are better than this. . . .

Senator Cory Booker: We in America are one precious same nation, but we have a wildly different set of experiences with the police. Where Black Americans live in fear of police interactions, disproportionally having our common ideals of fairness trampled. Where Black Americans disproportionately have our rights violated. Where Black Americans, disproportionally and unjustifiably, have violence, experience violence at the hands of the police. Where Black Americans unarmed or killed by police at grievous and wretches rates. In this moment in America, knowledge of this and acknowledgement of this is necessary, but it is not enough. Empathy, and sympathy, and words of caring for those who have died and suffered are necessary, but it's not enough. Having a nation that in all 50 States, millions of Americans of all ages, religious, and racial backgrounds are standing up and nonviolent protest has made this moment possible, but it's not enough. We must change laws and systems of accountability. We must pass legislation that makes our common values and our common ideals real in the law of our land. This bill focuses on accountability and transparency in polices. Specifically, the federal statute that governs police misconduct, section 242, it changes the difficult statutory standard of willfulness that makes holding police accountable too difficult, and it changes that standard from being willful to being reckless disregard. It also establishes transparency, making certification requirements that now vary by location where cities and towns do not share critical information with each other, making it far too easy for problematic officers to be fired in one town and easily hired in another. This bill closes a dangerous loophole by creating the first ever National Registry of Policeman's Conduct to better record and track police abuses to give transparency to local citizens, helping to create the necessary accountability.

I want to thank the leadership of Speaker Pelosi and Leader Schumer. I want to thank the head of the Congressional Black Caucus and all the members of the Black Caucus. I want to thank my partner, Kamala Harris, for her leadership in making a real piece of legislation sweeping and historic. And now we must deal with the work of making it the law of the land, of transforming the energy and the power, the empathy and the love of this moment into actual changes in American federal law. I'm honored to bring up my colleague, my friend, my sister, and my partner, Senator Kamala Harris.

Senator Kamala Harris: Thank you, brother Cory. Thank you to Speaker Pelosi, Leader Schumer, Leader Hoyer, Whip Clyburn, CBC Chair Karen Bass, my brother, Cory Booker, Chairman Nadler, and Chairman Jeffries, and everyone for the work that so many of you have been doing for decades. For decades. Shouting and passing or writing legislation, and requiring that America takes seriously this issue of policing and take seriously the issue that when the people are marching in the streets, it is because they are fully aware of the history of this issue in America, and they've had enough. So I thank all the leaders here for what you do. And we're here because Black Americans want to stop being killed.

Just last week, we couldn't even pass an anti-lynching bill in the United States Senate. So when we look at where we are now with this piece of legislation, we have to understand, yes, as a country, we've seen great progress, but just last week in the year of our Lord, 2020, we could not get an anti-lynching bill passed in the United States Senate. But we are here today with common sense solutions, to hold, at least at the federal level, to hold police accountable. But we know this is an issue that is not just at the federal level, it is at the state and local level as well. But we are here today to say in our position as leaders in our federal government, that reform and change must happen and it must happen now. And let's be clear, reforming policing is in the best interest of all Americans.

It is literally in the best interest of all Americans, because this is a basic matter of fairness, and as so many have said, justice. But to be clear, also, there is a broader issue that is not being addressed in this bill. And that is what we must do as a nation to truly achieve safe and healthy communities. Part of what has been upside down in policing policy in America is that we have confused having safe communities with hiring more cops on the street, as though that is the way to achieve safe communities. When in fact the real way to achieve safe and healthy communities is to invest in those communities, in affordable housing, in the ability for home ownership, jobs, funding our public schools, giving people access to capital so they can grow those small businesses that are part of the leadership and the health of these communities.

So ours is a bill that addresses a very specific matter under a larger umbrella of all that must be addressed. When we talk about the need for safety and safe in health communities in America, this specifically is a bill about accountability and consequence for bad behaviors by those who have been invested by society and the people with the ability to wear a badge and carry a gun. And let's be clear, many in America right now already live in places with minimal police presence. Go to any middle and upper class suburb and you will not see the kind of presence of police that you see in other neighborhoods, but you will also see in those communities that those families have jobs that allow them to pay the bills and keep a roof over their head. You will also see in those communities thriving schools, you will also see in those communities access to affordable healthcare or families that can afford access to healthcare.

So what we are doing today is saying that we need to have consequence and accountability in America for policing, but we also know that this is not the way that we are going to achieve healthy and safe communities, it is but a part of a much bigger issue that we still must address. So in closing, I'll just mention a few the other points that are in the bill that are very important. And I say this as a former prosecutor, we need a national use of force standard. Right now, the question asked if there is police misconduct and excessive force is to ask of that use of force, "Was it reasonable?" Well, as we all know, we can reason away just about anything the appropriate and fair question to ask is, "Was it necessary?" So part of what our bill will address is a national use of force standard, independent investigations, again, as a former prosecutor, I can say, no matter how well intentioned the prosecutor of a DA's office, when they are confronted with dealing with misconduct by a police officer who serves in a department they work with every day, at the very least, there will be an appearance of conflict, even when none is intended.

If a justice system is going to be robust and real, it must not only do justice, there must be an appearance of justice and confidence by the public that justice is being done in that place. So independent investigations and then the last piece that I'll add is the pattern and practice investigations. Under President Obama under General Holder, these were robust. Where when there was a finding or an accusation, that there was a pattern and practice within a law enforcement agency, the federal government would do investigations. Well, those under this current administration have practically been shut down. They need to be reinstated but also what we are saying is to give it teeth, in addition to what has been done in the past, we will grow on that progress by giving the Civil Rights Division of the Department of Justice subpoena power so when police departments do not comply with requests, they will be required to, by responding to a subpoena. And so my final point is, again, that it is time for this and I am so heartened by all of the colleagues we have in the United States Senate, Leader Schumer who have banded together in support of this, and there's more work to be done. . .

Print Citations

CMS: Bass, Karen, Nancy Pelosi, Chuck Schumer, Steny Hoyer, Cory Booker, and Kamala Harris. "Congressional Democrats Unveil Police Reform Bill in Press Conference." Press Conference at the U.S. House of Representatives, Washington, DC, June 8, 2020. In *The Reference Shelf: Representative American Speeches, 2019-2020,* edited by Annette Calzone, 65-71. Amenia, NY: Grey House Publishing, 2020.

MLA: Bass, Karen, Nancy Pelosi, Chuck Schumer, Steny Hoyer, Cory Booker, and Kamala Harris. "Congressional Democrats Unveil Police Reform Bill in Press Conference." U.S. House of Representatives, Washington, DC, 8 June 2020, Washington, DC. Press Conference. *The Reference Shelf: Representative American Speeches, 2019-2020,* edited by Annette Calzone, Grey House Publishing, 2020, pp. 65-71.

APA: Bass, K., N. Pelosi, C. Schumer, S. Hoyer, C. Booker, and K. Harris. (2020, June 8). Congressional Democrats unveil police reform bill in press conference. U.S. House of Representatives, Washington, DC. In Annette Calzone (Ed.), *The reference shelf: Representative American speeches, 2019-2020* (pp. 65-71). Amenia, NY: Grey House Publishing.

Press Conference on Protests in Seattle

By Jenny Durkan and Carmen Best

Seattle Mayor Jenny Durkan and Seattle Police Chief Carmen Best spoke at a press conference in June about the protests taking place in the city and about the autonomous zone. Durkan insisted that it was unconstitutional for President Donald Trump to send in the military to quell the protests, and Best commented on the need for de-escalation and establishing trust while at the same time maintaining public safety for all of Seattle's citiziens.

Jenny Durkan: [It is un]constitutional and illegal to send military to Seattle. If you don't believe me, you can take the word of a line of highly decorated generals who have said so and have rebuked him. I have spoken with Governor Inslee and together we will assure the people this will not be happening. Many people actually are afraid that it would happen because the President of the United States said it. We would like to be able to trust what the President of the United States says, but I want people to know there is no imminent threat of an invasion in Seattle. But just as we did at the beginning of this pandemic, and as we have done many times before, we will not wait for a change in Washington for Seattle to act. I know we have a lot of work to do, trust has been broken and it must be rebuilt. People's voices have been drowned out during this time and for several hundred years, we have allowed a system to build and promote racism to continue to benefit us. That will take years to dismantle, but we must start immediately, and I believe the rest of Seattle is ready to get to work.

I also want to get back to why we cannot lose sight of the conversation our community needs to be having. We can't lose this moment. From Black Lives Matter to the organizers on Capitol Hill to others, people are demanding change and we need to listen. Change at the city including SPD, City Council, City Attorney and me. Change on policing, education, healthcare and criminal justice system. Change at the county, change at public health, change at the state. We are seeing movement in ways we have not seen in decades and that's a good thing. This change has to be centered on the voices of community and what people need. We must empower community. I remain committed to listening and to working with community, including the organizers on Capitol Hill to reimagine how we do things as a city, how do we reinvest in community to address public health needs, education, and true economic justice? This will continue to build off some of the work we have done,

Press conference on June 11, 2020, in Seattle, Washington.

from free childcare to two years' free college for every public high school student, to jobs for our youth, to reforms in the criminal justice system. We will continue to build those programs and to make Seattle a more just and equitable place, and we will also continue to fund intervention programs so that more mental health professionals are on tap to reply to when people need them.

I've said it so many times over my career, when people call 911, we need to send them the help they need. That is not always a police officer and many times isn't. We have to reimagine our response to community and what they need in times of crisis. Our efforts going forward include investments, . . . re-imagining what we need to do with those investments and providing alternatives to incarceration and arrest. This year, we will invest $100 million in new community-based programs that serve the black community as well as the indigenous and communities of color.

Over the last week and including this afternoon, my office and I have prioritized having conversations with community leaders and residents about the changes they want to see in the city and about how they bring them about. Some of these conversations are very difficult and painful, but that kind of conversation has to happen in order for us to move forward. In many ways, the test is the more uncomfortable it is for me as mayor, probably the more important it is for it to happen. We're working on a range of proposals on what we've heard from community to dismantle systemic racism, but it can't come from the top down with us dictating what community needs. We have to listen, but we also have to act. Chief Best will address you now. Before I want to turn this over to her, I want to thank her for all of her work over the last few weeks. I know she and her department leaders and her officers have been working so hard and they've worked to adjust and improve every day and ultimately, I know that they are guided by doing all they can for the businesses and residents of Seattle. Thank you.

[Seattle Chief of Police Carmen] Best: Great. Thank you Mayor, and I'll start where you left off and just say that the men and women of the department have been working really hard tirelessly for several days while we go through trying to manage demonstrations and they've done incredible work trying to make sure that we address the needs of the community. This morning as you know I and several of my command staff entered the East Precinct just to see what the conditions were there. We have been operating from a position of trust and de-escalation. The demonstrators made it clear, the conflict was the fencing preventing them from marching, so we moved it. I want to allow peaceful demonstrations and resolve every situation with full awareness that sometimes there are clear threats to the facilities. You know a precinct burned in Minneapolis, a headquarters was ransacked in Portland, arson and looting in Downtown Seattle, bulletins from the FBI and chants at the East Precinct of burn it down. We took down the barricades anyway because we really wanted to establish trust. Instead of marching, the protesters, after complaining about police barricades, established their own barricades so the streets that we wanted to be clear, now they're no longer clear.

SPD has a responsibility to provide public safety services to the entire East Precinct and to the city. The actions of a small group cannot and should not deprive an entire segment of our community from public safety services. In the first day of the SPD not having access to the precinct, response times for crimes in progress were over 15 minutes, about three times as long as the average of every year. If that is your mother, your sister, your cousin, your neighbor's kid that is being raped, robbed, assaulted and otherwise victimized, you are not going to want to have to report that it took the police three times longer to get there to provide services to them. The difference in that amount of time could prevent someone's life and prevent a violent attack. It was never an option to have residents of the precinct, many of whom are members of our most marginalized communities by the way, waiting for an extra length of time for an officer to arrive to a violent crime in progress.

The Seattle Police Department stands open and ready to engage in dialog and action about how we can address that is inequalities and racism in the criminal justice system. We all know that over history when people have cried out for justice, when they've been black, when they've been Latino, when they've been LGBTQ or Asian, the police department and the police officers were often on the wrong side of good and often perpetuating the status quo. We have to acknowledge that history, a long history of abuses. I for one am specifically in tune with some of those issues. That doesn't mean we can't continue to evolve and change and do better and we're committed to doing that. I call on all of my colleagues as well, across the criminal justice system, prosecutors, judges and other elected officials, service providers and behavioral health providers, to join us with community in these conversations. It is especially important that the entire community is a part of the conversation.

Everyone shows . . . come out and they have been particularly concerned about what the death and the murder of George Floyd represents. What it represents is a history of black men dying at the hands of law enforcement in unprovoked or sometimes deemed as unprovoked ways. We have to acknowledge that, but that doesn't mean we throw the baby out with the bathwater. That doesn't mean that law enforcement isn't an important part in the fabric of society. It doesn't mean that we can't do better and it doesn't mean that many of the men and women right here in Seattle, right here in your police department, want to do better and want to have that opportunity. I've served here for 28 years. I love Seattle, I love the department, I love our community. My daughter, my son-in-law and my nephew were at those protests, have been at the demonstrations, both good and bad endings that is and they participate, so I care. My family cares. These things are important to us. So we want to make sure that we get it right. We will have to take some deep examination of what brought us to the events of the past two weeks.

It is time now to purposefully heal, to have reconciliation and to move forward together. We must do this for George Floyd and all the many other people who have suffered at the hands of police and we also must do it for everyone who has suffered at the hands of injustice and we must make sure that all of our officers are on board with moving forward and I believe that the men and women who work for the Seattle Police Department really are engaged and want it to be better and want this to be a better society. So on that note, I guess it's open for questions and you'll take care of that.

Speaker 3: Yes. So thank you Mayor, thank you Chief. The way we'll balance this is we will have two questions in the room and then we will take one from the Webex portal so I open it up to the room. I open it up to the mayor and the chief to acknowledge questions in the room.

Jenny Durkan: Chris.

[CNN news anchor Chris Cuomo]: So Chief, you've stood here on Friday and you said it was going to be your decision and your decision alone to use tear gas. Tear gas was deployed on Sunday. You released a video today to say that it was not your decision to close the East Precinct. So who is making tactical decisions right now for the Seattle Police Department?

Chief Best: So a couple of things, Chris. Those are two very different incidents. So for the tear gas, it was my decision. I think I prefaced that, I made it very clear that we did not want to use any of the pepper spray, flash bangs, blast balls or tear gas and we suspended the use for 30 days unless there was a life safety situation, and that was the exemption. I was keeping abreast of what was happening in the precinct. They had a shooting earlier in the day. At some point it got unruly. There was a man with a gun in the crowd. The officers felt like it was a life safety situation based on what was occurring and I concurred, and I own that decision. I made that decision and I will own any decision that I think is in the best interest of everyone's public safety. There's a lot of discussion about what less lethal what we call munitions will be used and how . . . use in the future and I hope to have the opportunity to engage in those conversations, but I totally own that decision.

In regards to the precinct, we were looking at … We had opened up the roads, we had decided to put some safety measures around the precinct to protect it. We were asked to do an operational plan in case we needed to leave. We got an update that there was the potential for fire, of course if the precinct goes down in fire, the whole block could potentially burn up. As they were moving things out, the decision was made to … As officers were taking things out of the precinct, they didn't want to come back into the precinct and many of them did not. So. . . evaluate exactly the pinpoint of why that changed, but it didn't come from me. We will review all of it.

Chris: So command staff made mad that decision to close the precinct?

Chief Best: We're looking into all of it, Chris, to see where it came from.

Chris: I mean –

Jenny Durkan: Wait a minute. We have so many people to get to Chris. We'll come back to you.

[KOMO News reporter Matt Markovich]: Madam.

Jenny Durkan: David, then two on the phone, then we'll come back to you Matt.

[Crosscut reporter David Kroman]: Well I want to ask about the Capitol Hill Zone. What's the plan? Are you going to … How long are you going to let it stay there? Are you going to let it stay indefinitely? People are wanting to turn the East Precinct into a community center. Is that on the table? What's going to happen?

Jenny Durkan: So the Capitol Hill area is … In fact, some of my family is up there right now. I think it has been described by the president and others as what it is not. It is not an armed Antifa militia no-go zone. It is a number of people are there. We have had ongoing communications with them, with the businesses, with the residents and we will make sure that we find some way for people to continue to protest peacefully while also getting ingress and egress. We've had blocks of Seattle and Capitol Hill shut down every summer for everything from Block Party to Pride. This is really not that much of an operational challenge but we want to make sure that the businesses and residents feel safe and we'll continue to move that forward.

David: Is the SPD going to try and move back into the East Precinct?

Jenny Durkan: We've talked about SPD moving in. They did the assessment today and there's going to be an ongoing assessment about when it would be safe and appropriate for them to move in there, including response times and the like. We don't want to introduce additional flashpoints. The chief has made it very clear when we had discussions last week that it was clear that those barriers were the flashpoint and needed to be removed and we want to make sure that moving forward, SPD is in the planning for Capitol Hall.

Jenny Durkan: Two on the phone.

Speaker 3: Thank you Chris. Thank you David. Thank you Mayor. Our first question will come from Hanna Scott, KIRO Radio. Hanna, the floor is yours. Hannah? The floor is yours.

[KIRO radio reporter] Hanna Scott: Sorry, there we go.

Speaker 3: Whenever you're ready.

Hanna Scott: All right, can you hear me?

Speaker 3: Yes we can.

Hanna Scott: Okay. For Chief Best, can you speak to any legitimate reports where there's been evidence found of people with arms extorting businesses or residents in the … What's now known as the Capitol Hill Autonomous Zone and for the mayor, … met with the protestors up there.

Jenny Durkan: I have not met with the protesters that are on Capitol Hill right now. I'll let the chief address the reports. My understanding is is that there have been some occasions of some property damage, vandalism, a fight but there's not been any serious incidents that have been documented but I'll let her confirm that.

Chief Best: Sure. Hi Hanna, we had heard through folks anecdotally that these things are occurring. Chief Nollette who's also here today gave a press conference and asked if anybody actually experienced that and reported it, then we would make sure that we have taken a report. We haven't had any formal reports of this occurring other than people have mentioned it through news media, social media posts, but no one's come forward for a police report. So if that does happen, we are encouraging people if they have experienced that to please notify us and we can follow up on it but that has not happened affirmatively.

Print Citations

CMS: Durkan, Jenny, and Carmen Best. "Press Conference on Protests in Seattle." Press conference in Seattle, WA, June 11, 2020. In *The Reference Shelf: Representative American Speeches, 2019-2020,* edited by Annette Calzone, 72-77. Amenia, NY: Grey House Publishing, 2020.

MLA: Durkan, Jenny, and Carmen Best. "Press Conference on Protests in Seattle." 11 June 2020, Seattle, WA. Press conference. *The Reference Shelf: Representative American Speeches, 2019-2020,* edited by Annette Calzone, Grey House Publishing, 2020, pp. 72-77.

APA: Durkan, J., & Best, C. (2020, June 11). Press conference on protests in Seattle. Seattle, WA. In Annette Calzone (Ed.), *The reference shelf: Representative American speeches, 2019-2020* (pp. 72-77). Amenia, NY: Grey House Publishing.

A Debate on Police Reform

By Kamala Harris and John Cornyn

A U.S. Senate debate on a Republican police reform bill raised issues about its efficacy, with Senator Kamala Harris insisting that the bill did not provide for transparency into police misconduct or for data collection on use of force or racial profiling, and it did not ban no knock warrants or choke holds. Senator John Cornyn commented that negotiations should occur not behind closed doors but rather be broadcast from the floor of the Senate to achieve some consensus about what the appropriate reforms should be.

Senator John Cornyn: Madam President, would the Senator yield for a question?

Senator Kamala Harris: When I'm finished I will. The Republican bill does not even provide a baseline for a discussion or amendment on police reform in that there are no mechanisms to hold law enforcement officers accountable in court for their misconduct. There is no transparency into police misconduct, which is necessary, of course, to enable communities to hold officers accountable. There is no requirement of data collection on all use of force incidents or on racial or religious profiling. There is no ban on harmful policing policies and practices such as racial and religious profiling, no knock warrants in drug cases. We're not banning all no knock warrants, no knock warrants in drug cases because Breonna Taylor would be alive today had that been the case. Choke holds, carotid holds, no reform of those issues in the Republican bill that's being offered, and there's no national standard for use of force. So, I'm happy to entertain the question from the Senator from Texas, and then I'll conclude my comments.

Senator John Cornyn: Thank you, Madam President. I wonder if the Senator would tell me the bill that the police act that it sounds like are the democratic conference intends to block tomorrow includes the antilynching legislation that you and Senator Booker have championed. Are you aware of that?

Senator Kamala Harris: The same one that Rand Paul obstructed a couple of weeks ago?, Yes I am aware of that.

Senator John Cornyn: So you're going to block . . . Madam President, so the senators are going to block their own anti-lynching bill by their vote tomorrow?

Senator Kamala Harris: Absolutely not and I think that it is important that we not distract the American people from the task at hand. We cannot pull out a specific component of this bill and leave everything else in the garbage bin. That is the

Debate on June 23, 2020, at the U.S. Senate, Washington, DC.

logical and actual and practical conclusion of where you're going with the suggestion that we would sacrifice issues like no knock warrants, issues like national standard for use of force, issues like the need for independent investigations of police misconduct, issues like pattern and practice investigations with subpoena power for the United States Department of Justice in sake of one. It's like asking a mother, save one of your children and leave the others.

Senator John Cornyn: Madam President, will the Senator yield for another question.

Senator Kamala Harris: Absolutely.

Senator John Cornyn: Madam President the Senator certainly is familiar with the rules of the Senate, which allows senators to offer amendments to improve legislation once we get on it, but if the democratic conference is going to prevent the Senate from actually getting on the bill, there's no opportunity for anyone, any Senator, you or any one of us, to offer amendments to improve it. And I would further ask the Senator, aren't you aware of the fact that there are 60 vote thresholds on the back end so that if we get on the bill and you don't like the way it turns out, that you can block it on the back end, but is the Senator where of those options that she has?

Senator Kamala Harris: Well, Senator Cornyn, you and I both serve, and we are honored to serve on the Senate Judiciary Committee as does Senator Booker, Senator Durbin. We all serve on the Judiciary Committee. The two Senate authors of this bill serve with you on the Senate Judiciary Committee. As you know, because we've been present together during our most recent hearings, we have asked that there would be a meaningful discussion of the Justice and Policing Act in that committee. None has occurred. So if we're going to talk about process, let us look at all the tools that are available to well-intentioned, well-meaning legislators if the goal is actually to solve and address the issue at hand. I've seen no evidence of that. I've seen no evidence of . . . In fact, what I've seen reading some of the newspapers, sometimes they get things wrong, but if they got it right, the Senate leader said that he has no interest in engaging in that kind of discussion or debate before putting the bill on the floor for a vote tomorrow.

Senator John Cornyn: Madam President, may I ask one last question of the Senator? What I'm trying to fathom Madam President is why the Senator would rather have these negotiations occur behind closed doors as opposed to here on the floor of the Senate for the American people to see broadcast on television. Don't you think that sort of interaction and debate and negotiation out in front of all 330 million Americans would be beneficial to healing our country and coming to some consensus about what the appropriate reforms should be.

Senator Kamala Harris: Indeed, that is the beauty of the Judiciary Committee. Our meetings are public meetings.

Senator Kamala Harris: I will now conclude my remarks by saying that I do believe now is the time for Congress to pass legislation that will bring real change and real improvement. It is time that we meet this moment and meet the movement that we are seeing outside of these doors. We are seeing people of every race, gender, and age, and religion marching together in unison as Americans. We are seeing people putting their bodies on the line in the face of more excessive force and tear gas to stand for equality for all people. The bill that is being offered for vote tomorrow does not in any way meet the needs of this moment, and the long-standing needs America has had for reform. I will therefore join Senator Schumer and Booker in not only sending a letter to Senator McConnell this morning demanding that the Senate vote on the Justice and Policing Act, but I will say that I fully intend to vote against the motion to proceed until, and unless, we as a body are prepared to offer meaningful, meaningful reforms upon which we can debate.

Senator Kamala Harris: But I will say also that one of the other problems with what is being offered by our colleagues across the aisle is it is not meeting the moment in terms of the need for reform. It is simply . . . It is basically they've constructed a confessional where there can be a confession of misdeeds after the fact, and that in no way meets the moment in terms of reforms that are necessary, and so in the words of my . . . immortal words of my great uncle, Sherman, God rest his soul, "That dog don't hunt." Thank you.

Print Citations

CMS: Harris, Kamala, and John Cornyn. "A Debate on Police Reform." Debate in the U.S. Senate, Washington, DC, June 23, 2020. In *The Reference Shelf: Representative American Speeches, 2019-2020,* edited by Annette Calzone, 78-80. Amenia, NY: Grey House Publishing, 2020.

MLA: Harris, Kamala, and John Cornyn. "A Debate on Police Reform." U.S. Senate, 23 June 2020, Washington, DC. Debate. *The Reference Shelf: Representative American Speeches, 2019-2020,* edited by Annette Calzone, Grey House Publishing, 2020, pp. 78-80.

APA: Harris, K., & Cornyn, J. (2020, June 23). A debate on police reform. U.S. Senate, Washington, DC. In Annette Calzone (Ed.), *The reference shelf: Representative American speeches, 2019-2020* (pp. 78-80). Amenia, NY: Grey House Publishing.

Portland Police Chief Press Conference

By Chuck Lovell

Portland Police Chief Chuck Lovell discussed the riots taking place in the city and the police response. While acknowledging the need for reforms and increased transparency, Lovell argued that the way to achieve that would not be through the Defund the Police movement. Lovell described the approach toward the community as one of de-escalation, committing resources to stopping criminal activity while not engaging with the many large peaceful protests calling for reform and relationship building. Lovell noted that these demands were being heard by the police department.

Chief Chuck Lovell: About the reforms and the advances and just giving the community the service that they really need and expect. We have a great partnership with OSP downtown. They have replaced the federal officers. And we have a long standing history of working closely with Oregon State Police and training with them. And the downtown activity has actually been pretty promising. So we're really happy for our partnership with Oregon State Police and also Multnomah County Sheriff's office. And to the officers that have been working, we're pushing almost 70 straight days of protest here in Portland. Officers are tired, and they keep coming back every night because they love this city. They're working hard to keep the city safe, protect people and give people the right to exercise their free speech, but also protect property from those who are committed to try to destroy it and to try to do things that are disruptive to the functioning of our beautiful city. So with that, I'll open it up for questions, but I just wanted to say thanks everyone for being here, and I'm happy to give all the local media folks some accessibility.

Speaker 2: Chief, you have retirements happening this month. Some have been scheduled for awhile. Are there officers who are taking early retirement or are some just saying I'm done and giving you notice?

Chief Chuck Lovell: Well, we've had, I want to say that the latest number I heard was about 46 projected retirements, and those are officers who've done their 25 years and are now ready to retire. But when you look at that number and that core of officers, you've got over 1,000 years of experience leaving the police bureau this month. And those are 46 veteran bodies who are able to work in their investigative assignments or on patrol. And then we have a cadre of officers who haven't even been to the Academy yet, and we've got about 100 I think that are still trainees.

And it takes an officer about two years to really be up and functioning, off

Press conference on August 5, 2020, in Portland, Oregon.

probation and able to go out and give service to the public. So I've heard, "Hey, you guys have 900 officers. Where are they going?" There's a lot that goes into that number. Some of those officers are just at the very beginning of their career. We have a lot who are leaving at the end of their career. So I think in the future, we'll kind of break down what those numbers look like in the more general sense. But yeah, this is going to be a big retirement for us, August.

Speaker 2: You have not seen officers telling you that they're just exhausted and this isn't the career for them anymore?

Chief Chuck Lovell: No, I think officers are exhausted, but we don't have people leaving early for that reason. We have dedicated officers. I mean, if you look at what's been going on here for the last 70 days, and we have people who show up every night to deal with these tumultuous situations. They come downtown to work or to one of our precincts to work, and they see hateful graffiti, and they still come back every day to give service to the community under what are really tough circumstances. It really affects their wellness and their families. And they love this city so much that they keep coming back and they keep serving. I'm very proud of them. I can't say enough how proud I am of their resilience and their dedication to Portland.

Nick: Chief, you mentioned nightly violence and response times. Can you spell out, do you think the nightly violence is having effects on response times? What does that affect and how does that work for those that don't know all the details?

Chief Chuck Lovell: Sure. Yeah, I do. And in the very general sense, we have officers assigned to answer 911 calls at precincts, and they have big areas that they cover. Night shift is the smallest shift we have, and we'll designate mobile field forces to come downtown to assist in the crowd control efforts or at precincts if that's where the resource is needed. But when we pull those resources to assist with the crowd control, it leaves very few cars in the precinct to answer 911 calls, sometimes just two or three cars. And if we get a shooting or a critical incident there that requires multiple cars, people aren't getting police service, and that's the real issue. And I think for us, there's a prevention piece. When the police are out and able to do proactive work, there's a prevention piece that I think is hard to quantify, but it's important. And I think right now that prevention piece is just not as efficient because of all the activity downtown or at the precincts that's drawn away from our resources.

Nick: Do you think there's a connection to the homicides and shootings, or do you attribute that to the GVRT going away? Can you talk about what you think the cause is of that?

Chief Chuck Lovell: I think that's probably twofold. I think both of those are probably factors. The Gun Violence Reduction Team did great work. They had relationships with people. They had knowledge of people. They had the ability to collect data. They interfaced with the Office of Violence Prevention, outreach workers, parole and probation. They had a structure that was focused on shootings and on gun violence. So absent that structure that we're dealing with now, all those people's jobs got harder. It's harder for probation and parole. It's harder for the Office of Violence

Prevention. It's harder for the outreach workers. And I think there's some deterrent piece there too. Knowing that they're no longer there, I think it gives people more… I'd say they're more emboldened maybe to be out with guns. They know there's not someone watching. There's no real deterrent there. And I think that's part of the issue with causing us to see the spike we have in July.

Speaker 2: Is there a chance they're coming back?

Chief Chuck Lovell: I think so. I hope so. I'm not sure, but I have dedicated some resources from patrol. As a chief of police when you see those numbers, it gives you a knot in your stomach. People are dying in your streets and you're responsible for the safety of the community. So I've dedicated resources from patrol to the detective division where the previous GVRT detectives are now housed to give support for followup to those investigations. It's that important to me.

Speaker 4: Chief, why do you think those numbers are up in homicides?

Chief Chuck Lovell: Well, I think, like I answered with Nick's question, I think the absence of the Gun Violence Reduction Team, the limited resources to do proactive stops and the amount of officers that we're dedicating to crowd control events and really the violent activity that we have to respond to, there's really less of a deterrent for people. And then when you do have shootings, sometimes you have retaliatory shootings and other things that if you had the GVRT resource, you could maybe try to prevent on the front end.

Speaker 4: Do you think it may be related to the pandemic and economy?

Chief Chuck Lovell: That's possible too. There's a lot of forces at play for us right now between the pandemic, people out of work, a lot of people with free time, the economy, the crowd control events, the violence. I think all of those probably play a role, but it's hard to quantify.

Speaker 5: What is the bureau's game plan in dealing with the nightly violence or the nightly protests that might involve violence?

Chief Chuck Lovell: Yeah. Our game plan is really to be as de-escalative as possible. We try to not be out where we are a target or visible where people want to provoke a response from us. We respond when people attempt burglaries, arsons, damage to property, things that would harm other people, fights breakout and things of that nature. And our approach is really to respond to criminal activity. Having Oregon State Police here has been very helpful. We've gotten help from Multnomah County Sheriff's office. But we've really been focused on using our resources to respond to the criminal activity. And there've been some really large peaceful protests where people have come out, they've listened and given speeches, they've marched to different parts of the city, and it's really required zero police interaction. And their voices are definitely being heard by us. And we want to get to the conversations, the reforms, the relationship buildings that a lot of the community is calling for.

Speaker 6: The mayor made a big deal when he was talking about his four step plan to get the streets of Portland back, he says getting rid of the feds was the biggest step. And he said or seemed to feel that that would make a big change. Now, we've also heard that if the streets of Portland don't calm back down, the feds say they will come back in. Do you have concerns that the feds will come back? And how, if the feds are gone, do we truly get the streets to calm down?

Chief Chuck Lovell: Yeah, I think the switch with OSP has been helpful, especially downtown at the federal building. I mean, we have a fair amount of federal buildings in Portland that have to be protected. For us, I think it's really focusing on how do we protect our infrastructure. Some of the focus has shifted from the downtown federal building to our precincts. Last night, we had a bunch of disturbing activity at our Portland Police Association office. So I think it's really our ability to keep Portlanders safe, one, but also to protect our valuable infrastructure as well. And I think having Oregon State Police here is helpful in that, but we have to figure out a way where we can secure those structures adequately and also at some point really allow the federal government to leave and our local assets to be able to maintain that.

Speaker 6: So the mayor and other federal officials have said it really lies on the shoulders of Portland. I guess the question is how? How do you ask or how do you expect Portlanders to help out getting this small group of agitators that you're talking about to step down?

Chief Chuck Lovell: Yeah, I think it does rely on Portlanders and I think it's Portlanders in a general sense, everyone from the person who owns a mom and pop store, to the big business owners, to faith leaders, all the way up to elected officials to really send a strong message that enough is enough. This is not forwarding the goals of things that are going to lead to better outcomes for people of color. This movement is very powerful and I feel like the violence has taken away from it in a really kind of concerning way. But I think it's really dependent on Portland as a community to really say we're not going to tolerate this. Businesses are struggling.

There's so much in our beautiful, vibrant city that has kind of been tainted a little bit by the national reputation that we've gotten over the past few weeks too. So I just want to make sure that I say what I can to support the officers that are out there doing the hard work to keep the city safe, but also encourage other people to really have a voice and say this is not what Portland's about, and this is not what we need right now in our city. We need to really be moving forward together on police reform and a whole bunch of other things that really are societal inequalities that we should be looking at fixing together. . . .

Speaker 9: I was going to ask. The narrative was, "Well, the Gun Violence Reduction Team had to go away because it intentionally or not was racist." It was profiling people that were black. And it sounds like . . . Well, do you disagree with that?

Chief Chuck Lovell: I disagree with that, yes. Yeah. I mean, the stop state of the numbers are the numbers, but I think if you look at major cities that do that type work, the numbers are similar. I mean, it's a hard thing to quantify because if you look at the victim side of that, you'll notice black people are overrepresented heavily on the victim side too. So when you're doing that type of work in the community, it's so hard because you are trying to respond to a societal issue in many ways, and when you do it and you have those numbers, people label you racist. And that's not the case.

Those officers that do that work, I can tell you, are the most caring people. They get up, leave their house in the middle of the night, go out and investigate these shootings. And they do it because they care about these families. They don't want to see another family the next night standing in the street with their loved one laying there. So, I would definitely disagree with that. And it's tough, when you do that work, those are kind of the numbers you have. And it's the case in a lot of major cities. . . .

I've been in Portland almost 20 years and with the police bureau just over 18. But I've never seen a summer like this. I mean, when I stepped into this role less than two months ago, it was the pandemic, it was really kind of the start of the George Floyd protest. Huge budget cuts were coming. And at the time, it was like, well, this job is going to be hard. And then you throw in the national press that we've gotten and then now the shootings, and it's very hard. But I think arresting people is a tactic that we use, but we've arrested over 400 people I think since these demonstrations have started. One, people don't stay in jail very long when they get arrested. And two, arrests have to be a deterrent kind of in the near term.

A lot of these cases aren't going to trial anytime soon also. This is not a situation where you can arrest your way out of it, I don't think. We're 70 days into it, and we still have violence taking place almost on a nightly basis. So, I think it's really going to be a community led effort where people just say enough is enough and we're tired of it. And we get the violent actors to stop coming out because they feel like, you know what, this is not going to be tolerated by the community.

Speaker 6: You said that you've talked to community members and you had that opportunity. Has anything come out of that that surprised you, that maybe you haven't thought of, or maybe you walked away still thinking about that one thing that they said that you'd be willing to share?

Chief Chuck Lovell: Yeah. I think the overarching thing is a lot of people, the defund, abolish police movement had gotten a fair amount of attention. A lot of the people I talked to, the vast majority, are like, "No, we need police. We need good, fair, just policing." And they feel like the ability to have that is there. And I think for me, I feel like the things I want to do to bring the police bureau and the community closer together, they need investment, not divestment. I mean, a lot of these things are relationship things, and relationships take time. We can't form a relationship with anyone if we don't spend time together. But in order to have that time, we have to have adequate staffing, we have to have the ability for officers to go out and contact people and spend time with them in situations that aren't immediate emergency critical situations.

And you look at the loss of things like the Youth Services Division and Gun Violence Reduction Team. Those were two of the units that we had that had some of the best relationships with people, and YSD in particular, young people. So, I mean, for me, I was really taken aback by the fact that the community is like, "No, we need you. We just want to make sure that you're giving us good, just policing." And for me, I feel like it's incumbent on me to have a police bureau that knows that the expectation is that they're here to care about the community first and foremost. And then to have things in place that when people do things that are outside our directives, policies and values, to catch it, and then have mechanisms to hold people in place. And I think that's kind of the accountability piece that goes along with community trust.

Print Citations

CMS: Lovell, Chuck. "Portland Police Chief Press Conference." Press conference in Portland OR, August 5, 2020. In *The Reference Shelf: Representative American Speeches, 2019-2020,* edited by Annette Calzone, 81-86. Amenia, NY: Grey House Publishing, 2020.

MLA: Lovell, Chuck. "Portland Police Chief Press Conference." 5 August 2020, Portland, OR. Press conference. *The Reference Shelf: Representative American Speeches, 2019-2020,* edited by Annette Calzone, Grey House Publishing, 2020, pp. 81-86.

APA: Lovell, C. (2020, August 5). Press conference of Portland police chief. Portland, OR. In Annette Calzone (Ed.), *The reference shelf: Representative American speeches, 2019-2020* (pp. 81-86). Amenia, NY: Grey House Publishing.

Addressing the Congregation of Grace Lutheran Church and Community Members

By Joe Biden

Addressing the community at the Grace Lutheran Church in Kenosha, Wisconsin, after the shooting of Jacob Blake by police officers, presidential candidate Joe Biden discussed the long history of racial injustice in the United States and his involvement with the early Civil Rights Movement, pledging to make police reform and racial equality priorities once elected. Biden acknowledged the role of hate in perpetuating racial inequites.

The words of a president matter. No matter if they're good, bad, or indifferent, they matter. No matter how competent or incompetent a president is, they can send the nation to war, they can bring peace, they can make markets rise or fall, and they can do things that I've observed can make a difference just by what they say. . . .

When I came home from law school, what happened was my last semester, the only two political heroes I ever had, both were assassinated. Dr. King and Bobby Kennedy. Matter of fact, Kennedy was assassinated the day I graduated. I came home and my city is the only city in the United States of America occupied by the military since reconstruction for 10 months. Every single corner with someone, a military person standing with a drawn bayonet. Not a joke, 10 months. I had a job with a good law firm, a well known law firm, one of the oldest law firms in the state. And after awhile, I concluded that I was in the wrong place. They were good people, but I quit and became a public defender.

I used to interview my clients in what they call the Northeast Corridor, where Amtrak runs from Washington to New York, that area goes right through my city. And I used to interview clients down in the basement of that train station before they were arraigned. . . . And we had the eighth largest black population of any state in the nation as the percent of population. And we were, to our great shame, a slave state, although we were one of those border states who fought in the side of the North, thank God.

But anyway, make a long story short, what happened was I thought black and whites would never be in my city, talk to each other again. And here I was then, literally 40 years later to the month, on January 17th, standing on a platform at that very same train station and looking out over called the East Side, which had been burned to the ground. Literally it had been completely leveled. When things get burned out,

Delivered on September 3, 2020, at Grace Lutheran Baptist Church, Kenosha, WI.

they come in and level everything. And then across the Christina River, they call the Third Street Bridge, it was all overwhelmingly 100% African American community. And I was standing on that platform January 17th, waiting for a black man to come 26 miles from Philadelphia to pick me up and take me on a train ride to Washington DC with 10,000 people standing down below cheering.

And my son Beau was alive then. He was the attorney general of the state of Delaware at the time. And my daughter, who's a social worker, ran the largest criminal justice program in the state. And my son, my middle son, who was running the World Food Health Program, The World Food Program USA, the largest program in the world. I call them up and all of a sudden it hit me. Here I was and that whole area has been rebuilt. And third street bridge is still in a little bit of trouble, but things have moved. And I said, "Don't tell me things can't change." I told them about the story. . . .

But I made a mistake about something. I thought you could defeat hate. Hate only hides. It only hides. And when someone in authority breathes oxygen under that rock, it legitimizes those folks to come on out, come out in front of the rocks. . . . And I hadn't planned on running for anything again after my son had died. . . . Until I saw those people coming out of Charlottesville, carrying torches, literally torches coming out of the fields. Close your eyes. Remember what you saw on television. Their veins bulging, their hateful speech, chanting the same antisemitic bile that was chanting in the streets of Germany in the 30s. On top of that, accompanied by white supremacists, Klu Klux Klan. A young woman was killed protesting those folks.

And the president of United States was asked. He was asked, "What do you think?" And he said something no president's ever, ever said. He said, "There are very fine people on both sides." No president has ever said anything like that. The generic point I'm making is not all his fault, but it legitimizes. It legitimizes the dark side of human nature.

And what it did though, it also exposed what had not been paid enough attention to, the underlying racism that is institutionalized in the United States still exists, has existed for 400 years. So what's happened is that we end up in a circumstance like you had here in Kenosha and have here in Kenosha. . . .

Well, I think we've reached an inflection point in American history. I honest to God believe we have an enormous opportunity now that the screen, the curtain's been pulled back, and just what's going on in the country, to do a lot of really positive things. As much as they say that Black Lives Matter has lost some standards since the president has gone on this rant about law and order, et cetera, still you have over 50% of the American people supporting it. It was up to 78. That's never happened before. People are beginning to see because of COVID who the people are out breaking their necks and risking their lives to keep them safe in their homes. . . .

Prison reform, there's a whole lot of forms it takes. But my view is we should turn prison reform, and I've been preaching this for the last five years, from prison punishment to reform. So for example, anybody serves their time in prison and they get out, they should be entitled to every single program that exists under the federal government. Why don't we want them getting a Pell Grant and going to school? Why don't we want them getting a job and being able to get public housing, housing subsidies? Why don't we want them qualifying for what used to be called food stamps? But right now, I wrote years ago with a guy named Specter, Senator from Pennsylvania, the Second Chance Act. Because right now we're in a situation where you get out of prison, and I think you all know this, you get a bus ticket and 25 bucks. By the way, 93% of everybody, 93 out of every 100 prisoners in prison are behind a city jail, a county jail, a state jail, not a federal prison. Barack were I are able to reduce the prison population federally by 38,000 folks. . . .

Right now in the United States of America, we don't have the kind of housing funding we had back in our administration earlier before that, even the Republican administrations. No one should have to pay more than 30% of their income to be able to live and have housing, including people on the street. That's why I proposed a $400 billion program to vastly increase available housing in America. And by the way, it's not a waste of money. Even the folks on Wall Street pointed out that will increase the GDP, make it grow. People will do better. People do better. . . .

Mental health. Mental health is a badly needed commodity right now. That's why in the Affordable Care Act, we insisted it be treated equally. There's no difference between a mental health problem and a physical health problem. They're both related to your health. They should be both covered. You talked about the whole idea of federal support clinics. We need community clinics. You guys are expected to do everything right now.

And Barb, you talked about rebuilding. Well, you know what? Let's get something straight here. Protesting is protesting, my buddy John Lewis used to say. But none of it justifies looting, burning or anything else. So regardless how angry you are, if you loot or you burn, you should be held accountable as someone who does anything else, period. It just cannot be tolerated across the board. . . .

Last piece, education. The idea in the United States of America, your education is determined by your zip code. Title one schools. You all know what a title one school is. Mostly in black and Hispanic neighborhoods, but also poor white neighborhoods where they can't afford the tax base. Title one schools are unable to get $15 billion a year to make up for the $200 billion gap that exists between them and other school districts, white school districts. Well, guess what? We moved that to $45 billion a year. It means I can put every three, four and five year old in school. . . .

We've also learned . . . And I'll end with this. . . . But this is important. Here's the deal. If you think about it, we've finally figured out drug abuse doesn't cause mental health problems. Mental health problems cause drug abuse. And if you don't detect the anxiety in children early and deal with it and treat it, you increase exponentially the prospect that they're going to in fact find themselves susceptible to what's happening in the community. . . .

Well, even though I've been involved with the African American community and the civil rights movement since I've been a junior in high school, desegregating movie theaters and the like, I can't understand what it's like to walk out the door or send my son out the door, or my daughter, and worry about just because they're Black, they may not come back. I can intellectually understand it, but I can't feel it.

I just spent an hour or more with the family [of Jacob Blake] as I got off the airplane. Had an opportunity to spend some time with Jacob on the phone. He's out of ICU. We spoke for about 15 minutes. His brother and two sisters, his dad and his mom on the telephone. And I spoke to them a lot before, but we spent some time together with my wife. And he talked about how nothing was going to defeat him, how whether he walked again or not, he was not going to give up. We talked about a Psalm and my . . . based on the 23rd Psalm. "May he raise you up with eagle's wings and bury you on the breath of dawn until we . . . And keep you and hold you in the palm of his hand until we meet again."

Well, I think, Alderman, what's been unleashed with a lot of people is they understand that fear doesn't solve problems. Only hope does. And if you give up hope, you might as well surrender. There's no real option. And as we talked, I listened to his mom. She was on the phone. She wasn't with Jacob, she was in the same location. And as I said, his dad, his son, his brother, two sisters, and a family lawyer, two family lawyers were there. And what I came away with was the overwhelming sense of resilience and optimism that they have about the kind of response they're getting. His mom talked about, we asked, my wife asked to say a prayer. And his mom said a prayer. She said, "I'm praying for Jacob, but I'm praying for the policemen as well. I'm praying that things change."

If you think a little bit about where we are right now, it's been a terrible, terrible wake up call that's gotten the rest of the nation to realize that the confluence of three things. One, the COVID crisis. Two, and we didn't have to have over six million people contract COVID. Over 186,000 dead and climbing. If we had acted, if we'd had just acted. It's been pointed out by the University of Columbia law school that if he had acted just one week earlier, 37,000 more people would have been alive. If he acted two weeks earlier, 51,000. Maybe 31 and 57 or 51 and . . . But the point is over 80,000 people would still be alive. You have to take responsibility if you're a leader, a president. Instead of saying, "I'm not responsible, didn't happen on my watch. I take no responsibility." . . .

When Dr. King, when he said, I know that's ancient history, you weren't even born. But when Bull Connor, I was in grade school when Bull Connor took those fire hoses and dogs on those Black women going to church in their Sunday best and little kids having the skin ripped off them by these high powered fire hoses, he thought he was putting a wooden stake in the heart of the civil rights movement. But in other parts of the country where they heard about this but didn't believe it ever happened, everybody turned on a black and white TV. And they saw it. Said, "Oh my god." Dr. King said it was a second emancipation. It got the Voting Rights Act, it got the Civil Rights Act. Didn't get us all the way there, but made progress.

And that young man stood there for eight minutes and I think it was 43 seconds watching, watching Floyd die, having his face pressed up against that curb. People not only United States, but all around the world said, "Oh my God. It really, really happens." When you had a man of his size and physicality calling for his mom, it struck a nerve that hadn't been struck before. It's awful it has to happen. But I think we're at one of those moments. We have this opportunity. If we don't let up, we don't let up.

There's a reason why this administration doesn't want to talk about it, wants to only talk about dividing the country and about law and order. They don't want to talk about all those people who have died from COVID. They don't want to talk about the fact that almost a million people again file for unemployment, don't have jobs. They don't want to talk about the fact that you have tens of thousands of businesses closing, maybe for good. They don't want to talk about the fact that the Congress passed legislation, Heroes Act, to provide money for states to be able to keep fire-fighters on the job, teachers on the job, first responders on the job, et cetera. They don't want to talk about that because they don't want to do it. They don't feel it's their obligation. So they're trying to divert us the attention it'd have.

If I get elected president, I promise you there will be a national commission on policing out of the White House where I'll bring everyone to the table, including police chiefs, including civil rights activists, including the NAACP, including the African, the Latino community. We're going to sit down there and we're going to work it out. Because a significant portion of the police are decent people, but no one, there's a lot of bad folks in every organization. . . .

We're in a situation now where we can not let up. We can not let up. Violence in any form is wrong. The idea that this president continues to try to divide us, gives succor to the white supremacists, talks about how there's really good people on both sides, talks in ways that are just absolutely, I've never used this regarding the president before, not only incorrect, but immoral and just simply wrong, simply wrong. And the one concern I have, and I understand it, is that people are going to be so frustrated, particularly in the communities that need the help the most, need to be treated most clearly and equally, are going to say, "It's not worth it at all. I'm not going to vote." . . .

America set its mind to something it's never, never, never, never, never failed. When we put our minds to and we do it together, never. We've gone through Wars and pestilence, plague. We've gone through a lot, and we're finally now getting to the point, we're going to be addressed the original sin of this country, 400 years old. It's the original sin, slavery, and all the vestiges of it. I'm not saying in four years, and this is not about a campaigning, I can't say if tomorrow God made me President, I can't guarantee you everything gets solved in four years. . . .

Print Citations

CMS: Biden, Joe. "Addressing the Congregation of Grace Lutheran Church and Community Members." Speech at Grace Lutheran Baptist Church, Kenosha, WI, September 3, 2020. In *The Reference Shelf: Representative American Speeches, 2019-2020,* edited by Annette Calzone, 87-92. Amenia, NY: Grey House Publishing, 2020.

MLA: Biden, Joe. "Addressing the Congregation of Grace Lutheran Church and Community Members." Grace Lutheran Baptist Church, 3 September 2020, Kenosha, WI.

Speech. *The Reference Shelf: Representative American Speeches, 2019-2020,* edited by Annette Calzone, Grey House Publishing, 2020, pp. 87-92.

APA: Biden, J. (2020, September 3). Speech to the congregation of Grace Lutheran Church and community members. Grace Lutheran Baptist, Kenosha, WI. In Annette Calzone (Ed.), *The reference shelf: Representative American speeches, 2019-2020* (pp. 87-92). Amenia, NY: Grey House Publishing.

Rally Speech in Latrobe, Pennsylvania

By Donald Trump

At a September rally in Pennsylvania, President Donald Trump criticized the Demo-cratic Party for not taking a stand against protests-turned-riots and against violent ex-tremists. He also discussed increased military spending, turning the corner with regard to COVID-19, and protecting American jobs. Trump came out in support of law en-forcement, advocating stiff penalties for vandalism and looting. He also discussed the border wall, immigration, and education.

I will keep your jobs in America, and I'll bring rioters, looters, violent extremists, anarchists, we will bring them to justice. That's what we're doing right now. We have over 400 right now under arrest. These are bad people.

Over the last three and a half years, we've secured America's borders, fixed our broken trade deals, rebuilt the United States military, obliterated the ISIS caliph-ate 100%, secured American energy independence, and built the single greatest economy in the history of the world, and now we're going to do it again. Have to do it again. Have to do it again. Got to do it again.

In the hopefully rounding the turn on the pandemic, we're rounding that turn, and vaccines are coming along great. The job that they've done, the doctors, every-body else, we're years ahead of schedule. Anybody else's President, you wouldn't be talking about vaccines for two or three years from now. I'll tell you right now. That I can tell you.

Biden will never be able to protect your jobs or your family. He is a puppet of the socialists, Marxists, and the cop-hating extremists. And they are cop-hating. And we love our law enforcement. We love our law enforcement. . . . I will tell you, the election that we have coming up is the single most important election in the history of this country.

They're going to raise your taxes. They're going to take away your guns. Really, if you look. And you know, they'll criticize me for saying this, the fake news media, which is back there, with their fake polls. The same as last year.

Again, if we didn't get hit by the plague from China, between us, I would have canceled Mr. Congressman, most of the rallies. I wouldn't have needed a rally. That's a little bit unfair, but that's okay. That's what China's done to our nation. They've screwed us for a long time on a lot of different ways. Never has anybody ripped off our nation like China, and I've taken in billions and billions of dollars. We

Delivered on September 3, 2020, at a Trump rally in Latrobe, PA.

never took in 25 cents from China. And I gave $28 billion, right, $28 billion to the farmers because they were targeted unfairly by China.

But for the entire summer, Biden was silent as far left rioters viciously attacked law enforcement in Democrat run cities all, burned down businesses, terrorized civilians, and just recently marched through the streets chanting, "Death to America." This is what we have. Death to America.

And by the way, we could end it like immediately. You saw what we did in Wisconsin. It ended. It took a while for the governor. You know, they have to ask us in. It's like, otherwise we have to do something much bigger and it's totally unnecessary. The National Guard is fantastic. I went to see them two days ago. Biden went there today. There was nobody there. There was nobody there. He was a little late. I was going to say, "Hey, listen, we ended that problem." But we could end it in Portland. Wise guys in Portland. Anarchists. They're agitators. They're looters. I'll tell you we could end it in Portland in a half an hour.

We did it in Seattle. We told them we're coming in. You either end it or were coming in. Congressman, we were going in the next day. We were all set. I was actually disappointed, to be honest. They ended it in Seattle. They took over 20% of the city. Do you believe this? And the mayor said, "No, it's going to be a summer of love." These people are crazy. So we end them very quickly. We end them very quickly. And now what we're doing is we're holding back funds for cities that don't know what they're doing, where they allow crime to run rampant.

And we put a 10-year prison sentence at anybody that knocks down a statue. I took out an old ordinance, a very old one, because today in Congress, you don't get things like that today. They think that you should just have no cash bail. They do the no cash bail. You kill somebody. There's no bail. Don't worry about it. Go out. But I took out an old ordinance. I gave a new executive order. It says 10 years in prison. And amazingly, amazingly, that was three and a half months ago. And they were having a big March on Washington, march elsewhere, and amazingly, that was the end of the statues coming down. No statutes.

And we're actually prosecuting people for having done it. We made it retroactive to the beginning. Terrible. Terrible. And by the way, the state statues and monuments, they have to do the same thing. It's real easy. But the rioters that want Biden to win, they want him to win because their agenda, it's what they want. It's the craziest thing I've ever seen. They both want to cut funding for police. They want to end that cash bail. They want to hire far left prosecutors and judges, and let the criminals run wild. The radical left District Attorney in Portland, Mike Schmidt, his name is, has released hundreds of rioters that announced that anyone arrested for interfering with police officers, disorderly conduct, criminal trespass, rioting, and other offenses will not be prosecuted under any circumstance. Oh, it's worse. It's worse.

Biden has pledged to appoint prosecutors who extend these insane far left policies nationwide. That's what he's done. That's called the manifesto. He agreed to all this stuff. The craziest thing, you're supposed to bring it to the right. He actually brought it further left. Bernie never dreamt that this was possible, crazy Bernie. Do you know crazy Bernie? I had a lot of his voters come to me four years ago, a big percentage. You know why? Because I agree with him and he agrees with me on one thing, trade. The trade. Because he knew that other countries are ripping us off and so did I. Nobody else got it. Especially Biden never got it.

And I will always defend law abiding citizens. That's why the rioters are voting for Biden and the law enforcement people, you know, we have it from everybody. We just got the sheriffs in Florida, all of them, all of them. We got Ohio. We got Texas. We got North Carolina. We got South Carolina. We got everybody. I see Rick Perry right there. Rick Perry, what are you doing here, Rick? Rick Perry, one of the greats. But they're all voting for me. . . . This election is about safety and this election is about jobs. . . .

The so-called Paris Climate Accord. It's a disaster, a death sentence. It's a death sentence for your energy jobs. I took it out. I withdrew from that calamity. Biden pledged to reinstate it. It's going to cost you billions and billions of dollars. You know what it really is? It's a way of really taking advantage of the United States. This is what it is. Last year I visited the Shell Petrochemical Plant in Beaver County. Anybody ever hear of Beaver County?

The largest investment in your state's history, all made possible by our pro-energy policies. Biden would wipe out that entire industry, killing the jobs of more than 600,000 Pennsylvania workers. It's probably 940,000 they say. Think of that. Also, prices and everything else. Now Biden today came out and said, "No, no, fracking's okay. It's okay? Did you see that? Fracking's okay. Because he was getting killed. And now we came out in favor of law enforcement.

The Democrats yesterday came out with a plan. Did you see it? Now, they're the DC Democrats. They want to change the name of the Washington Monument, perhaps take it down. Thomas Jefferson, pretty good Thomas Jefferson, right? You could forget about ever hearing that name again. Abraham Lincoln, you could forget about it. They want to take down all statues, all monuments in Washington.

And no oil, no guns, no God. I don't think George Washington running with Abraham Lincoln as his VP, he'll pick Abraham Lincoln as VP, is going to win in Texas, or in Pennsylvania, or any place else with those three things eliminated.

That's what they want to do. They want to take away your Second Amendment. If I weren't president, you would either have an obliterated Second Amendment or it would be gone entirely. I am standing between them and your Second Amendment. And that's it. That's it. They know.

It's just the craziest thing. Also, I am truly an environmentalist, but you have to understand. When we do things and they don't, and we clean, and it's very expensive to do that and they don't, and we have this massive planet, and China, India, Russia, Germany, all these places, it's fuming up and we're doing our job and beautiful. No, they have to do it also. Otherwise, it just doesn't work the way it's supposed to.

When asked whether he would be willing to destroy the jobs of hundreds of thousands of blue-collar workers to push his anti-energy agenda, you know what the answer is, right? It's the Green New Deal, right? This Green New Deal. This was made up by people that don't get it. Either that or people that just don't like our country very much. But Biden replied yes, he'll get rid of those jobs.

In less than four years we've achieved more than anyone thought possible. We passed massive tax cuts for hardworking families and we eliminated more regulations than any administration in the history of our country. I saved the U.S. auto industry by withdrawing from the last administration's job-killing catastrophe known as the Trans-Pacific Partnership. It would have been a catastrophe, not only for autos by the way, for everything else too. To protect our workers I imposed stiff tariffs on foreign aluminum and foreign steel. That kept you guys very busy. . . all over the place. This week my administration reached a breakthrough agreement to stop additional steel imports from Brazil and from Mexico for the rest of the year despite the USMCA, sometimes they get a little carried away and we have to do a little tariff action on them. So we stopped that. . . .

Earlier this year I kept my promise to the Commonwealth of Pennsylvania when we ended the NAFTA nightmare and signed the brand new U.S.-Mexico-Canada agreement into law which is in effect now and really doing well. Everyone said it will never happen, and I had great help from these gentlemen right here. I took the toughest ever action to stand up to China's pillaging, plundering and rampant theft of Pennsylvania and many other places, jobs. That's all throughout the world by the way but our states have been just pillaged by China and others. Joe Biden's agenda is made in China, my agenda is made in America.

After years and years of rebuilding other countries, we are finally rebuilding our country, it's called America First. We're America First, that's enough, and we're bringing our soldiers back home. You see what's going on. After 19 years in Afghanistan, far away places, to bring hope to our inner cities, I created opportunity zones, Tim Scott, great senator from South Carolina worked on it with me. Passed criminal justice reform, delivered permanent funding for historically black colleges and universities that Obama would never do and before the China virus we achieved the lowest African-American, Hispanic-American, Asian-American unemployment rates ever recorded by far. And they're now heading back in that direction quickly. Democrat politicians have failed the black community for decades, they've failed the Asian community, the Hispanic community. They failed women. The numbers on women's unemployment were the best in 61 years. Biden spent the last 47 years betraying the American people. He was always for things that you wouldn't want and now he's changing, "No, I never said that. I never said that." I've spent the last four years keeping my promises and delivering for the African-American community and for all communities and the best is yet to come.

Perhaps in no area have our opponents more thoroughly betrayed working families of all backgrounds and on the subject of immigration, we've been fighting for that. Under my administration we achieved the most secure border in American history. We ended catch and release, stopped asylum fraud, and we've deported 20,000 gang members and we get them out and we get them out fast. Thank you ICE. ICE and Border Patrol. ICE and Border Patrol.

We built 300 miles of border wall and we're adding 10 new miles every single week. Every week and the wall will be finished very soon and by the way, they keep saying, "But Mexico will be paying for the wall," and I said respectfully to Mexico but they will be paying for the wall. They understand that, they just don't want to write it and that's okay too. Because Mexico's treated us very well. The president of Mexico, right now they have 27,000 Mexican soldiers on our border guarding us from people coming in illegally into our country. We invested $2.5 trillion in the United States military and launched the first new branch of the United States Armed Forces in nearly 75 years since the Air Force and that's called the Space Force. . . .

I withdrew from the last administration's disastrous Iran nuclear deal, think of this. Obama paid $150 billion for a short-term deal. He gave $1.8 billion in cash. You ever see a million dollars like at a casino floor or something in $100 bills? It's a lot, it's like the size of this, right? Now think $1.8 billion. How did you guys allow that to happen? They said we all voted against it. I kept my promise, recognized the true capital of Israel. You never know nowadays, right? And I opened the U.S. embassy in Jerusalem. I recognized Israeli sovereignty over the Golan Heights. They've been trying to get that done for 52 years, I got it done immediately.

By the way, as far as the capital of Israel, Jerusalem, they've been talking about many, many presidents. They all promised it, nobody did it. I did it. We get things done, and we just did something that is incredible. Even the *New York Times* gave it good reviews, not good reviews, beyond good reviews. Tom Friedman gave it phenomenal reviews, you believe that? That's we achieved the first breakthrough in Middle East peace in decades, a deal with Israel and the UAE. It's a deal with Israel and the UAE and that's going to lead and I'm going to tell you we have representatives over right now and other people are saying we want to get in that deal. You'll have peace in the Middle East. We want to get the hell out. Let's get them all back. Let's get them all back. Don't forget, we're energy independent. There used to be a reason. Now we do have a reason, it's called Israel, and we have some very good partnerships over there. In all fairness we have some countries that have treated us very well and we're going to take care of those countries, but we are energy independent for the first time and that's a very good feeling.

Our military has never been stronger than it is now. It's new and it's beautiful and I told you we took over 100% of the ISIS caliphate in Iraq and Syria and we killed the founder and leader of ISIS al-Baghdadi, and separately, we killed the world's number one terrorist, number one terrorist for decades and decades, Qasem Soleimani. We killed Soleimani. It's a big step for the Middle East. We kept America out of wars. Remember they always said, "Oh, this Trump. He's radical, he's really, I mean he's off the … He's too radical. He'll get us in wars." I kept us out of wars, what happened with North Korea? Look, I get along with Kim Jong-un. They say, "That's terrible he gets along." No it's good if I get along. If I get along with Russia, is that a good thing or a bad thing? I think it's a good thing.

Together we've been rapidly fixing a half a century of disasters and Biden was there for every one of them. Joe Biden supported NAFTA, China's entry into the

World Trade. He supported the Korean deal, the Korean deal was so bad, it was so bad. This was a deal that was going to produce to South Korea done by Crooked Hillary Clinton, this was a deal that was going to produce 250,000 jobs. She said, "This will be 250,000," and she was right, for South Korea. It produced 250,000 jobs. For us, we got nothing. . . .

Just in closing, we will rapidly return to full employment, soaring wages and record prosperity. We will hire more police, increase penalties for assault on law enforcement. Surge federal prosecutors into high-crime communities and ban sanctuary cities. We will appoint prosecutors, judges, and justices who believe in enforcing the law, not their own political agenda. We will uphold religious liberty, free speech and the right to keep and bear arms.

America will land the first woman on the moon and the United States will be the first nation to land an astronaut on Mars. When I took over, NASA was dead. Now it's the most vibrant space center in the world, by far. We will restore patriotic education to our schools and we'll teach our children to love our country, honor our history and always respect our great American flag. We will live by the timeless words of our national motto, In God, We Trust. For years, you had a president who apologized for America. Now you have a president who is standing up for America.

Print Citations

CMS: Trump, Donald. "Rally Speech in Latrobe, Pennsylvania." Speech at Trump rally, Latrobe, PA, September 3, 2020. In *The Reference Shelf: Representative American Speeches, 2019-2020,* edited by Annette Calzone, 93-98. Amenia, NY: Grey House Publishing, 2020.

MLA: Trump, Donald. "Rally Speech in Latrobe, Pennsylvania." 3 September 2020, Latrobe, PA. Speech. *The Reference Shelf: Representative American Speeches, 2019-2020,* edited by Annette Calzone, Grey House Publishing, 2020, pp. 93-98.

APA: Trump, D. (2020, September 3). Speech at Trump rally, Latrobe, Pennsylvania. Latrobe, PA. In Annette Calzone (Ed.), *The reference shelf: Representative American speeches, 2019-2020* (pp. 93-98). Amenia, NY: Grey House Publishing.

4

The Great Divide—The 2020 Election

President-elect Joe Biden ran on a platform of defeating the coronavirus with science and unifying the nation.

Joe Biden and Kamala Harris Will Lead by Example

By Gretchen Whitmer

Michigan Governor Gretchen Whitmer came out in support of Joe Biden and Kamala Harris in the 2020 presidential race at the August Democratic National Convention, pointing out that they would lead by example and rely on science in combatting the COVID-19 pandemic. Whitmer sharply criticized the partisan politics and ego of President Donald Trump, insisting that Biden and former President Barack Obama, not Trump, had saved many American jobs.

I'm Governor Gretchen Whitmer, or, as Donald Trump calls me, that woman from Michigan. Tonight, I'm here at UAW Local 652 in Lansing, Michigan. Auto workers in this union and across our state could have lost their jobs if not for Barack Obama and Joe Biden. In 2009, the Obama-Biden administration inherited the worst economic crisis since the Great Depression, the auto industry in the brink of collapse, a million jobs at stake, but President Obama and Vice President Biden didn't waste time blaming anyone else or shirking their responsibility. They got to work. They brought together union members, companies, and lawmakers on both sides of the aisle, and they saved the auto industry.

When, you know, just a few months ago, as our nation began battling COVID-19, auto workers across Michigan spring into action, and they started making protective equipment for doctors and nurses on the front lines. Let me break it down. President Obama and Vice President Biden saved these auto workers livelihoods. Then these workers did their part to save American lives. That's the story of this great nation. Action begets action, progress begets progress. When we work together, we can accomplish anything. After all, democracy is a team sport, especially now.

It's crucial that we rally together to fight this virus and build our economy back better. From the jump, we took this pandemic seriously in Michigan. We listened to medical experts. We planned, and with a lot of work from the auto workers and too little help from the White House, we executed our plan. We saved thousands of lives. Just imagine if we had a national strategy, so everyone who needs a test gets one for free. So, everyone has access to a safe vaccine. So, our kids and educators have the resources they need to safely get back to school.

With Joe Biden and Kamala Harris in the White House, we will. Joe Biden and Kamala Harris will lead by example. It'll be science not politics or ego that will drive

---

Delivered on August 17, 2020, to the Democratic National Convention.

their decisions. They know the health of our people goes hand in hand with the strength of our economy. They know action begets action.

Over the past few months, we've learned what's essential, rising to the challenge, not denying it. We've learned who is essential to, not just the wealthiest among us, not a president who fights his fellow Americans rather than fight the virus that's killing us and our economy. It's the people put their own health at risk to care for the rest of us. They are the MVPs, the nurses and the doctors, the utility workers, truck drivers, and grocery clerks, the childcare workers, the parents, the teachers, the mail carriers and the auto workers. So many of these essential workers have lost their lives to COVID. Nearly a thousand healthcare workers, more than 170,000 people across America, including a five-year-old girl named Skylar from Detroit, whose mom is a police officer and dad is a firefighter.

Generation after generation, our nation has been defined by what we do or what we fail to do. So, for Skylar, for her parents and in the memory of all those we've lost, let us act, let us heal as one nation. Let us find strength to do the work.

Print Citations

CMS: Whitmer, Gretchen. "Joe Biden and Kamala Harris Will Lead by Example." Speech at the Democratic National Convention, August 17, 2020. In *The Reference Shelf: Representative American Speeches, 2019-2020,* edited by Annette Calzone, 101-102. Amenia, NY: Grey House Publishing, 2020.

MLA: Whitmer, Gretchen. "Joe Biden and Kamala Harris Will Lead by Example." Democratic National Convention, 17 August 2020. Speech. *The Reference Shelf: Representative American Speeches, 2019-2020,* edited by Annette Calzone, Grey House Publishing, pp. 101-102.

APA: Whitmer, G. (2020, August 17). Speech on Joe Biden and Kamala Harris will lead by example. Democratic National Convention. In Annette Calzone (Ed.), *The reference shelf: Representative American speeches, 2019-2020* (pp. 101-102). Amenia, NY: Grey House Publishing.

Acceptance Speech of the Democratic Vice Presidential Nominee

By Kamala Harris

Kamala Harris's acceptance of the vice presidential nomination at the August Democratic National Convention reflected on the sacrifices and dedication of many who came before her. Harris remarked on the 100th anniversary of the passage of the 19th Amendment and the journey from that moment to this, thanking the generations who paved the way for the leadership of Barack Obama and Hillary Clinton and for her own nomination as vice president.

That I am here tonight is a testament to the dedication of generations before me, women and men who believed so fiercely in the promise of equality, liberty, and justice for all. This week marks the 100th anniversary of the passage of the 19th Amendment, and we celebrate the women who fought for that right. Yet so many of the black women who helped secure that victory were still prohibited from voting long after its ratification, but they were undeterred. Without fanfare or recognition, they organized and testified and rallied and marched and fought, not just for their vote, but for a seat at the table. These women and the generations that followed worked to make democracy and opportunity real in the lives of all of us who followed. They paved the way for the trail-blazing leadership of Barack Obama and Hillary Clinton. And these women inspired us to pick up the torch and fight on. Women like Mary Church Terrell, Mary McLeod Bethune, Fannie Lou Hamer, and Diane Nash, Constance Baker Motley, and the great Shirley Chisholm.

We're not often taught their stories, but as Americans, we all stand on their own shoulders. And there's another woman whose name isn't known, whose story isn't shared, another woman whose shoulders I stand on. And that's my mother, Shyamala Gopalan Harris. She came here from India at age 19 to pursue her dream of curing cancer. At the University of California Berkeley, she met my father Donald Harris, who had come from Jamaica to study economics. They fell in love in that most American way while marching together for justice in the civil rights movement of the 1960s. In the streets of Oakland and Berkeley, I got a strollers-eye view of people getting into what the great John Lewis called good trouble. When I was five, my parents split and my mother raised us mostly on her own. Like so many mothers, she worked around the clock to make it work, packing lunches before we woke

---

Delivered on August 19, 2020, to the Democratic National Convention.

up and paying bills after we went to bed, helping us with homework at the kitchen table, and shuttling us to church for choir practice.

She made it look easy, though it never was. My mother instilled in my sister Maya and me the values that would chart the course of our lives. She raised us to be proud, strong Black women, and she raised us to know and be proud of our Indian heritage. She taught us to put family first, the family you're born into, and the family you choose. Family is my husband Doug, who I met on a blind date set up by my best friend. Family is our beautiful children, Cole and Ella who call me Momala. Family is my sister. Family is my best friend, my nieces, and my godchildren. Family is my uncles, my aunts, and my chithis.

Family is Mrs. Shelton, my second mother who lived two doors down and helped raise me. Family is my beloved Alpha Kappa Alpha, our Divine Nine, and my HBCU brothers and sisters. Family is the friends I turned to when my mother, the most important person in my life, passed away from cancer. And even as she taught us to keep our family at the center of our world, she also pushed us to see a world beyond ourselves. She taught us to be conscious and compassionate about the struggles of all people, to believe public service is a noble cause, and the fight for justice is a shared responsibility. That led me to become a lawyer, a district attorney, attorney general, and a United States Senator. And at every step of the way, I've been guided by the words I spoke from the first time I stood in a courtroom, "Kamala Harris for the people."

I have fought for children and survivors of sexual assault. I fought against transnational criminal organizations. I took on the biggest banks and helped take down one of the biggest for profit colleges. I know a predator when I see one. My mother taught me that service to others gives life purpose and meaning. And oh, how I wish she were here tonight, but I know she's looking down on me from above. I keep thinking about that 25 year old Indian woman, all of five feet tall, who gave birth to me at Kaiser hospital in Oakland, California. On that day, she probably could have never imagined that I would be standing before you now and speaking these words. I accept your nomination for Vice President of the United States of America.

I do so committed to the values she taught me, to the word that teaches me to walk by faith and not by sight, and to a vision passed on through generations of Americans, one that Joe Biden shares. A vision of our nation as a beloved community, where all are welcome, no matter what we look like, no matter where we come from, or who we love. A country where we may not agree on every detail, but we are united by the fundamental belief that every human being is of infinite worth, deserving of compassion, dignity, and respect. A country where we look out for one another, where we rise and fall as one, where we face our challenges and celebrate our triumphs together.

Today, that country feels distant. Donald Trump's failure of leadership has cost lives and livelihoods. If you're a parent struggling with your child's remote learning, or you're a teacher struggling on the other side of that screen, you know what we're doing right now is not working, and we are a nation that is grieving. Grieving the loss of life, the loss of jobs, the loss of opportunities, the loss of normalcy, and yes, the loss of certainty. And while this virus touches us all, we got to be honest. It is not an equal opportunity offender. Black, Latino, and Indigenous people are suffering and dying disproportionately. And this is not a coincidence. It is the effect of structural racism, of inequities in education and technology, healthcare and housing, job security and transportation.

The injustice in reproductive and maternal health care, in the excessive of force by police, and in our broader criminal justice system. This virus, it has no eyes, and yet it knows exactly how we see each other and how we treat each other. And let's be clear. There is no vaccine for racism. We have got to do the work for George Floyd, for Breonna Taylor, for the lives of too many others to name, for our children, and for all of us. We've got to do the work to fulfill that promise of equal justice under law, because here's the thing. None of us are free until all of us are free.

So we're at an inflection point. The constant chaos leaves us adrift. The incompetence makes us feel afraid. The callousness makes us feel alone. It's a lot, and here's the thing. We can do better, and deserve so much more. We must elect a president who will bring something different, something better, and do the important work. A president who will bring all of us together, Black, White, Latino, Asian, Indigenous, to achieve the future we collectively want. We must elect Joe Biden. And I will tell you, I knew Joe as vice president. I knew Joe on the campaign trail. And I first got to know Joe as the father of my friend. So Joe's son Beau and I served as attorneys general of our states Delaware and California.

During the great recession, he and I spoke on the phone nearly every day, working together to win back billions of dollars for homeowners from the big banks that foreclosed on people's homes. And Beau would I, we would talk about his family. How as a single father, Joe would spend four hours every day riding the train back and forth from Wilmington to Washington. Beau and Hunter got to have breakfast every morning with their dad. They went to sleep every night with the sound of his voice, reading bedtime stories.

And while they endured an unspeakable loss, those two little boys always knew that they were deeply, unconditionally loved. And what also moved me about Joe is the work that he did as he was going back and forth. This is the leader who wrote the Violence Against Women Act, and enacted the Assault Weapons Ban, who as vice president implemented the Recovery Act, which brought our country back from the great recessions. He championed the Affordable Care Act, protecting millions of Americans with preexisting conditions, who spent decades promoting American values and interests around the world. Joe, he believes we stand with our allies and stand up to our adversaries. Right now, we have a president who turns our tragedies into political weapons. Joe will be a president who turns our challenges into purpose. Joe will bring us together to build an economy that doesn't leave anyone behind, where a good paying job is the floor, not the ceiling.

Joe will bring us together to end this pandemic, and make sure that we are prepared for the next one. Joe will bring us together to squarely face and dismantle racial injustice, furthering the work of generations. Joe and I believe that we can build that beloved community. One that is strong and decent, just and kind. One in which we can all see ourselves. That's the vision that our parents and grandparents fought for. The vision that made my own life possible. The vision that makes the American promise, for all its complexities and imperfections, a promise worth fighting for. So make no mistake, the road ahead is not easy. We may stumble. We may fall short, but I pledge to you that we will act boldly and deal with our challenges honestly. We will speak truths, and we will act with the same faith in you that we ask you to place in us.

We believe that our country, all of us, will stand together for a better future. And we already are. We see it in the doctors, the nurses, the home healthcare workers, and frontline workers who are risking their lives to save people they've never met. We see it in the teachers and truck drivers, the factory workers and farmers, the postal workers and poll workers, all putting their own safety on the line to help us get through this pandemic. And we see it in so many of you who are working, not just to get us through our current crisis, but to somewhere better.

There's something happening all across our country. It's not about Joe or me. It's about you, and it's about us. People of all ages and colors and creeds who are, yes, taking to the streets, and also persuading our family members, rallying our friends, organizing our neighbors, and getting out the vote. And we have shown that when we vote, we expand access to healthcare, and expand access to the ballot box, and ensure that more working families can make a decent living. And I'm so inspired by a new generation. You, you are pushing us to realize the ideals of our nation, pushing us to live the values we share. Decency and fairness, justice, and love. You are patriots who remind us that to love our country is to fight for the ideals of our country.

In this election, we have a chance to change the course of history. We're all in this fight. You, me, and Joe, together. What an awesome responsibility. What an awesome privilege. So let's fight with conviction. Let's fight with hope. Let's fight with confidence in ourselves, and a commitment to each other, to the America we know is possible, the America we love. And years from now, this moment will have passed, and our children and our grandchildren will look in our eyes. And they're going to ask us, "Where were you when the stakes were so high?" They will ask us, "What was it like?" And we will tell them. We will tell them not just how we felt. We will tell them what we did. Thank you, God bless you, and God bless the United States of America.

Print Citations

CMS: Harris, Kamala. "Acceptance Speech of the Democratic Vice Presidential Nominee." Speech at the Democratic National Convention, August 19, 2020. In *The Reference Shelf: Representative American Speeches, 2019-2020*, edited by Annette Calzone, 103-107. Amenia, NY: Grey House Publishing, 2020.

MLA: Harris, Kamala. "Acceptance Speech of the Democratic Vice Presidential Nominee." Democratic National Convention, 19 August 2020. Speech. *The Reference Shelf: Representative American Speeches, 2019-2020*, edited by Annette Calzone, Grey House Publishing, 2020, pp. 103-107.

APA: Harris, K. (2020, August 19). Acceptance speech of the Democratic vice presidential nominee. Democratic National Convention. In Annette Calzone (Ed.), *The reference shelf: Representative American speeches, 2019-2020* (pp. 103-107). Amenia, NY: Grey House Publishing.

Acceptance Speech of the Republican Presidential Candidate

By Donald Trump

Incumbent President Donald Trump accepted the nomination as the Republican presidential candidate at the Republican National Convention in August 2020. Trump outlined his goals, stressing a strong economy, law-and-order values, and stopping the course of the COVID-19 pandemic. Trump spoke of rekindling faith in America's destiny, criticizing cancel culture and the Democratic Party for tearing down the United States.

Thank you very much. Thank you very much. Thank you very much.

Friends, delegates and distinguished guests, please. I stand before you tonight honored by your support, proud of the extraordinary progress we have made together over the last four incredible years and blooming with confidence in the bright future we will build for America over the next four years. . . .

My fellow Americans, tonight, with a heart full of gratitude and boundless optimism, I profoundly accept this nomination for president of the United States.

The Republican Party, the party of Abraham Lincoln, goes forward united, determined and ready to welcome millions of Democrats, independents and anyone who believes in the greatness of America and the righteous heart of the American people.

In the new term as president, we will again build the greatest economy in history, quickly returning to full employment, soaring incomes and record prosperity. We will defend America against all threats and protect America against all dangers. We will lead America into new frontiers of ambition and discovery, and we will reach four new heights of national achievement. We will rekindle faith in our values, new pride in our history and a new spirit of unity that can only be realized through love for our great country.

Because we understand that America is not a land cloaked in darkness. America is the torch that enlightens the entire world. Gathered here at our beautiful and majestic White House, known all over the world as the people's house, we cannot help but marvel at the miracle that is our great American story.

This has been the home of larger-than-life figures like Teddy Roosevelt and Andrew Jackson, who rallied Americans to bold visions of a bigger and brighter future. Within these walls lived tenacious generals like President Grant and Eisenhower,

Delivered on August 27, 2020, to the Republican National Convention.

who led our soldiers in the cause of freedom. From these grounds, Thomas Jefferson sent Lewis and Clark to chart our continent. In the depths of a bloody Civil War, President Abraham Lincoln looked out these very windows upon a half-completed Washington Monument and asked God and his Providence to save our nation. Two weeks after Pearl Harbor, Franklin Delano Roosevelt welcomed Winston Churchill, and just inside, they set our people on course to victory in the Second World War.

In recent months, our nation and the entire planet has been struck by a new and powerful invisible enemy. Like those brave Americans before us, we are meeting this challenge. We are delivering lifesaving therapies and will produce a vaccine before the end of the year, or maybe even sooner. We will defeat the virus and the pandemic and emerge stronger than ever before.

What united generations past was an unshakable confidence in America's destiny and an unbreakable faith in the American people. They knew that our country is blessed by God and has a special purpose in this world. It is that conviction that inspired the formation of our union, our westward expansion, the abolition of slavery, the passage of civil rights, the space program and the overthrow of fascism, tyranny, and communism. . . .

At no time before have voters faced a clearer choice between two parties, two visions, two philosophies or two agendas. This election will decide if we save the American dream or whether we allow a socialist agenda to demolish our cherished destiny. It will decide whether we rapidly create millions of high-paying jobs or whether we crush our industries and send millions of these jobs overseas, as has been foolishly done for many decades. Your vote will decide whether we protect law-abiding Americans or whether we give free rein to violent anarchists and agitators and criminals who threaten our citizens.

And this election will decide whether we will defend the American way of life or allow a radical movement to completely dismantle and destroy it. It won't happen. At the Democrat National Convention, Joe Biden and his party repeatedly assailed America as a land of racial, economic and social injustice, so tonight, I ask you a simple question: How can the Democratic Party ask to lead our country when it spent so much time tearing down our country? . . .

In the left's backward view, they do not see America as the most free, just and exceptional nation on Earth. Instead, they see a wicked nation that must be punished for its sins. Our opponents say that redemption for you can only come from giving power to them. This is a tired anthem spoken by every repressive movement throughout history, but in this country, we don't look to career politicians for salvation. In America, we do not turn to government to restore ourselves. We put our faith in almighty God. . . .

Four years ago, I ran for president because I cannot watch this betrayal of our country any longer. I could not sit by as career politicians let other countries take advantage of us on trade, borders, foreign policy and national defense. . . .

From the moment I left my former life behind—and it was a good life—I have done nothing but fight for you. I did what our political establishment never expected and could never forgive, breaking the cardinal rule of Washington politics. I kept my promise. Together we have ended the rule of the failed political class, and they are desperate to get their power back by any means necessary. You have seen that. They are angry at me because instead of putting them first, I very simply said, "America first."

Thank you. . . .

In recent months, our nation and the world has been hit by the once-in-a-century pandemic that China allowed to spread around the globe. They could have stopped it, but they allowed it to come out. . . .

Many Americans, including me—I have sadly lost friends and cherished loved ones to this horrible disease. As one nation, we mourn, we grieve, and we hold in our hearts forever the memories of all of those lives that have been so tragically taken so unnecessary.

In their honor, we unite in their memory. We will overcome it. And when the China virus hit, we launched the largest national mobilization since World War II, invoking the Defense Production Act. We produce the world's largest supply of ventilators. Not a single American who has needed a ventilator has been denied a ventilator. .. .

We shipped hundreds of millions of masks, gloves and gowns to our frontline health care workers to protect our nation's seniors. We rushed supplies, testing kits and personnel to nursing homes. We gave everything you can possibly give, and we're are still giving it because we are taking care of our senior citizens. . . .

The United States has among the lowest case fatality rates of any major country anywhere in the world. The European Union's case fatality rate is nearly three times higher than ours, but you don't hear that. They do not write about that. They don't want to write about that. They do not want you to know those things. Altogether, the nations of Europe have experienced a 30 percent greater increase in excess mortality than the United States. Think of that.

We enacted the largest package of financial relief in American history. Thanks to our Paycheck Protection Program, we have saved or supported more than 50 million American jobs. That's one of the reasons we're advancing so rapidly with our economy. Great job. As a result, we have seen the smallest economic contraction of any nation, and we are recovering at a much faster rate than anybody.

Over the past three months, we have gained over nine million jobs, and that is a record in the history of our country. Unfortunately, from the beginning, our opponents have shown themselves capable of nothing but a partisan ability to criticize. . . .

Most importantly, we are marshaling America's scientific genius to produce a vaccine in record time. Under Operation Warp Speed, we have three different vaccines in the final stage of trials right now, years ahead of what has been achieved before. Nobody thought it could be done this fast. Normally it would be years, and we did it in a matter of a few months. We are producing them in advance so hundreds of millions of doses can be quickly available. We have a safe and effective vaccine this year, and together we will crush the virus. . . .

Joe Biden may claim he is an ally of the light, but when it comes to his agenda, Biden wants to keep us completely in the dark. He doesn't have a clue. He has pledged a $4 trillion tax hike on almost all American families, which would totally collapse our rapidly improving economy, and once again record stock markets that we have right now will also collapse. That means your 401(k)s. That means all of the stocks that you have. . . .

Biden has promised to abolish the production of American oil, coal, shale and natural gas, laying waste to the economies of Pennsylvania, Ohio, Texas, North Dakota, Oklahoma, Colorado and New Mexico—destroying those states, absolutely destroying those states, and others.

Millions of jobs will be lost, and energy prices will soar. These same policies led to crippling power outages in California just last week. Everybody saw that. Tremendous power outage. Nobody's seen anything like it, but we saw it last week in California. How can Joe Biden claim to be an ally of the light when his own party can't even keep the lights on?

Joe Biden's campaign has even published a 110-page policy platform. You can't get away from this. Co-authored with far-left senator crazy Bernie Sanders. The Biden-Bernie manifesto calls for suspending all removals of illegal aliens, implementing nationwide catch and release, providing illegal aliens with free taxpayer-funded lawyers. Everybody gets a lawyer. Come over to our country—everybody has a lawyer. We have a lawyer for you. That's is all we need is more lawyers. . . .

He also supports deadly sanctuary cities that protect criminal aliens. He promised to end national security travel bans from jihadist nations, and he pledged to increase refugee admissions by 700 percent.

This is in the manifesto.

The Biden plan would eliminate America's borders in the middle of a global pandemic, and he is even talking about taking the wall down. How about that?

Biden also vowed to oppose school choice and close all charter schools, ripping away the ladder of opportunity for Black and Hispanic children. In a second term, I will expand charter schools and provide school choice to every family in America. And we will always treat our teachers with the tremendous respect that they deserve. Great people. Great, great people.

Joe Biden claims he has empathy for the vulnerable, yet the party he leads supports the extreme late-term abortion of defenseless babies, right up until the moment of birth. Democrat leaders talk about moral decency, but they have no problem with stopping a baby's beating heart in the ninth month of pregnancy. Democrat politicians refuse to protect innocent life, and then they lecture us about morality and saving America's soul. Tonight, we proudly declare that all children, born and unborn, have a God-given right to life.

During the Democrat convention, the words "under God" were removed from the Pledge of Allegiance. Not once, but twice. We will never do that. But the fact is, this is where they are coming from. Like it or not, this is where they are coming from. If the left gains power, they will demolish the suburbs, confiscate your guns, and appoint justices who will wipe away your second amendment and other constitutional freedoms.

Biden is a Trojan horse for socialism. If Joe Biden doesn't have the strength to stand up to wild eyed Marxists like Bernie Sanders and his fellow radicals, and there are many, there are many many, we see them all the time. It is incredible, actually. Then how is he ever going to stand up for you? He's not.

The most dangerous aspect of the Biden platform is the attack on public safety. The Biden-Bernie manifesto calls for abolishing cash bail, immediately releasing 400,000 criminals onto the streets and into your neighborhoods. When asked if he supports cutting police funding, Joe Biden replied, yes, absolutely. When Congresswoman Ilhan Omar called the Minneapolis Police Department "a cancer that is rotten to the root," Biden would not disavow her support and reject her endorsement. He proudly displayed it shortly later on his website. Displayed it in big letters.

Make no mistake, if you give power to Joe Biden, the radical left will defund police departments all across America. They will pass federal legislation to reduce law enforcement nationwide. They will make every city look like Democrat-run Portland, Oregon.

No one will be safe in Biden's America. My administration will always stand with the men and women of law enforcement. . . .

When there is police misconduct, the justice system must hold wrongdoers fully and completely accountable, and it will. But when we can never have a situation where things are going on as they are today, we must never allow mob rule. We can never allow mob rule.

In the strongest possible terms, the Republican Party condemns the rioting, looting, arson, and violence we have seen in Democrat-run cities all, like Kenosha, Minneapolis, Portland, Chicago, and New York, and many others, Democrat-run. . . .

Many things have a different name now, and the rules are constantly changing. The goal of cancel culture is to make Americans live in fear of being fired, expelled, shamed, humiliated, and driven from society as we know it. The far-left wants to coerce you into saying what you know to be false and scare you out of saying what you know to be true. Very sad. But on November 3, you can send them a very thundering message they will never forget.

Joe Biden is weak. He takes his marching orders from liberal hypocrites who drive their cities into the ground while fleeing from the scene of the wreckage. The same liberals want to eliminate school choice while they enroll their children into the finest private schools in the land. They want to open the borders while living in walled off compounds and communities and the best neighborhoods in the world. They want to defund the police while they have armed guards for themselves. This November, we must turn the page forever on this failed political class. . . .

For America, nothing is impossible.

Over the next four years, we will prove worthy of this magnificent legacy. We will reach stunning new heights, and we will show the world that for America there is a dream, and it is not beyond your reach. Together, we are unstoppable. Together, we are unbeatable. Because together, we are the proud citizens of the United States of America.

On November 3, we will make America safer. We will make America stronger. We will make America prouder. And we will make America greater than ever before. I am very proud to be the nominee of the Republican Party.

I love you all. God bless you, and God bless America.

Print Citations

CMS: Trump, Donald. "Acceptance Speech of the Republican Presidential Candidate." Speech at the Republican National Convention, August 27, 2020. In *The Reference Shelf: Representative American Speeches, 2019-2020,* edited by Annette Calzone, 108-113. Amenia, NY: Grey House Publishing, 2020.

MLA: Trump, Donald. "Acceptance Speech of the Republican Presidential Candidate." Republican National Convention, 27 August 2020. Speech. *The Reference Shelf: Representative American Speeches, 2019-2020,* edited by Annette Calzone, Grey House Publishing, 2020, pp. 108-113.

APA: Trump, D. (2020, August 27). Acceptance speech of the republican presidential candidate. Republican National Convention. In Annette Calzone (Ed.), *The reference shelf: Representative American speeches, 2019-2020* (pp. 108-113). Amenia, NY: Grey House Publishing.

Acceptance Speech of the Democratic Presidential Candidate

By Joe Biden

Former Vice President Joe Biden accepted the nomination as the Democratic presidential candidate at the August Democratic National Convention. Biden stressed unity, a dedication to science and transparency, addressing racial injustice, and overcoming the COVID-19 pandemic. Biden put forth his election as a return to decency and morality, stating that together there was no goal the American people could not achieve.

Good evening. Ella Baker, a giant of the civil rights movement, left us with this wisdom: Give people light and they will find a way.

Give people light.

Those are words for our time.

The current president has cloaked America in darkness for much too long. Too much anger. Too much fear. Too much division.

Here and now, I give you my word: If you entrust me with the presidency, I will draw on the best of us, not the worst. I will be an ally of the light, not of the darkness.

It's time for us, for We the People, to come together.

For make no mistake. United we can, and will, overcome this season of darkness in America. We will choose hope over fear, facts over fiction, fairness over privilege.

I am a proud Democrat, and I will be proud to carry the banner of our party into the general election. So, it is with great honor and humility that I accept this nomination for President of the United States of America.

But while I will be a Democratic candidate, I will be an American president. I will work as hard for those who didn't support me as I will for those who did.

That's the job of a president. To represent all of us, not just our base or our party. This is not a partisan moment. This must be an American moment.

It's a moment that calls for hope and light and love. Hope for our futures, light to see our way forward, and love for one another.

America isn't just a collection of clashing interests of Red States or Blue States.

We're so much bigger than that.

We're so much better than that.

Nearly a century ago, Franklin Roosevelt pledged a New Deal in a time of massive unemployment, uncertainty and fear.

Delivered on August 20, 2020, at the Democratic National Convention.

Stricken by disease, stricken by a virus, FDR insisted that he would recover and prevail, and he believed America could as well.

And he did.

And so can we.

This campaign isn't just about winning votes.

It's about winning the heart and, yes, the soul of America.

Winning it for the generous among us, not the selfish. Winning it for the workers who keep this country going, not just the privileged few at the top. Winning it for those communities who have known the injustice of the "knee on the neck." For all the young people who have known only an America of rising inequity and shrinking opportunity.

They deserve to experience America's promise in full.

No generation ever knows what history will ask of it. All we can ever know is whether we'll be ready when that moment arrives.

And now history has delivered us to one of the most difficult moments America has ever faced. Four historic crises. All at the same time. A perfect storm.

The worst pandemic in over 100 years. The worst economic crisis since the Great Depression. The most compelling call for racial justice since the '60s. And the undeniable realities and accelerating threats of climate change.

So, the question for us is simple: Are we ready?

I believe we are.

We must be.

All elections are important. But we know in our bones this one is more consequential.

America is at an inflection point. A time of real peril, but of extraordinary possibilities.

We can choose the path of becoming angrier, less hopeful and more divided. A path of shadow and suspicion.

Or we can choose a different path, and together, take this chance to heal, to be reborn, to unite. A path of hope and light. This is a life-changing election that will determine America's future for a very long time.

Character is on the ballot. Compassion is on the ballot. Decency, science, democracy. They are all on the ballot.

Who we are as a nation. What we stand for. And, most importantly, who we want to be. That's all on the ballot.

And the choice could not be clearer.

No rhetoric is needed.

Just judge this president on the facts.

Five million Americans infected with COVID-19.

More than 170,000 Americans have died.

By far the worst performance of any nation on Earth.

More than 50 million people have filed for unemployment this year.

More than 10 million people are going to lose their health insurance this year.

Nearly one in six small businesses have closed this year.

If this president is reelected, we know what will happen.

Cases and deaths will remain far too high.

More mom and pop businesses will close their doors for good.

Working families will struggle to get by, and yet, the wealthiest one percent will get tens of billions of dollars in new tax breaks.

And the assault on the Affordable Care Act will continue until it's destroyed, taking insurance away from more than 20 million people—including more than 15 million people on Medicaid—and getting rid of the protections that President Obama and I passed for people who suffer from a preexisting condition.

And speaking of President Obama, a man I was honored to serve alongside for eight years as Vice President, let me take this moment to say something we don't say nearly enough.

Thank you, Mr. President. You were a great president. A president our children could — and did—look up to.

No one will say that about the current occupant of the office.

What we know about this president is, if he's given four more years, he will be what he's been the last four years.

A president who takes no responsibility, refuses to lead, blames others, cozies up to dictators, and fans the flames of hate and division.

He will wake up every day believing the job is all about him. Never about you.

Is that the America you want for you, your family, your children?

I see a different America.

One that is generous and strong.

Selfless and humble.

It's an America we can rebuild together.

As president, the first step I will take will be to get control of the virus that's ruined so many lives.

Because I understand something this president doesn't.

We will never get our economy back on track, we will never get our kids safely back to school, we will never have our lives back, until we deal with this virus.

The tragedy of where we are today is it didn't have to be this bad.

Just look around.

It's not this bad in Canada. Or Europe. Or Japan. Or almost anywhere else in the world.

The president keeps telling us the virus is going to disappear. He keeps waiting for a miracle. Well, I have news for him, no miracle is coming.

We lead the world in confirmed cases. We lead the world in deaths. Our economy is in tatters, with Black, Latino, Asian American, and Native American communities bearing the brunt of it.

And after all this time, the president still does not have a plan. Well, I do.

If I'm president on Day One we'll implement the national strategy I've been laying out since March.

We'll develop and deploy rapid tests with results available immediately.

We'll make the medical supplies and protective equipment our country needs.

And we'll make them here in America. So we will never again be at the mercy of China and other foreign countries in order to protect our own people.

We'll make sure our schools have the resources they need to be open, safe and effective.

We'll put the politics aside and take the muzzle off our experts so the public gets the information they need and deserve. The honest, unvarnished truth. They can deal with that.

We'll have a national mandate to wear a mask—not as a burden, but to protect each other. It's a patriotic duty.

In short, I will do what we should have done from the very beginning.

Our current president has failed in his most basic duty to this nation.

He failed to protect us.

He failed to protect America.

And, my fellow Americans, that is unforgivable.

As president, I will make you this promise: I will protect America. I will defend us from every attack. Seen. And unseen. Always. Without exception. Every time.

Look, I understand it's hard to have hope right now.

On this summer night, let me take a moment to speak to those of you who have lost the most.

I know how it feels to lose someone you love. I know that deep black hole that opens up in your chest. That you feel your whole being is sucked into it. I know how mean and cruel and unfair life can be sometimes.

But I've learned two things. First, your loved ones may have left this Earth, but they never leave your heart. They will always be with you.

And second, I found the best way through pain and loss and grief is to find purpose.

As God's children each of us have a purpose in our lives.

And we have a great purpose as a nation: To open the doors of opportunity to all Americans. To save our democracy. To be a light to the world once again.

To finally live up to and make real the words written in the sacred documents that founded this nation that all men and women are created equal. Endowed by their Creator with certain unalienable rights. Among them life, liberty and the pursuit of happiness.

You know, my Dad was an honorable, decent man.

He got knocked down a few times pretty hard, but always got up. He worked hard and built a great middle-class life for our family.

He used to say, *"Joey, I don't expect the government to solve my problems, but I expect it to understand them."*

And then he would say: *"Joey, a job is about a lot more than a paycheck. It's about your dignity. It's about respect. It's about your place in your community. It's about looking your kids in the eye and saying, honey, it's going to be OK."*

I've never forgotten those lessons.

That's why my economic plan is all about jobs, dignity, respect and community.

Together, we can, and we will, rebuild our economy. And when we do, we'll not only build it back, we'll build it back better.

With modern roads, bridges, highways, broadband, ports and airports as a new foundation for economic growth. With pipes that transport clean water to every community. With 5 million new manufacturing and technology jobs so the future is made in America.

With a healthcare system that lowers premiums, deductibles and drug prices by building on the Affordable Care Act he's trying to rip away.

With an education system that trains our people for the best jobs of the 21st century, where cost doesn't prevent young people from going to college, and student debt doesn't crush them when they get out.

With childcare and eldercare that make it possible for parents to go to work and for the elderly to stay in their homes with dignity. With an immigration system that powers our economy and reflects our values. With newly empowered labor unions. With equal pay for women. With rising wages you can raise a family on. Yes, we're going to do more than praise our essential workers. We're finally going to pay them.

We can, and we will, deal with climate change. It's not only a crisis, it's an enormous opportunity. An opportunity for America to lead the world in clean energy and create millions of new good-paying jobs in the process.

And we can pay for these investments by ending loopholes and the president's $1.3-trillion tax giveaway to the wealthiest 1 percent and the biggest, most profitable corporations, some of which pay no tax at all.

Because we don't need a tax code that rewards wealth more than it rewards work. I'm not looking to punish anyone. Far from it. But it's long past time the wealthiest people and the biggest corporations in this country paid their fair share.

For our seniors, Social Security is a sacred obligation, a sacred promise made. The current president is threatening to break that promise. He's proposing to eliminate the tax that pays for almost half of Social Security without any way of making up for that lost revenue.

I will not let it happen. If I'm your president, we're going to protect Social Security and Medicare. You have my word.

One of the most powerful voices we hear in the country today is from our young people. They're speaking to the inequity and injustice that has grown up in America. Economic injustice. Racial injustice. Environmental injustice.

I hear their voices, and if you listen, you can hear them too. And whether it's the existential threat posed by climate change, the daily fear of being gunned down in school or the inability to get started in their first job—it will be the work of the next president to restore the promise of America to everyone.

I won't have to do it alone. Because I will have a great vice president at my side. Senator Kamala Harris. She is a powerful voice for this nation. Her story is the American story. She knows about all the obstacles thrown in the way of so many in our country. Women, Black women, Black Americans, South Asian Americans, immigrants, the left-out and left-behind.

But she's overcome every obstacle she's ever faced. No one's been tougher on the big banks or the gun lobby. No one's been tougher in calling out this current administration for its extremism, its failure to follow the law, and its failure to simply tell the truth. Kamala and I both draw strength from our families. For Kamala, it's Doug and their families.

For me, it's Jill and ours.

No man deserves one great love in his life. But I've known two. After losing my first wife in a car accident, Jill came into my life and put our family back together.

She's an educator. A mom. A military Mom. And an unstoppable force. If she puts her mind to it, just get out of the way. Because she's going to get it done. She was a great Second Lady and she will make a great First Lady for this nation; she loves this country so much.

And I will have the strength that can only come from family. Hunter, Ashley and all our grandchildren, my brothers, my sister. They give me courage and lift me up.

And while he is no longer with us, Beau inspires me every day.

Beau served our nation in uniform. A decorated Iraq war veteran.

So I take very personally the profound responsibility of serving as Commander in Chief.

I will be a president who will stand with our allies and friends. I will make it clear to our adversaries the days of cozying up to dictators are over.

Under President Biden, America will not turn a blind eye to Russian bounties on the heads of American soldiers. Nor will I put up with foreign interference in our most sacred democratic exercise—voting.

I will stand always for our values of human rights and dignity. And I will work in common purpose for a more secure, peaceful and prosperous world.

History has thrust one more urgent task on us. Will we be the generation that finally wipes the stain of racism from our national character?

I believe we're up to it.

I believe we're ready.

Just a week ago yesterday was the third anniversary of the events in Charlottesville. Remember seeing those neo-Nazis and Klansmen and white supremacists coming out of the fields with lighted torches? Veins bulging? Spewing the same anti-Semitic bile heard across Europe in the '30s?

Remember the violent clash that ensued between those spreading hate and those with the courage to stand against it?

Remember what the president said?

They were, quote, "very fine people on both sides."

It was a wakeup call for us as a country.

And for me, a call to action. At that moment, I knew I'd have to run. My father taught us that silence was complicity. And I could not remain silent or complicit.

At the time, I said we were in a battle for the soul of this nation.

And we are.

One of the most important conversations I've had this entire campaign is with someone who is too young to vote.

I met with 6-year-old Gianna Floyd, a day before her Daddy, George Floyd, was laid to rest.

She is incredibly brave.

I'll never forget.

When I leaned down to speak with her, she looked into my eyes and said, "Daddy changed the world."

Her words burrowed deep into my heart.

Maybe George Floyd's murder was the breaking point; maybe John Lewis' passing the inspiration.

However it has come to be, America is ready, in John's words, to lay down "the heavy burdens of hate at last" and to do the hard work of rooting out our systemic racism.

America's history tells us that it has been in our darkest moments that we've made our greatest progress. That we've found the light. And in this dark moment, I believe we are poised to make great progress again. That we can find the light once more.

I have always believed you can define America in one word: possibilities.

That in America, everyone, and I mean everyone, should be given the opportunity to go as far as their dreams and God-given ability will take them.

We can never lose that. In times as challenging as these, I believe there is only one way forward. As a united America. United in our pursuit of a more perfect Union. United in our dreams of a better future for us and for our children. United in our determination to make the coming years bright.

Are we ready? I believe we are.

This is a great nation.

And we are a good and decent people.

This is the United States of America.

And there has never been anything we've been unable to accomplish when we've done it together

The Irish poet Seamus Heaney once wrote:

> *"History says,*
> *Don't hope on this side of the grave,*
> *But then, once in a lifetime*
> *The longed-for tidal wave*
> *Of justice can rise up,*
> *And hope and history rhyme"*

This is our moment to make hope and history rhyme.

With passion and purpose, let us begin—you and I together, one nation, under God — united in our love for America and united in our love for each other.

For love is more powerful than hate.

Hope is more powerful than fear.

Light is more powerful than dark.

This is our moment.

This is our mission.

May history be able to say that the end of this chapter of American darkness began here tonight as love and hope and light joined in the battle for the soul of the nation.

And this is a battle that we, together, will win.

I promise you.

Thank you.

And may God bless you.

And may God protect our troops.

Print Citations

CMS: Biden, Joe. "Acceptance Speech of the Democratic Presidential Candidate." Speech at the Democratic National Convention, August 20, 2020. In *The Reference Shelf: Representative American Speeches, 2019-2020,* edited by Annette Calzone, 114-121. Amenia, NY: Grey House Publishing, 2020.

MLA: Biden, Joe. "Acceptance Speech of the Democratic Presidential Candidate." Democratic National Convention, 20 August 2020. Speech. *The Reference Shelf: Representative American Speeches, 2019-2020,* edited by Annette Calzone, Grey House Publishing, 2020, pp. 114-121.

APA: Biden, J. (2020, August 20). Acceptance speech of the democratic presidential candidate. Democratic National Convention. In Annette Calzone (Ed.), *The reference shelf: Representative American speeches, 2019-2020* (pp. 114-121). Amenia, NY: Grey House Publishing.

Do Not Let Them Take Away Your Power

By Barack Obama

Former President Barack Obama came out in support of Joe Biden and Kamala Harris at the Democratic National Convention, stressing the importance of this election to democracy itself. Obama condemned the performance of Donald Trump, citing a lack of leadership that had left too many Americans dead because of the pandemic, heavy job losses, and democratic institutions under threat as never before. Obama presented a Biden presidency as a return to normalcy and American values, one that would unify instead of divide the American people.

Good evening everybody. As you've seen by now, this isn't a normal convention. It's not a normal time. So tonight I want to talk as plainly as I can about the stakes in this election. Because what we do these next 76 days will echo through generations to come. I'm in Philadelphia where our Constitution was drafted and signed. It wasn't a perfect document. It allowed for the inhumanity of slavery and failed to guarantee women and even men who didn't own property the right to participate in the political process. But embedded in this document was a North Star that would guide future generations, a system of representative government, a democracy through which we could better realize our highest ideals. Through civil war and bitter struggles we improved this Constitution to include the voices of those who'd once been left out, and gradually we made this country more just and more equal and more free.

The one constitutional office elected by all of the people is the presidency. So at a minimum we should expect a president to feel a sense of responsibility for the safety and welfare of all 330 million of us, regardless of what we look like, how we worship, who we love, how much money we have, or who we voted for. But we should also expect a president to be the custodian of this democracy. We should expect that, regardless of ego, ambition, or political beliefs, the president will preserve, protect, and defend the freedoms and ideals that so many Americans marched for, went to jail for, fought for, and died for. I have sat in the oval office with both of the men who are running for president. I never expected that my successor would embrace my vision or continue my policies. I did hope, for the sake of our country, that Donald Trump might show some interest in taking the job seriously, that he might come to feel the weight of the office and discover some reverence for the democracy that had been placed in his care. But he never did. For close to four years now he has shown no interest in putting in the work, no interest in finding common ground,

Delivered on August 20, 2020, to the Democratic National Convention.

no interest in using the awesome power of his office to help anyone but himself and his friends, no interest in treating the presidency as anything but one more reality show that he can use to get the attention he craves.

Donald Trump hasn't grown into the job because he can't, and the consequences of that failure are severe. One hundred seventy thousand Americans dead. Millions of jobs gone while those at the top take more than ever. Our worst impulses unleashed, our proud reputation around the world badly diminished, and our democratic institutions threatened like never before. Now I know that in times as polarized as these most of you have already made up your mind. But maybe you're still not sure which candidate you'll vote for, or whether you'll vote at all. Maybe you're tired of the direction we're headed but you can't see a better path yet, or you just don't know enough about the person who wants to lead us there.

So let me tell you about my friend Joe Biden. Twelve years ago, when I began my search for a vice president, I didn't know I'd end up finding a brother. Joe and I come from different places, different generations. But what I quickly came to admire about Joe Biden is his resilience born of too much struggle, his empathy born of too much grief. Joe is a man who learned early on to treat every person he meets with respect and dignity, living by the words his parents taught him. No one's better than you, Joe, but you're better than nobody. That empathy, that decency, the belief that everybody counts—that's who Joe is. When he talks with someone who's lost her job Joe'll remember the night his father sat him down to say that he'd lost his. When Joe listens to a parent who's trying to hold it all together right now, he does it as a single dad who took the train back to Wilmington each and every night so he could tuck his kids into bed. When he meets with military families who've lost their hero he does it as a kindred spirit, the parent of an American soldier, somebody whose faith has endured the hardest loss there is. For eight years Joe was the last one in the room whenever I faced a big decision. He made me a better president. And he's got the character and the experience to make us a better country.

And in my friend Kamala Harris he's chosen an ideal partner who is more than prepared for the job. Someone who knows what it's like to overcome barriers and who's made a career fighting to help others live out their own American dream along with the experience needed to get things done. Joe and Kamala have concrete policies that will turn their vision of a better, fairer, stronger country into reality. They will get this pandemic under control, like Joe did when he helped me manage H1N1 and prevent an Ebola outbreak from reaching our shores. They'll expand health care to more Americans, like Joe and I did 10 years ago when he helped craft the Affordable Care Act and nailed down the votes to make it the law. They'll rescue the economy, like Joe helped me do after the Great Recession. I asked him to manage the Recovery Act, which jump-started the longest stretch of job growth in history. And he sees this moment now not as a chance to get back to where we were but to make long overdue changes so that our economy actually makes life a little easier for everybody, whether it's the waitress trying to raise a kid on her own or the shift worker always on the edge of getting laid off or the student figuring out how to pay for next semester's classes.

Joe and Kamala will restore our standing in the world. And as we've learned from this pandemic, that matters. Joe knows the world and the world knows him, knows that our true strength comes from setting an example that the world wants to follow. A nation that stands with democracy not dictators, a nation that can inspire and mobilize others to overcome threats like climate change and terrorism, poverty and disease. But more than anything what I know about Joe, what I know about Kamala, is that they actually care about every American and that they care deeply about this democracy. They believe that in a democracy the right to vote is sacred and we should be making it easier for people to cast their ballots, not harder. They believe that no one, including the president, is above the law and that no public official, including the president, should use their office to enrich themselves or their supporters. They understand that in this democracy the commander-in-chief does not use the men and women of our military, who are willing to risk everything to protect our nation, as political props to deploy against peaceful protesters on our own soil. They understand that political opponents aren't un-American just because they disagree with you, a free press isn't the enemy but the way we hold officials accountable, that our ability to work together to solve big problems like a pandemic depend on a fidelity to facts and science and logic and not just making stuff up.

None of this should be controversial. These shouldn't be Republican principles or Democratic principles. They are American principles. But at this moment, this president and those who enable him have shown they don't believe in these things. Tonight I'm asking you to believe in Joe and Kamala's ability to lead this country out of these dark times and build it back better. But here's the thing: no single American can fix this country alone, not even a president. Democracy was never meant to be transactional—you give me your vote I make everything better—it requires an active and informed citizenry. So I'm also asking you to believe in your own ability, to embrace your own responsibility as citizens, to make sure that the basic tenets of our democracy endure. Because that's what's at stake right now: our democracy.

Look, I understand why a lot of Americans are down on government. The way the rules have been set up and abused in Congress make it easier for special interests to stop progress than to make progress. Believe me, I know it. I understand why a white factory worker who's seen his wages cut or his job shipped overseas might feel like the government no longer looks out for him and why a black mom might feel like it never looked out for her at all. I understand why a new immigrant might look around this country and wonder whether there's still a place for him here, why a young person might look at politics right now, the circus of it all, the meanness and the lies and conspiracy theories, and think what is the point. Well here's the point. This president and those in power, those who benefit from keeping things the way they are, they are counting on your cynicism. They know they can't win you over with their policies, so they're hoping to make it as hard as possible for you to vote and to convince you that your vote does not matter. That is how they win. That is how they get to keep making decisions that affect your life and the lives of the people you love. That's how the economy will keep getting skewed to the wealthy and well-connected, how our health systems will let more people fall through the cracks. That's how a democracy withers until it's no democracy at all. And we cannot let that happen.

Do not let them take away your power. Do not let them take away your democracy. Make a plan right now for how you are going to get involved and vote. Do it as early as you can, and tell your family and friends how they can vote, too. Do what Americans have done for over two centuries when faced with even tougher times than this, all those quiet heroes who found the courage to keep marching, keep pushing in the face of hardship and injustice. Last month we lost a giant of American democracy in John Lewis. And some years ago I sat down with John and a few remaining leaders of the early civil rights movement. One of them told me he never imagined he'd walk into the White House and see a president who looked like his grandson. And then he told me that he had looked it up and it turned out that on the very day that I was born he was marching into a jail cell trying to end Jim Crow segregation in the South.

What we do echoes through generations. Whatever our backgrounds, we are all the children of Americans who fought the good fight, great grandparents working in fire traps and sweatshops without rights or representation, farmers losing their dreams to dust, Irish and Italians and Asians and Latinos told to go back where you come from. Jews and Catholics, Muslims and Sikhs, made to feel suspect for the way they worshipped. Black Americans chained and whipped and hanged, spit on for trying to sit at lunch counters, beaten for trying to vote. If anyone had a right to believe that this democracy did not work and could not work it was those Americans. Our ancestors, they were on the receiving end of a democracy that had fallen short all their lives. They knew how far the daily reality of America strayed from the myth, and yet instead of giving up, they joined together. And they said somehow, some way, we are going to make this work. We are going to bring those words in our founding documents to life.

I have seen that same spirit rising these past few years, folks of every age and background who packed city centers and airports and rural roads so that families wouldn't be separated, so that another classroom wouldn't get shot up, so that our kids won't grow up on an uninhabitable planet. Americans of all races joining together to declare in the face of injustice and brutality at the hands of the state that black lives matter. No more but no less, so that no child in this country feels the continuing sting of racism. To the young people who led us this summer telling us we need to be better in so many ways, you are this country's dreams fulfilled. Earlier generations had to be persuaded that everyone has equal worth. For you it's a given, a conviction. And what I want you to know is that for all its messiness and frustrations, your system of self-government can be harnessed to help you realize those convictions for all of us. You can give our democracy new meaning, you can take it to a better place.

You're the missing ingredient, the ones who will decide whether or not America becomes the country that fully lives up to its creed. That work will continue long after this election, but any chance of success depends entirely on the outcome of this election. This administration has shown it will tear our democracy down if that's what it takes for them to win. So we have to get busy building it up by pouring all our efforts into these 76 days and by voting like never before for Joe and Kamala and candidates up and down the ticket, so that we leave no doubt about what this country that we love stands for today and for all our days to come. Stay safe, god bless, hey thanks for watching.

Print Citations

CMS: Obama, Barack. "Do Not Let Them Take Away Your Power." Speech at the Democratic National Convention, August 20, 2020. In *The Reference Shelf: Representative American Speeches, 2019-2020,* edited by Annette Calzone, 122-126. Amenia, NY: Grey House Publishing, 2020.

MLA: Obama, Barack. "Do Not Let Them Take Away Your Power." Democratic National Convention, 20 August 2020. Speech. *The Reference Shelf: Representative American Speeches, 2019-2020,* edited by Annette Calzone, Grey House Publishing, v, pp. 122-126.

APA: Obama, B. (2020, August 20). Speech on do not let them take away your power. Democratic National Convention. In Annette Calzone (Ed.), *The reference shelf: Representative American speeches, 2019-2020* (pp. 122-126). Amenia, NY: Grey House Publishing.

America Is Not a Racist Country

By Nikki Haley

Former United Nations Ambassador Nikki Haley spoke in support of President Donald Trump's candidacy at the 2020 Republican National Convention, drawing a parallel to the 1984 convention when UN ambassador Jean Kirkpatrick had also called out the Democratic Party for always blaming America first. Haley noted that Trump always put America first, and she went on to comment that America is not a racist country, drawing on her own experience as the daughter of immigrants from India.

Good evening. I'm Nikki Haley, and it's great to be back at the Republican National Convention. I'll start with a little story. It's about an American ambassador to the United Nations, and it's about a speech she gave to this convention. She called for the reelection of the Republican president she served, and she called out his Democratic opponent, a former vice president from a failed administration.

That ambassador said, and I quote, "Democrats always blame America first." The year was 1984, the president was Ronald Reagan, and ambassador Jean Kirkpatrick's words are just as true today. Joe Biden and the Democrats are still blaming America first. Donald Trump has always put America first, and he has earned four more years as president. It was an honor of a lifetime to serve as the United States ambassador to the United Nations. Now, the UN is not for the faint of heart. It's a place where dictators, murderers, and thieves denounce America, and then put their hands out and demand that we pay their bills.

Well, President Trump put an end to all of that. With his leadership, we did what Barack Obama and Joe Biden refused to do. We stood up for America and we stood against our enemies. Obama and Biden let North Korea threaten America. President Trump rejected that weakness, and we passed the toughest sanctions on North Korea in history. Obama and Biden let Iran get away with murder and literally sent them a plane full of cash.

President Trump did the right thing and ripped up the Iran nuclear deal. Obama and Biden led the United Nations to denounce our friend and ally, Israel. President Trump moved our embassy to Jerusalem, and when the UN tried to condemn us, I was proud to cast the American veto. This president has a record of strength and success. The former vice president has a record of weakness and failure. Joe Biden is good for Iran and ISIS, great for communist China. And he's a godsend to everyone who wants America to apologize, abstain, and abandon our values.

Delivered on August 24, 2020, to the Republican National Convention.

Donald Trump takes a different approach. He's tough on China, and he took on ISIS and won, and he tells the world what it needs to hear. At home, the president is the clear choice on jobs in the economy. He's moved America forward, while Joe Biden has held America back. When Joe was VP, I was governor of the great state of South Carolina. We had a pretty good run, manufacturers of all kinds flock to our state from overseas, creating tens of thousands of American jobs.

People were referring to South Carolina as the beast of the Southeast, which I loved. Everything we did happened in spite of Joe Biden and his old boss. We cut taxes, they raised them. We slashed red tape, they piled on more mandates. And when we brought in good paying jobs, Biden and Obama sued us. I fought back and they gave up.

A Biden-Harris administration would be much, much worse. Last time, Joe's boss was Obama. This time it would be Pelosi, Sanders, and the squad. Their vision for America is socialism. And we know that socialism has failed everywhere. They want to tell Americans how to live, what to think, they want a government take-over of healthcare. They want to ban fracking and kill millions of jobs. They want massive tax hikes on working families. Joe Biden, and the socialist left, would be a disaster for our economy. But president Trump is leading a new era of opportunity.

Before communist China gave us the coronavirus, we were breaking economic records left and right. The pandemic has set us back, but not for long. President Trump brought our economy back before and he will bring it back again. There's one more important area where the president is right. He knows that political correctness and cancel culture are dangerous and just plain wrong. In much of the Democratic Party, it's now fashionable to say that America is racist. That is a lie.

America is not a racist country. This is personal for me. I am the proud daughter of Indian immigrants. They came to America and settled in a small southern town. My father wore a turban, my mother wore a saree. I was a brown girl in a black and white world. We faced discrimination and hardship, but my parents never gave in to grievance and hate. My mom built a successful business. My dad taught 30 years at a historically black college, and the people of South Carolina chose me as their first minority and first female governor.

America is a story that's a work in progress. Now is the time to build on that progress and make America even freer, fairer, and better for everyone. That's why it's so tragic to see so much of the Democratic Party turning a blind eye towards riots and rage. The American people know we can do better. And of course we value and respect every black life. The black cops who've been shot in the line of duty, they matter.

The black, small business owners who've watched their life's work go up and flames, they matter. The black kids who've been gunned down on the playground, their lives matter too. And their lives are being ruined and stolen by the violence on our streets. It doesn't have to be like this. It wasn't like this in South Carolina, five years ago. Our state came face-to-face with evil: a white supremacist walked into Mother Emmanuel Church during Bible study. Twelve African-Americans pulled up a chair and prayed with him for an hour. Then he began to shoot. After that horrific tragedy, we didn't turn against each other.

We came together, black and white, Democrat and Republican. Together, we made the hard choices needed to heal and removed a divisive symbol peacefully and respectfully. What happened then should give us hope now. America isn't perfect, but the principles we hold dear are perfect. If there's one thing I've learned, it's that even on our worst day, we are blessed to live in America. It's time to keep that blessing alive for the next generation.

This president and this party are committed to that noble task. We seek a nation that rises together, not falls apart in anarchy and anger. We know that the only way to overcome America's challenges is to embrace America's strengths. We are striving to reach a brighter future, where every child goes to a world-class school chosen by their parents. Where every family lives in a safe community with good jobs, where every entrepreneur has the freedom to achieve and inspire. Where every believer can worship without fear, and every life is protected. Where every girl and boy, every woman and man of every race and religion has the best shot at the best life.

In this election, we must choose the only candidate who has and who will continue delivering on that vision. President Trump and Vice President Pence have my support and America has our promise. We will build on the progress of our past and unlock the promise of our future. That future starts when the American people reelect President Donald Trump. Thank you, good night, and may God always bless America.

Print Citations

CMS: Haley, Nikki. "America Is Not a Racist Country." Speech at the Republican National Convention, August 24, 2020. In *The Reference Shelf: Representative American Speeches, 2019-2020,* edited by Annette Calzone, 127-129. Amenia, NY: Grey House Publishing, 2020.

MLA: Haley, Nikki. "America Is Not a Racist Country." Republican National Convention, 24 August 2020. Speech. *The Reference Shelf: Representative American Speeches, 2019-2020,* edited by Annette Calzone, Grey House Publishing, 2020, pp. 127-129.

APA: Haley, N. (2020, August 24). Speech on America is not a racist country. Republican National Convention. In Annette Calzone (Ed.), *The reference shelf: Representative American speeches, 2019-2020* (pp. 127-129). Amenia, NY: Grey House Publishing.

Acceptance Speech of the Republican Vice Presidential Nominee

By Mike Pence

In his speech accepting the vice presidential nomination, Mike Pence warned that what was at stake in this election was whether America would remain America or be fundamentally transformed by what he described as the radical agenda of the Democratic Party. Pence cautioned against a federal government overly involved in Americans' lives and spoke in support of freedom of religion and freedom of school choice.

Mike Pence: Good evening, America. It's an honor to speak to you tonight from the hallowed grounds of Fort McHenry, the site of the very battle that inspired the words of our National anthem. Those words have inspired this land of heroes in every generation since. It was on this site, 206 years ago, when our young Republic heroically withstood a ferocious naval bombardment from the most powerful empire on earth. They came to crush our revolution, to divide our nation, and to end the American experiment.

The heroes who held this fort took their stand for life, liberty, freedom, and the American flag. And those ideals have defined our nation, but they were hardly ever mentioned at last week's Democratic National Convention. Instead, Democrats spent four days attacking America. Joe Biden said that we were living through a season of darkness, but as President Trump said, where Joe Biden sees American darkness, we see American greatness. In these challenging times, our country needs a president who believes in America, who believes in the boundless capacity of the American people, to meet any challenge, defeat any foe, and defend the freedoms we hold dear.

America needs four more years of President Donald Trump in the White House. Before I go further, allow me to say a word to the families and communities in the path of Hurricane Laura. Our prayers are with you tonight and our administration is working closely with authorities in the states that will be impacted. FEMA has mobilized resources and supplies for those in harm's way. This is a serious storm and we urge all those in the affected areas to heed state and local authorities. Stay safe and know that we'll be with you every step of the way to support, rescue, respond and recover in the days and weeks ahead. That's what Americans do.

Four years ago I answered the call to join this ticket because I knew that Donald Trump had the leadership and the vision to make America great again. And for

Delivered on August 26, 2020, to the Republican National Convention.

the last four years, I've watched this president endure unrelenting attacks, but get up every day and fight to keep the promises that he made to the American people. So with gratitude for the confidence President Donald Trump has placed in me, the support of our Republican party, and the grace of God, I humbly accept your nomination to run and serve as Vice President of the United States. Serving the American people in this office has been a journey I never expected. It's a journey that would not have been possible without the support of my family, beginning with my wonderful wife, Karen. She's a lifelong school teacher, an incredible mother to our three children, and she is one outstanding Second Lady of the United States. I'm so proud of her. And we couldn't be more proud of our three children, Marine Corps Captain Michael J. Pence and his wife, Sarah; our daughter, Charlotte Pence Bond, an author and the wife to Lieutenant Henry Bond, who is currently deployed and serving our in the United States Navy; and our youngest, a recent law school grad, our daughter Audrey and her fiancé, who, like so many other Americans, had to delay their wedding this summer. But we can't wait for Dan to be a part of our family. In addition to my wife and kids, the person who shaped my life the most is also with us tonight, my mom, Nancy. She is the daughter of an Irish immigrant, 87 years young, and mom follows politics very closely. And the truth be told, sometimes I think I'm actually her second favorite candidate on the Trump-Pence ticket. Thank you, mom. I love you.

Over the past four years, I've had the privilege to work closely with our president. I've seen him when the cameras are off. Americans see President Trump in lots of different ways, but there's no doubt how President Trump sees America. He sees America for what it is: a nation that has done more good in this world than any other, a nation that deserves far more gratitude than grievance, and if you want a president who falls silent when our heritage is demeaned or insulted, he's not your man. Now, we came by very different routes to this partnership. And some people think we're a little bit different. But you know, I've learned a few things watching him, watching him deal with all that we've been through over the past four years. He does things in his own way, on his own terms. Not much gets past him. And when he has an opinion, he's liable to share it. He certainly kept things interesting. But more importantly, President Donald Trump has kept his word to the American people. In a city known for talkers, President Trump is a doer, and few presidents have brought more independence, energy or determination to that office.

Four years ago, we inherited a military hollowed out by devastating budget cuts, an economy struggling to break out of the slowest recovery since the Great Depression, ISIS controlled a land mass twice the size of Pennsylvania, and we witnessed a steady assault on our most cherished values: freedom of religion and the right to life. That's when President Donald Trump stepped in. And from day one he kept his word. We rebuilt our military. This President signed the largest increase in our national defense since the days of Ronald Reagan and created the first new branch of our armed forces in 70 years, the United States Space Force. And with that renewed energy, we also returned American astronauts to space on an American rocket for the first time in nearly 10 years.

After years of scandal that robbed our veterans of the care that you earned in the uniform of the United States, president Trump kept his word again. We reformed the VA and Veterans Choice is now available for every veteran in America. Our armed forces and our veterans fill this land of heroes, and many join us tonight in this historic fort. Tonight, we have among us four recipients of the Medal of Honor, six recipients of the Purple Heart, a Gold Star Mother of a gallant naval seaman, and wounded warriors from Soldier Strong, a group that serves our injured veterans every day. We are honored by your presence, and we thank you for your service.

With heroes just like these, we defend this nation every day. Under this Commander In Chief, we've taken the fight to radical Islamic terrorists on our terms, on their soil. Last year, American armed forces took the last inch of ISIS territory, crushed their caliphate and took down their leader without one American casualty. I was there when President Trump gave the order to take out the world's most dangerous terrorist. Iran's top general will never harm another American, because Qasem Soleimani is gone. My fellow Americans, you deserve to know, Joe Biden criticized President Trump following those decisions, decisions to rid the world of two terrorist leaders.

But it's not surprising, because history records that Joe Biden even opposed the operation that took down Osama bin Laden. It's no wonder that the Secretary of Defense, under the Obama-Biden administration, once said that Joe Biden has been, and I quote, wrong on nearly every major foreign policy and national security issue over the past four decades. We've stood up to her enemies and we've stood with our allies. Like when President Trump kept his word and moved the American embassy to Jerusalem, the capital of the State of Israel, setting the stage for the first Arab country to recognize Israel in 26 years.

Closer to home, we appointed more than 200 conservative judges to our federal courts. We supported the right to life and all the God-given liberties enshrined in our constitution, including the Second Amendment right to keep and bear arms. When it came to the economy, President Trump kept his word and then some. We passed the largest tax cut and reform in American history. We rolled back more federal red tape than any administration ever had. We unleashed American energy and fought for free and fair trade. In our first three years, businesses, large and small, created more than 7 million good-paying jobs, including 500,000 manufacturing jobs all across America.

Our country became a net exporter of energy for the first time in 70 years. Unemployment rates for African-Americans and Hispanic-Americans hit the lowest level ever recorded. On this 100th anniversary of a woman's right to vote, I'm proud to report that under President Donald Trump, we achieved the lowest unemployment rate for women in 65 years, and more Americans working, than ever before. In our first three years, we built the greatest economy in the world. We made America great again. Then the coronavirus struck from China. Before the first case of the coronavirus spread within the United States, the president took unprecedented action and suspended all travel from China, the second largest economy in the world.

Now, that action saved untold American lives, and I can tell you firsthand, it bought us invaluable time to launch the greatest national mobilization since World War II. President Trump marshaled the full resources of our federal government from the outset. He directed us to forge a seamless partnership with governors across America, in both political parties. We partnered with private industry to reinvent testing and produce supplies that were distributed to hospitals around the land. Today, we're conducting more than 800,000 tests a day, and we have coordinated the delivery of billions of pieces of personal protective equipment for our amazing doctors, nurses, and healthcare workers.

We saw to the manufacture of 100,000 ventilators in a hundred days, and no one who required a ventilator was ever denied a ventilator in the United States. We built hospitals, surged military medical personnel, and enacted an economic rescue package that saved 50 million American jobs. As we speak, we're developing a growing number of treatments, known as therapeutics, including convalescent plasma, that are saving lives all across America. Now, last week Joe Biden said that no miracle is coming. But what Joe doesn't seem to understand, is that America is a nation of miracles, and I'm proud to report that we're on track to have the world's first safe, effective coronavirus vaccine by the end of this year.

After all the sacrifice in this year like no other, and all the hardship, we're finding our way forward again. But tonight our hearts are with all the families that have lost loved ones and have family members still struggling with serious illness. In this country, we mourn with those who mourn. We grieve with those who grieve. This night, I know that millions of Americans will pause and pray for God's comfort for each of you. Our country doesn't get through such a time, unless its people find strength within. The response of doctors, nurses, first responders, farmers, factory workers, truckers, and everyday Americans who put the health and safety of their neighbors first has been nothing short of heroic.

Veronica Saez put on her scrubs every day. Day in and day out, went to work in one of New York City's busiest hospitals. She stayed on the job, put in the long hours until it was done, and then got back in her neighborhood and helped neighbors and friends struggling. Her brother William is a New York City firefighter, and they're both emblematic of heroes all across this country. They're with us tonight. I say to them, and to all of you, you have earned the admiration of the American people, and we will always be grateful for your service and care.

Thanks to the courage and compassion of the American people, we're slowing the spread, we're protecting the vulnerable, and we're saving lives and we're opening up America again. Because of the strong foundation that President Trump poured in our first three years, we've already gained back 9.3 million jobs in the last three months alone. And we're not just opening up America again, we're opening up America's schools, and I'm proud to report that my wife Karen, that schoolteacher I've been married to, will be returning to her classroom next week. And so to all of our heroic teachers and faculty and staff, thank you for being there for our kids. We're going to stay with you every step of the way.

In the days ahead as we open up America again, I promise you, we'll continue to put the health of America first, and as we work to bring this economy back, we all have a role to play and we all have a choice to make. On November 3 you need to ask yourself, who do you trust to rebuild this economy? A career politician who presided over the slowest economic recovery since the Great Depression? Or a proven leader who created the greatest economy in the world? The choice is clear, to bring America all the way back, we need four more years of President Donald Trump in the White House.

My fellow Americans, we're passing through a time of testing, but in the midst of this global pandemic, just as our nation had begun to recover, we've seen violence and chaos in the streets of our major cities. President Trump and I will always support the right of Americans to peaceful protest. But rioting and looting is not peaceful protest. Tearing down statues is not free speech and those who do so will be prosecuted to the fullest extent of the law.

Last week, Joe Biden didn't say one word about the violence and chaos engulfing cities across this country, so let me be clear. The violence must stop, whether in Minneapolis, Portland, or Kenosha, too many heroes have died defending our freedom to see Americans strike each other down. We will have law and order on the streets of this country for every American of every race and creed and color. President Trump and I know that the men and women that put on the uniform of law enforcement are the best of us. Every day, when they walk out that door, they consider our lives more important than their own. People like Dave Patrick Underwood, an officer in the Department of Homeland Security's federal protective service, who was shot and killed during the riots in Oakland, California. Dave's heroism is emblematic of the heroes that serve in blue every day, and we're privileged tonight to be joined by his sister Angela. Angela, we say to you, we grieve with your family, and America will never forget or fail to honor Officer Dave Patrick Underwood.

The American people know we don't have to choose between supporting law enforcement and standing with our African-American neighbors to improve the quality of their lives, education, jobs, and safety. And from the first days of this administration, we've done both. And we will keep supporting law enforcement and keep supporting our African-American and minority communities across this land for four more years.

Now Joe Biden says that America is systemically racist and that law enforcement in America has, and I quote, "an implicit bias against minorities." When asked whether he'd support cutting funding to law enforcement, Joe Biden replied, "Yes. Absolutely." Joe Biden would double down on the very policies that are leading to violence in America's cities. The hard truth is you won't be safe in Joe Biden's America. Under President Trump, we will always stand with those who stand on the thin blue line. And we're not going to defund the police, not now, not ever.

My fellow Americans we're passing through a time of testing, but soon we will come to a time for choosing. Joe Biden has referred to himself as a transition candidate, and many were asking, transition to what? Last week, Democrats didn't talk very much about their agenda, and if I were them I wouldn't either. Bernie Sanders did tell his followers that Joe Biden would be the most liberal president in modern times. In fact, he said that "many of the ideas he fought for that just a few years ago were considered radical are now mainstream in the Democratic Party." At the root of their agenda is the belief that America is driven by envy, not aspiration. That millions of Americans harbor ill will toward our neighbors instead of loving our neighbors as ourselves. The radical left believes that the federal government must be involved in every aspect of our lives to correct those American wrongs. They believe the federal government needs to dictate how Americans live, how we should work, how we should raise our children—and in the process deprive our people of freedom, prosperity and security. Their agenda is based on government control. Our agenda is based on freedom.

Where President Trump cut taxes, Joe Biden wants to raise taxes by nearly $4 trillion. Where this president achieved energy independence for the United States, Joe Biden would abolish fossil fuels, end fracking, and impose a regime of climate change regulations that would drastically increase the cost of living for working families. Where we fought for free and fair trade and this president stood up to China and ended the era of economic surrender, Joe Biden has been a cheerleader for communist China. He wants to repeal all the tariffs that are leveling the playing field for American workers, and he actually criticized President Trump for suspending all travel to China at the outset of this pandemic.

Joe Biden is for open borders, sanctuary cities, free lawyers and healthcare for illegal immigrants. And President Trump, he secured our border and built nearly 300 miles of that border wall. Joe Biden wants to end school choice, and President Trump believes that every parent should have the right to choose where their children go to school, regardless of their income or area code. President Trump has stood without apology for the sanctity of human life every day of this administration. Joe Biden, he supports taxpayer funding of abortion right up to the moment of birth. When you consider their agenda, it's clear. Joe Biden would be nothing more than a Trojan horse for the radical left.

The choice in this election has never been clearer and the stakes have never been higher. Last week, Joe Biden said democracy is on the ballot, and the truth is our economic recovery is on the ballot. Law and order are on the ballot. But so are things far more fundamental and foundational to our country. In this election it's not so much whether America will be more conservative or more liberal, more Republican or more Democrat. The choice in this election is whether America remains America. It's whether we will leave to our children and our grandchildren a country grounded in our highest ideals of freedom, free markets and the unalienable right to life and Liberty, or whether we will leave them a country that's fundamentally transformed into something else.

We stand at a crossroads, America. President Trump has set our nation on a path of freedom and opportunity. Joe Biden would set America on a path of socialism and decline, but we're not going to let it happen. President Donald Trump believes in America and in the goodness of the American people, the boundless potential of every American to live out their dreams and freedom. Every day, President Trump has been fighting to protect the promise of America. Every day our president has been fighting to expand the reach of the American dream. Every day, President Donald Trump has been fighting for you, and now it's our turn to fight for him.

On this night in the company of heroes, I'm deeply grateful. Deeply grateful for the privilege of serving as vice president of this great nation and to have the opportunity to serve again. I pray to be worthy of it and I will give that duty all that's in me. In the year 2020, the American people have had more than our share of challenges, but thankfully we have a president with the toughness, energy, and resolve to see us through. Now, those traits actually run in our national character. As the invading force learned on approach to this fort in September of 1814, against fierce and sustained bombardment, our young country was defended by heroes, not so different from those who are with us tonight. The enemy was counting on them to quit, but they never did. Fort McHenry held, and when morning came, our flag was still here.

My fellow Americans, we're going through a time of testing, but if you look through the fog of these challenging times, you will see, our flag is still there today. That star spangled banner still waves over the land of the free and the home of the brave. From these hallowed grounds, American patriots in generations gone by did their part to defend freedom. Now it's our turn. So let's run the race marked out for us. Let's fix our eyes on Old Glory and all she represents. Let's fix our eyes on this land of heroes and let their courage inspire. Let's fix our eyes on the author and perfector of our faith and our freedom, and never forget that where the spirit of the Lord is there is freedom. That means freedom always wins.

My fellow Americans, thank you for the honor of addressing you tonight and the opportunity to run and serve again as your vice president. I leave here today inspired and I leave here today, more convinced than ever that we will do in our time as Americans have done throughout our long and storied past, we will defend our freedom and our way of life. We will re-elect our president and principled Republican leaders across the land and with President Donald Trump in the White House for four more years, and with God's help, we will make America great again, again. Thank you. God bless you, and God bless the United States of America.

Print Citations

CMS: Pence, Mike. "Acceptance Speech of the Republican Vice Presidential Nominee." Speech at the Democratic National Convention, August 19, 2020. In *The Reference Shelf: Representative American Speeches, 2019-2020,* edited by Annette Calzone, 130-136. Amenia, NY: Grey House Publishing, 2020.

MLA: Pence, Mike. "Acceptance Speech of the Republican Vice Presidential Nominee." Democratic National Convention, 19 August 2020. Speech. *The Reference Shelf: Representative American Speeches, 2019-2020,* edited by Annette Calzone, Grey House Publishing, 2020, pp. 130-136.

APA: Pence, Mike. (2020, August 19). Acceptance speech of the Republican vice presidential nominee. Democratic National Convention. In Annette Calzone (Ed.), *The reference shelf: Representative American speeches, 2019-2020* (pp. 130-136). Amenia, NY: Grey House Publishing.

Final Presidential Debate Highlights

By Donald Trump and Joe Biden

The final presidential debate in October 2020 highlighted the very different personalities of the two candidates as well as their obvious animosity toward one another. A discussion of the important issues facing the country quickly degenerated into an exchange of insults, as the moderator tried to keep order amid interruptions and crosstalk. Among other things, Biden focused on Trump's performance during the COVID-19 pandemic, while Trump criticized Biden's socialist agenda.

Moderator Kristen Welker: The . . . country is heading into a dangerous new phase. . . . How would you lead the country during this next stage of the coronavirus crisis?

Donald Trump: So as you know, 2.2 million people modeled out, were expected to die. We closed up the greatest economy in the world in order to fight this horrible disease that came from China. It's a worldwide pandemic. It's all over the world. . . The excess mortality rate is way down and much lower than almost any other country. And we're fighting it and we're fighting it hard. . . . We have a vaccine that's coming. It's ready. It's going to be announced within weeks. And it's going to be delivered. We have Operation Warp Speed, which is the military is going to distribute the vaccine. . . . I can tell you from personal experience, I was in the hospital. I had it and I got better. . . . And I got better very fast or I wouldn't be here tonight. And now they say I'm immune. Whether it's four months or a lifetime, nobody's been able to say that, but I'm immune. More and more people are getting better. We have a problem that's a worldwide problem. . . . If you take a look at what we've done in terms of goggles and masks and gowns and everything else, and in particular ventilators we're now making ventilators all over the world, thousands and thousands a month distributing them all over the world. It will go away. And as I say, we're rounding the turn. We're rounding the corner. It's going away. . . .

Joe Biden: 220,000 Americans dead. . . . Anyone who's responsible for that many deaths should not remain as president of the United States of America. We're in a situation where there are a thousand deaths a day now. A thousand deaths a day. And there are over 70,000 new cases per day. . . . The expectation is we'll have another 200,000 Americans dead between now and the end of the year. If we just wore these masks, the president's own advisors have told him, we can save 100,000 lives. And we're in a circumstance where the president thus far and still has no . . .

Delivered on October 22, 2020, at Belmont University, Nashville, Tennessee.

comprehensive plan. . . . What I would do is make sure we have everyone encouraged to wear a mask all the time. I would make sure we move into the direction of rapid testing. . . . I would make sure that we set up national standards as to how to open up schools and open up businesses so they can be safe. . . . We're in a situation now where the *New England Medical Journal*, one of the serious, most serious journals in the whole world, said for the first time ever that the way this president has responded to this crisis has been absolutely tragic. . . .

Kristen Welker: President Trump, . . .you also said a vaccine will be coming within weeks. Is that a guarantee?

Donald Trump: No, it's not a guarantee, but it will be by the end of the year. But I think it has a good chance. There are two companies, I think within a matter of weeks and it will be distributed very quickly. . . .

Kristen Welker: Vice President Biden, . . .what steps would you take to give Americans confidence in a vaccine if it were approved?

Joe Biden: Make sure it's totally transparent. Have the scientists of the world see it, know it, look at it, go through all the processes. And by the way, this is the same fellow who told you, "This is going to end by Easter" last time. This is the same fellow who told you that, "Don't worry, we're going to end this by the summer." We're about to go into a dark winter, a dark winter and he has no clear plan. And there's no prospect that there's going to be a vaccine available for the majority of the American people before the middle of next year. . . . Number one, he says that we're learning to live with it. People are learning to die with it. You folks home will have an empty chair at the kitchen table this morning. That man or wife going to bed tonight and reaching over to try to touch, there out of habit, where their wife or husband was, is gone. Learning to live with it. . . .

Donald Trump: Excuse me. I take full responsibility. It's not my fault that it came here. It's China's fault. And you know what? It's not Joe's fault that it came here either. It's China's fault. They kept it from going into the rest of China for the most part, but they didn't keep it from coming out to the world, including Europe and ourselves.

Joe Biden: The fact is that when we knew it was coming, when it hit, what happened? What did the President say? He said, "Don't worry. It's going to go away. It'll be gone by Easter. Don't worry. Warm weather. Don't worry. Maybe inject bleach." He said he was kidding when he said that, but a lot of people thought it was serious. A whole range of things the President has said, even today, he thinks we are in control. We're about to lose 200,000 more people.

Donald Trump: Look, perhaps just to finish this, I was kidding on that, but just to finish this, when I closed he said I shouldn't have closed. And that went on for months. Nancy Pelosi said the same thing. She was dancing on the streets in Chinatown, in San Francisco. But when I closed, he said, "This is a terrible thing, you xenophobic." I think he called me racist even, because I was closing it to China. Now he says I should have closed it earlier. Joe, it doesn't.

Joe Biden: I didn't say either of those things.

Donald Trump: You certainly did. You certainly did. . . . By the way, I will say this, if you go and look at what's happened to New York, it's a ghost town. It's a ghost town. And when you talk about plexiglass, these are restaurants that [are] dying. These are businesses with no money. Putting up plexiglass is unbelievably expensive, and it's not the answer. I mean, you're going to sit there in a cubicle wrapped around with plastic. These are businesses that are dying, Joe. You can't do that to people. You just can't. Take a look at New York and what's happened to my wonderful city. For so many years, I loved it. It was vibrant. It's dying. Everyone's leaving New York.

Joe Biden: Take a look at what New York has done in terms of turning the curve down, in terms of the number of people dying. And I don't look at this in terms of the way he does, blue states and red states. They're all the United States. And look at the states that are having such a spike in the coronavirus. They're the red states, they're the states in the Midwest, they're the states in the upper Midwest. That's where the spike is occurring significantly. But they're all Americans. They're all Americans. And what we have to do is say, wear these masks, number one. Make sure we get the help that the businesses need. That money's already been passed to do that. It's been out there since the beginning of the summer, and nothing's happened.

Donald Trump: Kristen, New York has lost more than 40,000 people, 11,000 people in nursing homes. . . . When you say spike, take a look at what's happening in Pennsylvania where they've had it closed. Take a look at what's happening with your friend in Michigan, where her husband's the only one allowed to do anything. It's been like a prison. Now, it was just ruled unconstitutional. Take a look at North Carolina, they're having spikes and they've been closed, and they're getting killed financially. We can't let that happen, Joe. You can't let that happen. We have to open up. And we understand the disease. We have to protect our seniors. We have to protect our elderly. We have to protect especially our seniors with heart problems and diabetes problems. And we will protect. We have the best testing in the world by far. That's why we have so many cases.

Kristen Welker: Let me follow up with you before we move on to our next section. President Trump, this week, you called Dr. Anthony Fauci, the nation's best known infectious disease expert "a disaster." You described him and other medical experts as "idiots." If you're not listening to them, who are you listening to?

Donald Trump: I'm listening to all of them, including Anthony. I get along very well with Anthony. . . . But he did say, "Don't wear masks." He did say, as you know, "This is not going to be a problem." I think he's a Democrat, but that's okay. He said, "This is not going to be a problem. We are not going to have a problem at all." When Joe says that I said, Anthony Fauci said, and others, and many others. And I'm not knocking him, nobody knew. Look, nobody knew what this thing was. Nobody knew where it was coming from, what it was. We've learned a lot. But Anthony said "Don't wear masks," now he wants to wear masks. Anthony also said, if you look back, exact words, here's his exact words. "This is no problem. This is going to go away soon." So he's allowed to make mistakes. He happens to be a good person.

Kristen Welker: Vice President Biden, your response quickly, and then we're going to move on to the next section.

Joe Biden: My response is that think about what the President knew in January and didn't tell the American people. He was told this was a serious virus that spread in the air, and it was much worse, much worse, than the flu. He went on record and said to one of your colleagues, recorded, that in fact he knew how dangerous it was but he didn't want to tell us. He didn't want to tell us because he didn't want us to panic. He didn't want us . . . . Americans don't panic. He panicked. But guess what, in the meantime, we find out in the *New York Times* the other day, that in fact his folks went to Wall Street and said, "This is a really dangerous thing." And a memo out of that meeting—not from his administration, but from some of the brokers—said, "Sell short, because we've got to get moving. It's a dangerous problem." . . .

Kristen Welker: All right. Let's move on to American families.

Donald Trump: Kristen.

Kristen Welker: Very quickly, 10 seconds, President Trump.

Donald Trump: They tried to meet with him [Kim Jong-un]. He wouldn't do it. He didn't like Obama. He didn't like him. He wouldn't do it.

Kristen Welker: Okay, I've got to give him a chance to respond to that before we move on.

Donald Trump: I know for a fact. They tried. We wouldn't do it. And that's okay. You know what? North Korea, we're not in a war. We have a good relationship. People don't understand. Having a good relationship with leaders of other countries is a good thing.

Kristen Welker: President Trump, we have to move on, because we have a lot of questions to get to. Your response.

Joe Biden: We had a good relationship with Hitler before he, in fact, invaded Europe, the rest of Europe. Come on. The reason he would not meet with President Obama is because President Obama said, "We're going to talk about denuclearization. We're not going to legitimize you and we're going to continue to push stronger and stronger sanctions on you." That's why he wouldn't meet with us.

Kristen Welker: All right, let's move on.

Donald Trump: And it didn't happen.

Kristen Welker: Let's move on and talk about American families.

Donald Trump: Excuse me. He left me a mess. Kristen.

Kristen Welker: President Trump. Okay

Donald Trump: They left me a mess. North Korea was a mess, and in fact, if you remember the first two or three months. It was a very dangerous period in my first three months before we worked things out a little bit.

Kristen Welker: Okay.

Donald Trump: There was a very day. They left us a mess, and Obama would be, I think, the first to say it, was the single biggest problem he thought that our country.

Kristen Welker: Okay, let's move on to American families and the economy. One of the issues that's most important to them is healthcare, as you both know. Today, there was a key vote on a new Supreme Court Justice, Amy Coney Barrett, and healthcare is at the center of her confirmation fight. Over 20 million Americans get their health insurance through the Affordable Care Act. It's headed to the Supreme Court and your administration, Mr. President, is advocating for the court to overturn it. If the Supreme Court does overturn that law, there's 20 million Americans could lose their health insurance almost overnight. So what would you do if those people have their health insurance taken away? You have two minutes uninterrupted.

Donald Trump: First of all, I've already done something that nobody thought was possible. Through the legislature, I terminated the individual mandate. That is the worst part of Obamacare, as we call it. The individual mandate where you have to pay a fortune for the privilege of not having to pay for bad health insurance, I terminated. It's gone. Now, it's in court, because Obamacare is no good. But then I made a decision, run it as well as you can, to my people, great people, run it as well as you can. I could have gone the other route and made everybody very unhappy. They ran it. Premiums are down. Everything's down. Here's the problem. No matter how well you run it, it's no good. What we'd like to do is terminate it. We have the individual mandate done. I don't know that it's going to work. If we don't win, we will have to run it and we'll have Obamacare, but it'll be better run. But it no longer is Obamacare, because without the individual mandate, it's much different. . . . Pre-existing conditions will always stay. What I would like to do is a much better healthcare, much better. We'll always protect people with pre-existing. So I'd like to terminate Obamacare, come up with a brand new, beautiful healthcare. The Democrats will do it, because there'll be tremendous pressure on them. And we might even have the House by that time. And I think we're going to win the House. You'll see, but I think we're going to win the House. But come up with a better healthcare, always protecting people with pre-existing conditions. And one thing very important, we have 180 million people out there that have great private healthcare. Far more than we're talking about with Obamacare. Joe Biden is going to terminate all of those policies. These are people that love their healthcare. People that have been successful, middle-income people, been successful. They have 180 million plans, 180 million people, families. Under what he wants to do, which will basically be socialized medicine, he won't even have a choice, they want to terminate 180 million plans. We have done an incredible job at healthcare, and we're going to do even better. Just you watch.

Kristen Welker: Okay. Vice President Biden, yes, this is for you. Your healthcare plan calls for building on Obamacare. So my question is, what is your plan if the law is ruled unconstitutional by the Supreme Court? You have two minutes uninterrupted.

Joe Biden: What I'm going to do is pass Obamacare with a public option, and become Bidencare. The public option is an option that says that if you in fact do not have the wherewithal, if you qualify for Medicaid and you do not have the wherewithal in your state to get Medicaid, you automatically are enrolled, providing competition for insurance companies. That's what's going to happen. Secondly, we're going to make sure we reduce the premiums and reduce drug prices by making sure that there's competition, that doesn't exist now, by allowing Medicare to negotiate drug prices with the insurance companies. Thirdly, the idea that I want to eliminate private insurance, the reason why I had such a fight with 20 candidates for the nomination was I support private insurance. That's why. Not one single person with private insurance would lose their insurance under my plan, nor did they under Obamacare. They did not lose their insurance unless they chose they wanted to go to something else. . . . Lastly, we're going to make sure we're in a situation that we actually protect pre-existing. There's no way he can protect pre-existing conditions. None, zero. You can't do it in the ether. He's been talking about this for a long time. He's never come up with a plan. I guess we're going to get the pre-existing condition plan the same time we got the infrastructure plan that we waited for since '17, '18, '19, and '20. I still have a few more minutes. I know you're getting anxious. The fact is that he's already cost the American people, because of his terrible handling of the COVID virus and economic spillover. 10 million people have lost their private insurance, and he wants to take away 22 million more people who have it under Obamacare and over 110 million people with pre-existing conditions. And all the people from COVID are going to have pre-existing conditions, what are they going to do?

Kristen Welker: President Trump [is] accusing you of wanting socialized medicine. What do you say to people who have concerns that your healthcare plan, which includes a government insurance option, takes the country one step closer to a healthcare system run entirely by the government?

Joe Biden: I say it's ridiculous. It's like saying that the fact that there's a public option that people can choose, that makes it a socialist plan. Look, the difference between the president and I. . . . I think healthcare is not a privilege, it's a right. Everyone should have the right to have affordable healthcare, and I am very proud of my plan. It's gotten endorsed by all the major labor unions, as well as a whole range of other people who, in fact, are concerned in the medical field. This is something that's going to save people's lives. And this is going to give some people an opportunity to have healthcare for their children. How many of you at home are worried and rolling around in bed tonight, wondering what in God's name you're going to do if you get sick, because you've lost your health insurance and your company's gone under? We have to provide health insurance for people at an affordable rate, and that's what I do.

Kristen Welker: President Trump-

Donald Trump: Excuse me. He was there-

Kristen Welker: . . . your response.

Donald Trump: . . . for 47 years. He didn't do it. He was now there as vice president for eight years. And it's not like it was 25 years ago. It was three and three quarters. . . . It was just a little while ago, right? Less than four years ago. He didn't do anything. He didn't do it. He wants socialized medicine. And it's not that he wants it. His vice president, she is more liberal than Bernie Sanders and wants it even more. Bernie Sanders wants it. The Democrats want it. You're going to have socialized medicine, just like you want it with fracking. "We're not going to have fracking. We're going to stop fracking. We're going to stop fracking." Then he goes to Pennsylvania after he gets a nomination, where he got very lucky to get it. And he goes to Pennsylvania, and he says, "Oh, we're going to have fracking." And you never ask that question. And by the way, so far, I respect very much the way you're handling this, I have to say.

Joe Biden: By the way-

Donald Trump: But somebody should ask the question.

Joe Biden: You can ask it.

Donald Trump: He goes for a year, there will be no fracking.

Kristen Welker: We do have a number-

Donald Trump: There will be no petroleum-

Kristen Welker: We have a number of topics we're going to get to.

Donald Trump: No, no. But that's a big question.

Kristen Welker: We're going to get to a number of topics-

Donald Trump: It's the same thing with socialized medicine.

Joe Biden: I have to respond to healthcare.

Kristen Welker: Vice President, your response please.

Joe Biden: My response is, people deserve to have affordable healthcare, period. Period, period, period. And the Biden care proposal will in fact provide for that affordable healthcare, lower premiums. What we're going to do is going to cost some money. It's going to cost over $750 billion over 10 years to do it. And they're going to have lower premiums. You can buy into the better plans, the cheaper plans, lower your premiums, deal with unexpected billing, and have your drug prices drop significantly. He keeps talking about it. He hasn't done a thing for anybody on healthcare. Not a thing.

Donald Trump: Kristen, when he says-

Kristen Welker: Very quickly, then I want to talk about what's happening on Capitol Hill.

Donald Trump: When he says public option, he's talking about socialized medicine and healthcare. When he talks about a public option, he's talking about destroying your Medicare, totally destroying-

Joe Biden: Wrong.

Donald Trump: . . . and destroying your Social Security. And this whole country will come down. Bernie Sanders tried it in his state.

Joe Biden: Bernie.

Donald Trump: He tried it in his state. His governor was a very liberal governor. They wanted to make it work.

Kristen Welker: Okay. Let's hear-

Donald Trump: It was impossible to work.

Kristen Welker: Let's let Vice President Biden respond-

Donald Trump: It doesn't work.

Joe Biden: He's a very confused guy. He thinks he's running against somebody else. He's running against Joe Biden. I beat all those other people because I disagreed with them. Joe Biden, he's running against. And the idea that we're in a situation that is going to destroy Medicare. . . .This is the guy that the actuary of Medicare said, "If in fact . . ." That's Social Security. "If in fact he continues his plan to with-hold the tax on Social Security, Social Security will be bankrupt by 2023 with no way to make up for it." This is the guy who's tried to cut Medicare. The idea that Donald Trump is lecturing me on Social Security and Medicare? Come on.

Donald Trump: He tried to get rid of-

Kristen Welker: 10 seconds, Mr. President, and then I have to go to another question.

Donald Trump: He tried to hurt Social Security years ago. Years ago. Go back and look at the records. He tried to hurt Social Security years ago. One thing. But this is the guy-

Kristen Welker: All right. Let's move on. I'm going to move on.

Donald Trump: . . . that when they announced last week-

Kristen Welker: Mr. President, I have to move on to the next question or else we're not going to have time to talk about it.

Donald Trump: They say the stock market will boom if I'm elected. If he's elected, the stock market will crash.

Kristen Welker: Okay. Let's move on to the next question.

Donald Trump: The biggest analysts are saying that.

Joe Biden: May I respond?

Kristen Welker: Very quickly.

Joe Biden: Look, the idea that the stock market is booming is his only measure of what's happening. Where I come from in Scranton and Claymont, the people don't live off of the stock market. Just in the last three years, during this crisis, the billion-aires in this country made, according to Wall Street, 700 billion more dollars. 700 billion more dollars. Because that's his only measure. What happens to the ordinary people out there? What happens to them?

Print Citations

CMS: Trump, Donald, and Joe Biden. "Final Presidential Debate Highlights." Speech at Belmont University, Nashville, Tennessee, October 22, 2020. In *The Reference Shelf: Representative American Speeches, 2019-2020,* edited by Annette Calzone, 137-145. Amenia, NY: Grey House Publishing, 2020.

MLA: Trump, Donald, and Joe Biden. "Final Presidential Debate Highlights." Belmont University, Nashville, Tennessee, 22 October 2020. Debate. *The Reference Shelf: Representative American Speeches, 2019-2020,* edited by Annette Calzone, Grey House Publishing, 2020, pp. 137-145.

APA: Trump, D., and J. Biden . (2020, October 22). Final presidential debate highlights. Belmont University, Nashville, Tennessee. In Annette Calzone (Ed.), *The reference shelf: Representative American speeches, 2019-2020* (pp. 137-145). Amenia, NY: Grey House Publishing.

President-Elect Joe Biden and Vice President-Elect Kamala Harris Acceptance Speech after Winning the 2020 Presidential Race

By Joe Biden and Kamala Harris

Joe Biden and Kamala Harris addressed the American people regarding their victory in the 2020 presidential election. Both stressed the importance of fighting for democratic values and of protecting the integrity of the country's democratic institutions. Biden and Harris promised a period of healing America's differences, and of leading by example, not might, on the international stage.

Kamala Harris: Good evening. Good evening. Good evening. Thank you. Thank you. Good evening. Thank you. Good evening. So Congressman John Lewis, Congressman John Lewis, before his passing, wrote, "Democracy is not a state. It is an act." What he meant was that America's democracy is not guaranteed. It is only as strong as our willingness to fight for it, to guard it and never take it for granted.

Protecting our democracy takes struggle, it takes sacrifice, but there is joy in it and there is progress, because we, the people, have the power to build a better future. When our very democracy was on the ballot in this election, with the very soul of America at stake, and the world watching, you ushered in a new day for America.

To our campaign staff and volunteers, this extraordinary team, thank you for bringing more people than ever before into the democratic process and for making this victory possible. To the poll workers and election officials across our country, who have worked tirelessly to make sure every vote is counted, our nation owes you a debt of gratitude. You have protected the integrity of our democracy.

And to the American people who make up our beautiful country, thank you for turning out in record numbers to make your voices heard.

Audience: Yes!

Kamala Harris: I know times have been challenging, especially the last several months, the grief, sorrow, and pain, the worries and the struggles, but we have also witnessed your courage, your resilience, and the generosity of your spirit. For four years, you marched and organized for equality and justice for our lives and for our planet.

Delivered on November 7, 2020, at the Chase Center on the Riverfront, Wilmington Delaware.

Then you voted and you delivered a clear message. You chose hope and unity, decency, science, and, yes, truth. You chose Joe Biden as the next president of the United States of America. Joe is a healer, a uniter, a tested and steady hand, a person whose own experience of loss gives him a sense of purpose that will help us as a nation reclaim our own sense of purpose, and a man with a big heart who loves with abandon.

It's his love for Jill, who will be an incredible First Lady. It's his love for Hunter and Ashley and his grandchildren and the entire Biden family. While I first knew Joe as vice president, I really got to know him as the father who loved Beau, my dear friend who we remember here today.

And to my husband Doug and our children Cole and Ella and my sister Maya and our whole family, I love you all more than I can ever express. We are so grateful to Joe and Jill for welcoming our family into theirs on this incredible journey. And to the woman most responsible for my presence here today, my mother, Shyamala Gopalan Harris, who is always in our hearts.

When she came here from India at the age of 19, she maybe didn't quite imagine this moment. But she believed so deeply, and in America, where a moment like this is possible. And so, I am thinking about her and about the generations of women, Black women, Asian, white, Latina, Native American women who, throughout our nation's history, have paved the way for this moment tonight, women who fought and sacrificed so much for equality and liberty and justice for all, including the Black women who are often too often overlooked, but so often prove they are the backbone of our democracy.

All the women who have worked to secure and protect the right to vote for over a century, 100 years ago with the 19th Amendment, 55 years ago with the Voting Rights Act, and now in 2020 with a new generation of women in our country who cast their ballots and continue the fight for their fundamental right to vote and be heard.

Tonight I reflect on their struggle, their determination, and the strength of their vision to see what can be unburdened by what has been. I stand on their shoulders. What a testament it is to Joe's character, that he had the audacity to break one of the most substantial barriers that exist in our country and select a woman as his vice president.

But while I may be the first woman in this office, I will not be the last, because every little girl watching tonight sees that this is a country of possibilities. To the children of our country, regardless of your gender, our country has sent you a clear message: dream with ambition, lead with conviction, and see yourselves in a way that others may not, simply because they've never seen it before. But know that we will applaud you every step of the way.

And to the American people, no matter who you voted for, I will strive to be a vice president like Joe was to President Obama, loyal, honest, and prepared, waking up every day thinking of you and your family, because now is when the real work begins, the hard work, the necessary work, the good work, the essential work to save lives and beat this epidemic, to rebuild our economy so it works for working people, to root out systemic racism in our justice system and society, to combat the climate crisis, to unite our country and heal the soul of our nation. The road ahead will not be easy, but America is ready, and so are Joe and I.

We have elected a president who represents the best in us, a leader the world will respect and our children will look up to, a commander-in-chief who will respect our troops and keep our country safe, and a president for all Americans.

Audience: Yes!

Kamala Harris: And it is now my great honor to introduce the President-elect of the United States of America, Joe Biden.

Joe Biden: Hello, my fellow Americans and the people who brought me to dance, Delawareans. I see my buddy Senator Tom Carper down there and I think Senator Coons is there and I think the governor's around. Is that Ruth Ann?

Audience: Yes, it is!

Joe Biden: And now former governor Ruth Ann Minner. Most importantly, my sisters-in-law and my sister Valerie. Anyway, folks, the people of this nation have spoken. They've delivered us a clear victory, a convincing victory, a victory for we the people. We've won with the most votes ever cast for a presidential ticket in the history of the nation, 74 million.

Well, I must admit it surprised me. Tonight, we've seen all over this nation, all cities in all parts of the country, indeed across the world, an outpouring of joy, of hope, renewed faith, and tomorrow bring a better day. I'm humbled by the trust and confidence you've placed in me.

I pledge to be a president who seeks not to divide but unify, who doesn't see red states and blue states, only sees the United States, and work with all my heart, with the confidence of the whole people, to win the confidence of all of you. For that is what America, I believe, is about. It's about people. And that's what our administration will be all about.

I sought this office to restore the soul of America, to rebuild the backbone of this nation, the middle class, and to make America respected around the world again and to unite us here at home. It's the honor of my lifetime that so many millions of Americans have voted for that vision. Now the work of making that vision is real. It's a task, the task, of our time.

Folks, as I said many times before, I'm Jill's husband, and I would not be here without her love and tireless support of Jill, and my son Hunter and Ashley, my daughter, and all our grandchildren and their spouses and all our family. They're in my heart.

Jill's a mom, a military mom, an educator. She's dedicated her life to education. But teaching isn't just what she does. It's who she is. For American educators, this is a great day for you all. You're going to have one of your own in the White House. Jill's going to make a great First Lady. I'm so proud of her.

I'll have the honor of serving with a fantastic vice president. You just heard from Kamala Harris, who makes history as the first woman, first Black woman, the first woman from South Asian descent, the first daughter of immigrants ever elected in this country.

Don't tell me it's not possible in the United States. It's long overdue. We're reminded tonight of those who fought so hard for so many years to make this happen. But once again, America's bent the arc of the moral universe, more toward justice. Kamala, Doug, like it or not, you're family. You've become an honorary Biden. There's no way out.

To all those of you who volunteered and worked the polls in the middle of this pandemic, local elected officials, you deserve a special thanks from the entire nation. To my campaign team and all the volunteers, and all who gave so much of themselves to make this moment possible, I owe you. I owe you. I owe you everything.

All those who supported us, I'm proud of the campaign we built and ran. I'm proud of the coalition we put together, the broadest and most diverse coalition in history. Democrats, Republicans, independents, progressives, moderates, conservatives, young, old, urban, suburban, rural, gay, straight, transgender, white, Latino, Asian, Native American. I mean it, especially in those moments and especially for those moments when this campaign was at its lowest ebb, the African American community stood up again for me. You've always had my back, and I'll have yours.

I said at the outset I wanted this campaign to represent and look like America. We've done that. Now that's what I want the administration to look like and act like.

For all those of you who voted for President Trump, I understand the disappointment tonight. I've lost a couple of times myself. But now let's give each other a chance. It's time to put away the harsh rhetoric, lower the temperature, see each other again, listen to each other again. To make progress, we have to stop treating our opponents as our enemies. They are not our enemies. They're Americans. They're Americans.

The Bible tells us to everything, there's a season, a time to build, a time to reap and a time to sow, and a time to heal. This is the time to heal in America.

Now this campaign is over, what is the will of people? What is our mandate? I believe it's this: American have called upon us to marshal the forces of decency, the forces of fairness, to marshal the forces of science and the forces of hope in the great battles of our time, the battle to control the virus, the battle to build prosperity, the battle to secure your family's healthcare, the battle to achieve racial justice and root out systemic racism in this country.

And the battle to save our planet by getting climate under control. The battle to restore decency, defend democracy, and give everybody in this country a fair shot. That's all they're asking for: a fair shot.

Folks, our work begins with getting COVID under control. We cannot repair the economy, restore our vitality, or relish life's most precious moments, hugging our grandchildren, our children on our birthdays, weddings, graduations, all the moments that matter most to us until we get it under control.

On Monday, I will name a group of leading scientists and experts as transition advisors, to help take the Biden-Harris COVID plan and convert it into an action blueprint that will start on January the 20th, 2021. That plan will be built on bed-rock science. It will be constructed out of compassion, empathy, and concern. I will spare no effort, none, or any commitment to turn around this pandemic.

Folks, I'm a proud Democrat, but I will govern as an American president. I'll work as hard for those who didn't vote for me as those who did. Let this grim era of demonization in America begin to end here and now.

The refusal of Democrats and Republicans to cooperate with one another is not some mysterious force beyond our control, it's a decision, a choice we make. If we can decide not to cooperate, then we can decide to cooperate.

I believe that this is part of the mandate given to us from the American people. They want us to cooperate in their interests, and that's the choice I'll make. I'll call on Congress, Democrats and Republicans alike, to make that choice with me.

The American story is about slow yet steadily widening the opportunities in America. Make no mistake, too many dreams have been deferred for too long. We must make the promise of the country real for everybody, no matter their race, their ethnicity, their faith, their identity, or their disability.

Folks, America has always been shaped by inflection points by moments in time where we've made hard decisions about who we are and what we want to be: Lincoln in 1860 coming to save the union, FDR in 1932 promising a beleaguered country a new deal, JFK in 1960 pledging a new frontier, and 12 years ago when Barack Obama made history and told us, yes, we can.

Well, folks, we stand at an inflection point. We have an opportunity to defeat despair, to build a nation of prosperity and purpose. We can do it. I know we can.

I've long talked about the battle for the soul of America. We must restore the soul of America. Our nation is shaped by the constant battle between our better angels and our darkest impulses, and what presidents say in this battle matters. It's time for our better angels to prevail.

Tonight, the whole world is watching America, and I believe, at our best, America is a beacon for the globe. We will lead not only by the example of our power, but by the power of our example.

I know I've always believed, and many of you heard me say it, I've always believed we can define America in one word: possibilities. That in America everyone should be given an opportunity to go as far as their dreams and God-given ability will take them.

You see, I believe in the possibilities of this country. We're always looking ahead, ahead to an America that's freer and more just, ahead to an America that creates jobs with dignity and respect, ahead to an America that cures diseases like cancer and Alzheimer's, ahead to an America that never leaves anyone behind, ahead to an America that never gives up, never gives in.

This is a great nation. It's always been a bad bet to bet against America. We're good people. This is the United States of America. There's never been anything, never been anything, we've been not able to do when we've done it together.

Folks, in the last days of the campaign, I began thinking about a hymn that means a lot to me and my family, particularly my deceased son, Beau. It captures the faith that sustains me and which I believe sustains America. I hope, and I hope, we can provide some comfort and solace to the 230,000 Americans who've lost a loved one due to this terrible virus this year. My heart goes out to each and every one of you. Hopefully this hymn gives you solace as well.

It goes like this. "And he will raise you up on eagle's wings, bear you on the breath of dawn, and make you just shine like the sun, and hold you in the palm of His hand." Now together on eagle's wings, we embark on the work that God and history have called upon us to do.

With full hearts and steady hands, with faith in America and in each other, with love of country, a thirst for justice, let us be the nation that we know we can be, a nation united, a nation strengthened, a nation healed, the United States of America.

Ladies and gentlemen, there's never, never, been anything we've tried we've not been able to do. Remember, as my grandpappy said when I walked out of his home, when I was a kid up in Scranton, he said, "Joey, keep the faith." And our grandmother, when she was alive, she yelled, "No, Joey. Spread it."

Spread the faith. God love you all. May God bless America and may God protect our troops. Thank you, thank you, thank you.

Print Citations

CMS: Biden, Joe, and Kamala Harris. "President-Elect Joe Biden and Vice President-Elect Kamala Harris Acceptance Speech after Winning the 2020 Presidential Race." Speech at the Chase Center on the Riverfront, Wilmington, Delaware, November 7, 2020. In *The Reference Shelf: Representative American Speeches, 2019-2020,* edited by Annette Calzone, 146-151. Amenia, NY: Grey House Publishing, 2020.

MLA: Biden, Joe, and Kamala Harris. "President-Elect Joe Biden and Vice President-Elect Kamala Harris Acceptance Speech after Winning the 2020 Presidential Race." Chase Center on the Riverfront, Wilmington, Delaware, 7 November 2020. Speech. *The Reference Shelf: Representative American Speeches, 2019-2020,* edited by Annette Calzone, Grey House Publishing, 2020, pp. 146-151.

APA: Biden, J., and K. Harris. (2020, November 7). President-elect Joe Biden and vice president-elect Kamala Harris acceptance speech after winning the 2020 presidential race. Chase Center on the Riverfront, Wilmington, Delaware. In Annette Calzone (Ed.), *The reference shelf: Representative American speeches, 2019-2020* (pp. 146-151). Amenia, NY: Grey House Publishing.

President Trump Is 100% within His Rights to Investigate Voting Irregularities

By Mitch McConnell

In the wake of claims of election uncertainty and voter fraud, Senate Majority Leader Mitch McConnell stated that President Trump's campaign had the legal right to look into claims of irregularities. McConnell went on to explain that the election process was designed to work through such concerns and that transparency was important.

Mitch McConnell: So it's time. Let's talk about where we are now. According to preliminary results, voters across the nation elected and re-elected Republican senators to a degree that actually stunned prognosticators. Likewise, the American people seem to have reacted to House Democrats' radicalism and obstruction by shrinking the speaker's majority and electing more Republicans.

And then there's the presidential race. Obviously, no states have yet certified their election results. We have at least one or two states that are already on track for a recount. And I believe the president may have legal challenges underway in at least five states.

The core principle here is not complicated. In the United States of America, all legal ballots must be counted and illegal ballots must not be counted. The process should be transparent or observable by all sides, and the courts are here to work through concerns. Our institutions are actually built for this. We have the system in place to consider concerns, and President Trump is 100% within his rights to look into allegations of irregularities and weigh his legal options.

Let's go back 20 years ago. 20 years ago when Florida came down to a very thin margin, we saw Vice President Gore exhaust the legal system and wait to concede until December. More recently, weeks after the media had called President Bush's re-election in 2004, Democrats baselessly disputed Ohio's electors and delayed the process here in Congress. In 2016, election law saw recounts or legal challenges in several states.

If any major irregularities occurred this time of a magnitude that would affect the outcome, then every single American should want them to be brought to light, and if the Democrats feel confident they have not occurred, they should have no reason to fear any extra scrutiny. We have the tools and institutions we need to address any concerns. The president has every right to look into allegations and to request recounts under the law. And notably, the Constitution gives no role in

Delivered on November 9, 2020, at the U.S. Senate, Washington, DC.

this process to wealthy media corporations. The projections and commentary of the press do not get veto power over the legal rights of any citizen, including the president of the United States.

Print Citations

CMS: McConnell, Mitch. "President Trump Is 100% within His Rights to Investigate Voting Irregularities." Speech at the U.S. Senate, Washington, DC, November 9, 2020. In *The Reference Shelf: Representative American Speeches, 2019-2020,* edited by Annette Calzone, 152-153. Amenia, NY: Grey House Publishing, 2020.

MLA: McConnell, Mitch. "President Trump Is 100% within His Rights to Investigate Voting Irregularities." U.S. Senate, Washington, DC, 9 November 2020. Speech. *The Reference Shelf: Representative American Speeches, 2019-2020,* edited by Annette Calzone, Grey House Publishing, 2020, pp. 152-153.

APA: McConnell, Mitch. (2020, November 9). President Trump is 100% within his rights to investigate voting irregularities. U.S. Senate, Washington, DC. In Annette Calzone (Ed.), *The reference shelf: Representative American speeches, 2019-2020* (pp. 152-153). Amenia, NY: Grey House Publishing.

Congressional Democratic Leaders News Conference on COVID-19 and Election Results

By Nancy Pelosi and Chuck Schumer

During a briefing on the coronavirus pandemic, the 2020 general election, and the House agenda, House Speaker Pelosi (D-CA) called on Senate Republicans to pass coronavirus relief legislation and Senator Schumer (D-NY) asked his Republican colleagues to accept the results of the 2020 election and start to work with President-elect Joe Biden.

Nancy Pelosi: Good morning everyone. It is an honor to welcome the Democratic leader in the Senate, Chuck Schumer. Welcome Mr. Leader. . . . Words have power. When the president speaks, his words have power. He has said things recently that are disconcerting. Numbers have eloquence, too. Yesterday our patients suffered a horrifying 144,000 new infections recorded. The eighth straight day of over 100,000 cases being reported. More than 65,000 Americans are hospitalized with COVID. A new record that threatens to overwhelm our hospitals in rural areas particularly. The devastating milestone of 10 million Americans . . . has been passed. . . . Sixty-five thousand people—more than 10 million Americans affected. More than 144,000 Americans have died. More than 20 million Americans are on unemployment. America has one million fewer teachers than a year ago. That is why we keep saying, Honor our heroes. Eight million people have fallen into poverty, and 17 million children in America are food-insecure. This is a red alert and all hands on deck. It should have been a long time ago. The president and the Republicans in Congress have ignored by delay, distortion, denial, doubts have been cast. What are they doing? Continuing to ignore in spite of these numbers. That should be so compelling. Every kind of avoidance of taking responsibility has been witnessed. Every chance we have for testing, tracing, treatment, mask wearing, separation, sanitation, what science tells us to do, they have ignored. Their contempt for science and disdain for government—science says wear a mask, the government says let's enforce that—science and governance is not what they are about. What that is, is they are engaged in an absurd circus right now, refusing to accept reality. Republicans are simply pretending, proceeding without recognizing what our responsibility is and making it even harder to address the masses—the massive health and economic crisis we are

Delivered on November 12, 2020, at the U.S. House of Representatives, Washington, DC.

facing. Ascertainment of major harm caused to the presidential transition is another subject. Right now we are talking about addressing the crisis, the pandemic. If we do so scientifically—we will be able to open our economy . We will be able to open our schools safely. We will be able to do so in a way that recognizes the tragedy that has befallen us in our country because of the Republican denial of science and disdain for governance. Stop the circus and get to work on what really matters to the American people: their health, and economic security. With that I'm pleased to yield to Mr. Schumer.

Chuck Schumer: Thank you . . . Speaker. It is good to be back. Good morning. This is a great—a moment of great national challenge. COVID-19 is surging, small businesses are shuttering, families are struggling, people continue to lose jobs and not gain new ones. We just had a divisive and hard-fought presidential election. Instead of working to pull the country back together so that we can fight our common enemy, COVID-19, Republicans in Congress are spreading conspiracy theories, denying realities, and poisoning the well of our democracy. The Republicans should stop their shenanigans about an election that Trump has already lost and focus their attention on the immediate issue at hand, providing relief to a country living through the COVID health and economic crises. When it comes to the election, Republicans, congressional Republicans don't have the evidence. They don't have the proof. They don't have anything, neither does the president. Congressional Republicans are deliberately casting doubt on our elections for no other reason than fear of Donald Trump. These Republicans are all auditioning for profiles in cowardice. This morning I have a simple message for Senate Republicans. The election is over. It wasn't close. Trump lost. Joe Biden will be the next president of the United States, Kamala Harris will be the next vice president of the United States. Senate Republicans, stop denying reality. Stop deliberately sowing doubt about our democratic process and start focusing on COVID. The Republican refusal to deal with reality is hurting our country in many ways. Fighting the health crisis of COVID, improving our economy, and not compromising on national security. It is time to move on and get to work for the American people. I want to be clear: the election is not in doubt. This is nothing more than a temper tantrum by Republicans, nothing more than a pathetic political performance for an audience of one, President Trump. This is nothing, Republicans, like the 2000 election, when it came down to one state and the difference between candidates was only 537 votes. Joe Biden's victory in the Electoral College has been secured by several states with tens of thousands of votes. Joe Biden leads in Wisconsin by 20,000; Pennsylvania 50,000; Michigan, 146,000. That is the fact. Biden has one. Nothing Republicans or Trump can do can change that. Legal claims by the president and his Republican allies are being left out of court. The *New York Times* called election officials from both parties in every state in the country. Not one reported any evidence of fraud or irregularities. These lawsuits have less than a snowball's chance in hell in succeeding. Let me speak to my colleagues in the Senate once again. Joe Biden has won. Move on and work with us to solve the COVID crisis. Let us bring the country together and get things done. Every day, as the Speaker mentioned, hundreds of thousands are getting sick, thousands are dying. We don't have time for these kinds of games. The American people are waiting for relief from the COVID virus. Republicans refused to take comprehensive action that meets the needs of the country. The virus—it is laser focused on health care issues that are at the heart of this pandemic. The Heroes Act does something that is vital, it strengthens Medicaid and improves access to health care coverage, support for hospitals. At a time when COVID is raging, health care expansion should be at the top of the list. These are the issues we should be discussing and debating. The Heroes Act should be the starting point, not an emaciated bill that prioritizes corporations and leaves American families as an afterthought. Every day that goes by without the Republican Party accepting the results of this election is another day Americans' faith in democracy declines. The longer Senate Republicans play this sad game, democracy declines. The longer Senate Republicans play this sad game, the longer the COVID crises.

Print Citations

CMS: Pelosi, Nancy, and Chuck Schumer. "Congressional Democratic Leaders News Conference on COVID-19 and Election Results." Press Conference at the U.S. House of Representatives, Washington, DC, November 12, 2020. In *The Reference Shelf: Representative American Speeches, 2019-2020,* edited by Annette Calzone, 154-156. Amenia, NY: Grey House Publishing, 2020.

MLA: Pelosi, Nancy, and Chuck Schumer. "Congressional Democratic Leaders News Conference on COVID-19 and Election Results." U.S. House of Representatives, Washington, DC, 12 November 2020. Press Conference. *The Reference Shelf: Representative American Speeches, 2019-2020,* edited by Annette Calzone, Grey House Publishing, 2020, pp. 154-156.

APA: Pelosi, N., and C. Schumer. (2020, November 12). Congressional Democratic leaders news conference on COVID-19 and election results. U.S. House of Representatives, Washington, DC. In Annette Calzone (Ed.), *The reference shelf: Representative American speeches, 2019-2020* (pp. 154-156). Amenia, NY: Grey House Publishing.

Key Cabinet Picks Announcement

By Joe Biden and Kamala Harris

Joe Biden and Kamala Harris announced the appointees and nominations for key cabinet positions on November 24, 2020, marking the first stage of the transition to a Biden presidency. Biden promised to work with global allies and reassert America's role as a global leader without getting involved in unnecessary military conflicts. At the same time, he pledged to address such threats as terrorism and extremism, nuclear proliferation, and the cyber threats in emerging technologies that spread authoritarianism.

Joe Biden: Everybody, okay. Well, good afternoon, everyone. Today, I'm pleased to announce nominations and staff for critical foreign policy national security positions in my administration. It's a team that will keep our country and our people safe and secure. And it's a team that reflects the fact that America is back, ready to lead the world, not retreat from it. Once again sit at the head of the table. Ready to confront our adversaries and not reject our allies. Ready to stand up for our values. In fact, in calls from world leaders that I've had, about 18 or 20 so far, I'm not sure the exact number, in the week since we won the election, I've been struck by how much they're looking forward to the United States reasserting its historic role as a global leader, both in the Pacific, as well as the Atlantic, all across the world.

The team meets this moment, this team behind me. They embody my core beliefs that America is strongest when it works with its allies. Collectively, this team has secured some of the most defining national security and diplomatic achievements in recent memory, made possible through decades of experience working with our partners. That's how we truly keep America safe, without engaging in needless military conflicts, and our adversaries in check, and terrorists at bay. And that's how we counter terrorism and extremism, control this pandemic and future ones, deal with crisis, nuclear proliferation, cyber threats in emerging technologies that spread authoritarianism, and so much more.

And while this team has unmatched experience and accomplishments, they also reflect the idea that we cannot meet these challenges with old thinking and unchanged habits. For example, we're going to have the first woman lead the intelligence community, the first Latino and immigrant to lead the Department of Homeland Security, and a groundbreaking diplomat at the United Nations. We're going to have a principle on the National Security Council who's full-time job is to

---

Delivered on November 24, 2020, at the Queen Theater, Wilmington, DE.

fight climate change. For the first time ever that will occur. And my national security team will be coordinated by one of the youngest national security advisors in decades.

Experience and leadership, fresh thinking and perspective, and an unrelenting belief in the promise of America. I've long said that America leads not only by the example of our power, but by the power of our example. And I'm proud to put forward this incredible team that will lead by example.

As Secretary of State, I nominate Tony Blinken. He's one of the better prepared for this job. No one's better prepared in my view. He will be the Secretary of State who previously served in top roles on Capitol Hill, in the White House and in the State Department. He delivered for the American people in each place. For example, leading our diplomatic efforts and the fight against ISIS, strengthening America's alliance and positions in the Asian-Pacific, guiding our responses to the global refugee crisis with compassion and determination. And he will rebuild morale and trust in the State Department, where his career in government began.

And he starts off with the kind of relationships around the world that many of his predecessors have had to build over the years. I know, I've seen him in action. Tony's been one of my closest and most trusted advisors. I know him and his family, immigrants and refugees, a Holocaust survivor, who taught him to never take for granted the very idea of America as a place of possibilities. Possibilities. Tony is ready on day one.

As Secretary for Homeland Security, I nominate Alejandro Mayorkas. This is one of the hardest jobs in government, a gigantic agency. The DHS Secretary needs to keep us safe from threats at home and from abroad and it's the job that plays a critical role in fixing our broken immigration system. After years of chaos, dysfunction and absolute cruelty a DHS, I'm proud to nominate an experienced leader who has been hailed by both Democrats and Republicans. Ally as he goes by is a former US attorney, former Director of US Citizenship and Immigration Services, and a former DHS Deputy Secretary. Helped implement DACA, prevented attacks on the homeland, enhanced our cybersecurity, helped communities recover from natural disaster, combated Ebola and Zika. And while DHS affects everyone, given it's critical role in immigration matters I'm proud that for the first time ever the department will be led by an immigrant, a Latino, who knows that we are a nation of laws and values. And one more thing, today's his birthday. Happy birthday, man, happy birthday. He's 21.

As a Director of National Intelligence, I nominate Avril Haine, the first woman ever to hold this post. To lead our intelligence community I didn't pick a politician or a political figure. I picked a professional. She's eminently qualified. Former Deputy Director of the CIA, former Deputy National Security Advisor to President Obama, and a fierce advocate for telling the truth and leveling with her decisions with the decision makers, straight up, nothing unnecessary. I know because I've worked with her for over a decade. Brilliant, humble, can talk literature and theoretical physics, fixing cars, flying planes, running a bookstore cafe, all in a single conversation, because she's done all that. And above all, if she gets word of a threat coming to our shores, like another pandemic or a foreign interference in our elections, she will not stop raising alarms until the right people take action. People will be able to take her word because she always calls it as she sees it. I believe we are safer with Avril on a watch. I think she can make a great contribution.

And as United States Ambassador to the United Nations I nominate Linda Thomas Greenfield. A seasoned and distinguished diplomat with 35 years in the foreign service who never forgot where she came from, growing up in segregated, Louisiana, the eldest of eight, her dad couldn't read or write, but she said he was the smartest person she knew. First in her family to graduate from high school, then college, with the whole world literally ahead of her as her dad and mom taught her to believe. Post in Switzerland, Pakistan, Kenya, The Gambia, Nigeria, Jamaica, Liberia, where she was known as the people's ambassador. Willing to meet with anyone, an ambassador, a student, working people struggling to get by, and always treating them with the same level of dignity and respect. She was our top State Department official in charge of African policy during the Ebola crisis. She received overwhelming support from her fellow career foreign service officers. And she'll be a cabinet status because I want to hear her voice on all the major foreign policy discussions we have.

And my National Security Advisor, I choose Jake Sullivan. He's once in a generation intellect with experience and temperament for one of the toughest jobs in the world. When I was Vice President, he served as my National Security Advisor. He was a top advisor to Secretary of State Clinton. He helped lead the early negotiations that led to the Iran nuclear deal. He helped broker the Gaza ceasefire in 2012, played a key role in Asia Pacific rebalance in our administration, and in this campaign for the presidency he served as one of my most trusted advisors on both foreign and domestic policy, including help me develop our COVID-19 strategy. Jake understands my vision, that economic security is national security, and it helps steer what I call a foreign policy for the middle class, for families like his growing up in Minnesota, where he was raised by parents who were educators, and taught him the values of hard work, decency, service and respect.

What that means is to win the competition for the future we need to keep us safe and secure, and build back better than ever. We need to invest in our people, sharpen our innovative edge, unite the economic might of our democracies around the world to grow the middle class, and reduce inequity and do things like counter predatory trade practices of our competitors and our adversaries.

And before I talk about the final person today, let me talk about this new position. For the first time ever the United States will have a full-time climate leader who'll participate in ministerial level meetings. And that's a fancy way of saying they'll have a seat at every table around the world. For the first time ever, there will be a principal on the NASA Security Council who can make sure climate change is on the agenda in the situation room. For the first time ever, we will have a Presidential Envoy on climate. He will be matched with high level White House climate policy coordinator and policymaking structure to be announced in December. And that'll lead efforts here in the United States to combat the climate crisis, mobilize action, to meet the existential threat that we face. Let me be clear. I don't for a minute underestimate the difficulties of meeting my bold commitments to fighting climate change. But at the same time, no one should underestimate for a minute my determination to do just that.

And as for the man himself, if I had a former secretary of state who helped negotiate the Paris Climate Accord, or a former presidential nominee, or a former leading Senator, or the head of a major climate organization for the job, that would show my commitment to the United States and the whole world. The fact that I picked the one person who was all of these things speaks unambiguously to my commitment. The world will know that with one of my closest friends, John Kerry, he's speaking for America on one of the most pressing threats of our time. No one I trust more.

To this team, I thanked them for accepting this call to service. And for their families, I thank you all for your sacrifice. We could not do this without you, in my view. Together, these public servants will restore America globally, it's global leadership, and it's moral leadership. And will ensure that our service members, diplomats, and intelligence professionals can do their job free of politics. They'll not only repair, they'll also reimagine American foreign policy and NASA security for the next generation. And they'll tell me what I need to know, not what I want to know, what I need to know. To the American people, this team will make us proud to be Americans. And as more states certify the results of this election, there's progress to wrap up our victory.

I'm pleased to have received the ascertainment from GSA to carry out a smooth and peaceful transition of power so our teams can prepare to meet the challenges at hand, to control the pandemic, to build back better, and to protect the safety and security of the American people. And to the United States Senate, I hope these outstanding nominees received a prompt hearing and that we can work across the aisle in good faith to move forward for the country. Let's begin that work to heal and unite, to heal and unite America as well as the world. I want to thank you all. May God bless you. May God protect our troops. And now I turn this over, this new team, starting with our next secretary of state, Tony Blinken. Get my mask here, Tony, so I don't get in trouble. And we're going to clean off the podium. . . .

Kamala Harris: . . . Congratulations, Mr. President-elect, on bringing together this extraordinary team. I have always believed in the nobility of public service and these Americans embody it. Their lives and careers are a Testament to the dedication, sacrifice, and commitment to civic responsibility that has strengthened our democracy and kept America's promise alive for more than 200 years.

President-elect Biden and I have long known that when we were elected, we would inherit a series of unprecedented challenges upon walking into the White House. Addressing these challenges starts with getting this pandemic under control, opening our economy responsibly, and making sure it works for working people. And we also know that our challenges will require us here at home to overcome those issues that block our ability to proceed.

Our challenge here is a necessary foundation for restoring and advancing our leadership around the world. And we are ready for that work. We will need to reassemble and renew America's alliances, rebuild and strengthen the national security and foreign policy institutions that keep us safe and advance our nation's interests. And confront and combat the existential threat of climate change that endangers us all.

I take these issues very seriously. My whole career has been about keeping people safe from serving as district attorney to California's Attorney General to the United States Senate, where I have served on the Intelligence and Homeland Security committees. I've come to know firsthand the gravity of the challenges and threats facing the United States. And over the past few months, I've also come to know the sound judgment, expertise, and character of the people on this stage. I can say with confidence that they are to a person, the right women and men for these critical positions. And I look forward to working alongside them on behalf of the American people. And on behalf of a president who will ask tough questions, demand that we be guided by facts and expect our team to speak the truth no matter what. A president who will be focused on one thing and one thing only, doing what is best for the people of the United States of America.

When Joe asked me to be his running mate, he told me about his commitment, to making sure we selected a cabinet that looks like America, that reflects the best of our nation. And that's what we have done. Today's nominees and appointees come from different places. They bring a range of different life and professional experiences and perspectives. And they also share something else in common, and unwavering belief in America's ideals and unshakeable commitment to democracy, human rights, and the rule of law. And they understand the indispensable role of America's leadership in the world. These women and men are patriots and public servants to their core. And they are leaders, the leaders we need to meet the challenges of this moment and those that lie ahead. Thank you.

Print Citations

CMS: Biden, Joe, and Kamala Harris. "Key Cabinet Picks Announcement." Public Address at the Queen Theater, Wilmington, DE, November 24, 2020. In *The Reference Shelf: Representative American Speeches, 2019-2020,* edited by Annette Calzone, 157-161. Amenia, NY: Grey House Publishing, 2020.

MLA: Biden, Joe, and Kamala Harris. "Key Cabinet Picks Announcement ." Queen Theater, Wilmington, DE, 24 November 2020. Public Adress. *The Reference Shelf: Representative American Speeches, 2019-2020,* edited by Annette Calzone, Grey House Publishing, 2020, pp. 157-161.

APA: Biden, J., and K. Harris. (2020, November 24). Key Cabinet picks announcement. Queen Theater, Wilmington, DE. In Annette Calzone (Ed.), *The reference shelf: Representative American speeches, 2019-2020* (pp. 157-161). Amenia, NY: Grey House Publishing.

5
Other Significant Events in 2020

by U.S. National Archives, via Wikimedia

Ruth Bader Ginsburg, who passed away in September 2020, delivered an address on the centennial of the Nineteenth Amendment in February.

Key Moments from the Donald Trump Impeachment Trial Final Day

By U.S. Senate

The divide between the House of Representatives and the Senate over the impeachment of President Donald Trump came through in the speeches delivered by members of Congress on the final day of the Senate trial. Kamala Harris called the trial a miscarriage of justice, while Lamar Alexander contended that the evidence did not meet the Constitution's high bar for an impeachable offense.

Kamala Harris: Thank you. Mr. President, when the framers wrote the constitution, they didn't think someone like me would serve as the United States Senator, but they did envision someone like Donald Trump being President of the United States. Someone who thinks he is above the law and that rules don't apply to him. So they made sure our democracy had the tool of impeachment to stop that kind of abuse of power.

The House managers have clearly laid out a compelling case and evidence of Donald Trump's misconduct. They have shown that the President of the United States of America withheld military aid and a coveted White House meeting for his political gain. He wanted a foreign country to announce, not actually conduct, announce an investigation into his political rivals. And then he refused to comply with congressional investigations into his misconduct. And unfortunately a majority of United States senators, even those who concede that what Donald Trump did was wrong, are nonetheless going to refuse to hold him accountable.

The Senate trial of Donald Trump has been a miscarriage of justice. Donald Trump is going to get away with abusing his position of power for personal gain, abusing his position of power to stop Congress from looking into his misconduct, and falsely claiming he's been exonerated. He's going to escape accountability because a majority of senators have decided to let him. They voted repeatedly to block key evidence like witnesses and documents that could have shed light on the full truth, and we must recognize that still in America there are two systems of justice, one for the powerful and another for everyone else.

So let's speak the truth about what our two systems of justice actually mean in the real world. It means that in our country, too many people walk into courthouses and face systemic bias. Too often they lack adequate legal representation, whether they are overworked, underpaid, or both. It means that a young man named Emmett

Delivered on February 5, 2020, at the U.S. Senate, Washington, DC.

Till was falsely accused and then murdered, but his murderer didn't have to spend a day in jail. It means that four young black men had their lives taken and turned upside down after being falsely accused of a crime in Groveland, Florida. It means that right now, too many people in America are sitting in jail without having yet been convicted of a crime, but simply because they cannot afford bail. And it means that future Presidents of the United States will remember that the United States Senate failed to hold Donald Trump accountable and they will be emboldened to abuse their power knowing there will be no consequence.

Donald Trump knows all this better than anybody. He may not acknowledge that we have two systems of justice, but he knows the institutions in this country, be it courts or the Senate are set up to protect powerful people like him. He told us as much when regarding the sexual assault of women. He said, quote, when you're a star, they let you do it. You can do anything. He said that Article Two of the United States constitution gives him as president the right to do whatever he wants. Trump has shown us through his words and actions that he thinks he is above the law and when the American people see the president acting as though he is above the law, it understandably leaves them feeling untrustful of our system of justice, distrustful of our democracy. When the United States Senate refuses to hold him accountable, it reinforces that loss of trust in our system.

Now, I'm under no illusion that this body is poised to hold this president accountable, but despite the conduct of the United States Senate in this impeachment trial, the American people must continue to strive toward the more perfect union that our constitution promises. And it's going to take all of us in every state, every town, everywhere to continue fighting for the best of who we are as a country. We each have an important role to play in fighting for those words inscribed on that United States Supreme Court equal justice under law.

Frederick Douglass, who like many, I consider to be one of the founders of our nation, wrote that quote, the whole history of the progress of human liberty, that all concessions yet made to her august claims have been born of earnest struggle.

The impeachment of Donald Trump has been one of those earnest struggles for liberty. And this fight like so many before it, it has been a fight against tyranny. This struggle has not been an easy one and it has left too many people across our nation feeling cynical. For too many people, this trial confirms something they've always known that the real power in this country lies not with them, but with just a few people who advance their own interest at the expense of others' needs. For many, the injustice in this trial is yet another example of the way that our system of justice has worked or more accurately failed to work. But here's the thing, Frederick Douglass also told us that quote, if there is no struggle, there is no progress. He went on to say, power concedes nothing without a demand. And he said it never did and it never will.

In order to wrestle power away from the few people at the very top who abuse their power, the American people are going to have to fight for the voice of the people and the power of the people. We must go into the darkness to shine a light and we cannot be deterred and we cannot be overwhelmed and we cannot ever give up on our country. We cannot ever give up on the ideals that are the foundation for our system of democracy. We can never give up on the meaning of true justice and it is part of our history, our past, clearly our present, and our future that in order to make these values real, in order to make the promise of our country real, we can never take it for granted. There will be moments in time, in history where we experienced incredible disappointment, but the greatest disappointment of all will be if we give up. We cannot ever give up fighting for who we know we are. And we must always see who we can be unburdened by who we have been. That is the strength of our nation.

So after the Senate votes today, Donald Trump will want American people to feel cynical. He will want us not to care. He will want us to think that he is all powerful and we have no power. But we're not going to let him get away with that. We're not going to give him what he wants, because the true power and potential of the United States of America resides not with the president, but with the people, all the people. So in our long struggle for justice, I will do my part by voting to convict this lawless president and remove him from office. And I urge my colleagues to join me on the right side of history. I yield the floor. . . .

Doug Jones: Thank you, Mr. President. Mr. President, on the day I was sworn in as a United States Senator, I took an oath to protect and defend the constitution. Just last month, at the beginning of the impeachment trial, I took a second oath to do fair and impartial justice according to the same constitution I swore to protect. . . .

I'm reminded of Robert Kennedy's words that were mentioned in this trial. "Few men are willing to brave the disapproval of their fellows, the censure of their colleagues, the wrath of their society. Moral courage is a rarer commodity than bravery in battle or great intelligence. Yet it is the one essential vital quality for those who seek to change a world that yields most painfully to change." Candidly to my colleagues on both sides of the aisle, I fear that moral courage, country before party, is a rare commodity these days.

We can write about it and talk about it in speeches and in the media, but it is harder to put into action when political careers may be on the line. Nowhere is the dilemma more difficult than in an impeachment of the President of the United States. Very early on in this process, I implored my colleagues on both sides of the aisle, in both houses of Congress, to stay out of their political and partisan corners.

Many did, but so many did not. Even the media continually view this entire process through partisan political eyes and how it may or may not affect an election. That is unfortunate. The country deserves better and we must find a way to move beyond such partisan divides. The solemn oaths that I have taken have been my guides during what has been a difficult time for the country, my state, and for me personally.

I did not run for the Senate hoping to participate in the impeachment trial of a duly elected president, but I cannot and will not shrink from my duty to defend the constitution and to do impartial justice. In keeping with my oath as Senator and my oath to do impartial justice, I resolve that throughout this process I would keep an open mind, to consider the evidence without regard to political affiliation and to hear all of the evidence before making a final decision on either charge against the President.

I believe that my votes later today will reflect that commitment. With the eyes of history upon us, I'm acutely aware of the precedence that this impeachment trial will set for future presidencies and congresses. Unfortunately, I do not believe that those precedents are good ones. I am particularly concerned that we have now set a precedent that the Senate does not have to go forward with witnesses or review documents, even when those witnesses have firsthand information and the documents would allow us to test not just the credibility of witnesses but also test the words of counsel of both parties.

It is my firm belief that the American people deserve more. In short, witnesses and documents would provide the Senate and the American people with a more complete picture of the truth and I believe the American people deserve nothing less. That's not to say, however, that there is not sufficient evidence in which to render a judgment. There is. As a trial lawyer, I once explained this process to a jury as like putting together the pieces of a puzzle. When you open the box and spread all the pieces on the table, it's just an incoherent jumble.

But one by one you hold those pieces up and you hold them next to each other and see what fits and what doesn't. And even if, as was often the case in my house growing up, you're missing a few pieces, even important ones, you more often than not see the picture. As I've said many times, I believe the American people deserve to see a completed puzzle, a picture with all of the pieces, pieces in the form of documents and witnesses with relevant firsthand information, which would have provided valuable context, corroboration or contradiction to that which we have heard. But even with missing pieces, our common sense and life's experiences allow us to see the picture as it comes into full view.

Throughout the trial one piece of evidence continued to stand out for me. It was the President's statement that under the constitution we have article two and I can do anything I want. That seems to capture this President's belief about the presidency, that he has unbridled power, unchecked by Congress or the judiciary or anyone else. That view, dangerous as it is, explains the President's actions toward Ukraine and Congress.

The sum of what we've seen and heard is unfortunately a picture of a President who has abused the great power of his office for personal gain. A picture of a President who has placed his personal interest well above the interest of the nation and in so doing threatened our national security, the security of our European allies and the security of Ukraine. The evidence clearly proves that the President used the weight of his office and the weight of the United States government to seek, to coerce a foreign government, to interfere in our election for his personal political benefit.

His actions were more than simply inappropriate. They were an abuse of power. When I was a lawyer for the Alabama Judicial Inquiry Commission, there was a saying that the Chairman of the Inquiry Commission and one of Alabama's great judges used to say, Randall Cole. Judge Cole used to say about judges who strayed from the canons of ethics that the judge left his post. Sadly, President Trump left his post with regard to the withholding of military aid to Ukraine and a White House visit for the new Ukrainian President.

And in so doing, he took the great powers of the office of the President of the United States with him. Impeachment is the only check on such presidential wrong-doing. The second article of impeachment, obstruction of Congress, gave me more pause. I've struggled to understand the House's strategy and their failure to fully pursue documents and witnesses and wished that they had done more.

However, after careful consideration of the evidence developed in the hearings, the public disclosures, the legal precedents in the trial, I believe that the President deliberately and unconstitutionally obstructed Congress by refusing to cooperate with the investigation in any way. While I am sensitive to protecting the privileges and immunities afforded to the President and his advisors, I believe it's critical to our constitutional structure that we also protect the authorities of the Congress of the United States.

Here it was clear from the outset that the President had no intention whatsoever of accommodating Congress when he bought both witnesses and documents from being produced. In addition, he engaged in a course of conduct to threaten poten-tial witnesses and smear the reputations of the civil servants who did come forward and provide testimony. The President's actions demonstrate a belief that he is above the law, that Congress has no power whatsoever in questioning or examining his ac-tions and that all who do so do so at their peril.

That belief, unprecedented in history of this country, simply must not be permit-ted to stand. To do otherwise risks guaranteeing that no future whistleblower or wit-ness will ever come forward and no future President, Republican or Democrat, will be subject to congressional oversight as mandated by the constitution, even when the president has so clearly abused his office and violated the public trust.

Accordingly, I will vote to convict the president on both articles of impeachment. In doing so, I am mindful that in a democracy there is nothing more sacred than the right to vote and respecting the will of the people. But I'm also mindful that when our founders wrote the constitution, they envisioned a time, or at least a possibil-ity, that our democracy would be more damaged if we fail to impeach and remove a President. Such is the moment in history that we face today. The gravity of this moment, the seriousness of the charges and the implication for future presidencies and congresses all contributed to the difficulty with which I've arrived at my deci-sion. . . .

Lamar Alexander: Thank you, Madame President. Madame President, in this im-peachment proceeding I worked with other senators to make sure that we had the right to ask for more documents and witnesses, but there was no need for more evidence to prove something that I believed had already been proven and that did not meet the United States Constitution's high bar for an impeachable offense. There was no need for more evidence to prove that the president asked Ukraine to investigate Joe Biden and his son, Hunter. He said this on television on Octo-ber 3rd, 2019, and he said it during his July 25th, 2019 telephone call with the president of Ukraine. There was no need for more evidence to conclude that the president withheld United States aid, at least in part, to pressure Ukraine to investigate the Bidens. The House managers had proved this with what they called a "Mountain of overwhelming evidence." One of the managers said it was proved beyond the shadow of a doubt. There was no need to consider further the frivolous second article of impeachment that would remove from the president, and future presidents, remove from this president for asserting his constitutional prerogative to protect confidential conversations with his close advisors. It was inappropriate for the president to ask a foreign leader to investigate his political opponent and to withhold United States aid to encourage this investigation. When elected officials inappropriately interfere with such investigations, it undermines the principle of equal justice under the law.

But Madame President, the Constitution does not give the Senate the power to remove the president from office and ban him from this year's ballot simply for actions that are inappropriate. The question then is not whether the president did it, but whether the United States Senate or the American people should decide what to do about what he did. I believe that the Constitution clearly provides that the people should make that decision in the presidential election that began on Monday in Iowa.

The Senate has spent 11 long days considering this mountain of evidence, the arguments of the House managers, the president's lawyers, their answers to senator's questions and the House record. Even if the house charges were true, they don't meet the Constitution's "Treason, bribery or other high crimes and misdemeanors," standard for impeachable offense. The framers believed that there never ever should be a partisan impeachment. That is why the Constitution requires a two-thirds vote of the Senate to convict. Yet not one House Republican voted for these articles. If this shallow, hurried and wholly partisan impeachment were to succeed, it would rip the country apart, pouring gasoline on the fire of cultural divisions that already exists. It would create a weapon of perpetual impeachment to be used against future presidents whenever the House of Representatives is of a different political party. Our founding documents provide for duly elected presidents who serve, "With the consent of the governed," not at the pleasure of the United States Congress. Let the people decide.

A year ago at the Southeastern Conference basketball tournament, a friend of 40 years sitting in front of me turned to me and said, "I'm very unhappy with you for voting against the president." She was referring to my vote against the president's decision to spend money that Congress hadn't appropriated to build the border wall. I believe then and now that the United States Constitution gives to the Congress the exclusive power to appropriate money. This separation of powers creates checks and balances in our government that preserves our individual liberty by not allowing, in that case, the executive to have too much power. I replied to my friend, "Look, I was not voting for or against the president. I was voting for the United States Constitution." Well, she wasn't convinced. Now this past Sunday walking my dog, Rufus, in Nashville, I was confronted by a neighbor who said she was angry and crushed by my vote against allowing more witnesses in the impeachment trial. "The Senate should remove the president for extortion," she said. I replied to her, "I was not voting for or against the president. I was voting for the United States Constitution, which in my view, does not give the Senate the power to remove a president from his office and from this year's election ballot simply for actions that are inappropriate."

The United States Constitution says a president may be convicted only for treason, bribery, and other high crimes and misdemeanors. President Trump's actions regarding Ukraine are a far cry from that. Plus I said, "Unlike the Nixon impeachment, when almost all Republicans voted to initiate an impeachment inquiry, not one single Republican voted to initiate this impeachment inquiry against President Trump. The Trump impeachment," I said to her, "was a completely partisan action, and the framers of the United States constitution, especially James Madison, believed we should never ever have a partisan impeachment. That would undermine the separation of powers by allowing the House of Representatives to immobilize the executive branch as well as the Senate by a perpetual partisan series of impeachments." Well, she was not convinced.

When our country was created there never had been anything quite like it, a democratic Republic with a written constitution. Perhaps its greatest innovation was the separation of powers among the presidency, the Supreme Court, and the Congress. The late Justice Scalia said of this checks and balances, "Every tin-horn dictator in the world today, every president for life, has a bill of rights. What has made us free is our Constitution." What he meant was what makes the United States different and protects our individual liberty is the separation of powers and the checks and balances in our constitution. The goal of our founders was not to have a king as chief executive on the one hand, or not to have a British-style parliament on the other, which could remove our chief executive or prime minister or the majority or no confidence vote.

The principle reason our constitution created a United States Senate is so that one body of Congress can pause and resist the excesses of the executive or popular passions that can run through the House of Representatives like a freight train. The language of the Constitution of course is subject to interpretation, but on some things his words are clear. The president cannot spend money that Congress doesn't appropriate, that's clear. And the Senate can't remove a president for anything less than treason, bribery, high crimes, and misdemeanors and two thirds of us, the senators, must agree on that. That requires a bipartisan consensus. We senators take an oath to base our decisions on the provisions of our constitution, which is what I have endeavored to do during this impeachment proceeding.

Print Citations

CMS: U.S. Senate. "Key Moments from the Donald Trump Impeachment Trial Final Day." Speeches at the U.S. Senate, Washington, DC, February 5, 2020. In *The Reference Shelf: Representative American Speeches, 2019-2020,* edited by Annette Calzone, 165-172. Amenia, NY: Grey House Publishing, 2020.

MLA: U.S. Senate. "Key Moments from the Donald Trump Impeachment Trial Final Day." U.S. Senate, 5 February 2020, Washington, DC. Speeches. *The Reference Shelf: Representative American Speeches, 2019-2020,* edited by Annette Calzone, Grey House Publishing, 2020, pp. 165-172.

APA: U.S. Senate. (2020, February 5). Speeches on key moments from the Donald Trump impeachment trial final day. U.S. Senate, Washington, DC. In Annette Calzone (Ed.), *The reference shelf: Representative American speeches, 2019-2020* (pp. 165-172). Amenia, NY: Grey House Publishing.

On the Centennial of Women's Right to Vote

By Ruth Bader Ginsburg

Supreme Court Justice Ruth Bader Ginsburg spoke about the 100th anniversary of women being granted the right to vote in February. Her comments touch on her personal experience, some of the related cases she has heard over the years, and her dissent collar, among other things. Her remarks reflect her signature style in interpreting the law.

Yes. My mother was 18 when the 19th amendment became a part of the Constitution. So when she was 15 and 16, she took part in the parades in New York. . . .

The notorious RBG was created by a second-year law student, it was the year the Supreme Court decided the Shelby County case, which codified the key provision in the Voting Rights Act of 1965. The law was passed in 1965, it was renewed periodically with large majorities on both sides of the aisle, and recently being renewed it was attacked on the ground that the formula, the way the Voting Rights Act worked was, if you had a record of keeping African Americans from voting, you could not pass any new election law without pre-clearing it either with the Civil Rights Division of the Department of Justice or a three-judge Federal District Court in D.C. That provided a check on laws that were aimed at suppressing minority voters, you couldn't pass the law unless you had it pre-cleared. The law was attacked as obsolete. The argument was that some states that might have discriminated in 1965 are no longer denying African Americans the right to vote. There was a built-in check in the statute to take care of that kind of situation. It was a bear-out provision. It said that if you had a clean record for X number of years, you can apply to be released from preclearance. But the majority of minds thought the formula was obsolete, it needed to be done over. One of the points that I made in my dissent was, what member of our Congress is going to stand up and say my state or my city or my county is still keeping African Americans from voting, so please keep us out of the preclearance system. That was not going to happen. If you think about, who knows a little more about the political world, the Congress or the Court, the Congress said we want the Voting Rights Act, it is working well, and the Court said, you cannot have it. If you talk about judicial activism, here is a law that Congress overwhelmingly passed and the Court nullified it. This second-year student was angry about the decision, she thought here is a piece of legislation that is really working and the Supreme Court stopped it. And then she thought more, and decided that anger is a

---

Delivered on February 10, 2020, on C-Span, Washington, DC.

useless emotion, it just gets [you] riled up but it does not move you forward. So she wanted to do something positive, and she took, not my full dissenting opinion but the announcement of my dissent that I read from the bench in the Shelby County case and put it on some kind of blog or tumblr.

Anyway, the second-year student paired with a journalist and they wrote a book called *The Notorious RBG*, which is now an exhibition that is traveling around the country. It was most recently in Philadelphia, and currently it is in Chicago, it will be some months from now in New York. So now there is a *Notorious RBG* adult reader and a *Notorious RBG* for young readers, and many children's books, coloring books.

I should say something that you didn't mention before. *On the Basis of Sex*, which the script writer for that, by the way, was my nephew, and when we asked him, Why did you choose the *Moritz* case, because it was not reviewed by the Supreme Court, and his answer was because he wanted the film to be as much the story of a marriage as the story of the development of a legal strategy. I think he succeeded in that. But before *On the Basis of Sex* there was a documentary called *RBG* done by Betsy West and Julie Cohen, years before, those two women had done a special for PBS about the women's movement, the revived women's movement starting in the late sixties and continuing through the seventies. They interviewed all kinds of people for it, people on both sides. So there was an interview with Phyllis Schlafly, who single-handedly brought down the Equal Rights Amendment. . . . And I was one of the people interviewed for *Makers*, so the people who created that documentary decided they would like to do one. It focused on the American civil issue litigation efforts in the 1970s to invigorate the equal protection clause so that it worked for women and men.

I do have a dissent collar. Years ago, *Glamour* magazine gave me a Lifetime Achievement Award, and it was a bag filled with goodies. And one of them was that dissent collar. I thought it looked just right for dissent. (laughs) Nowadays I get a call, or at least once a week, I get two things: I get collars and I get scrunchies.

I will start at the end. Marty was a superb cook, and when we were married we spent the first two years, and he was in military service, in Oklahoma. And there, Marty had been originally [a] chemistry major until . . . golf practice interfered with chemistry labs, so then he switched [to] government, which was my subject. My cousin sent him, as a joke, an English translation of the great *Escoffier Cookbook*. Marty started with a basic stock and he worked his way, I still have the book, food stains all over it. But we had an arrangement where I was the everyday cook; Marty was the weekend and company cook. I was never allowed to cook for company. I had seven things that I made, they all came out of a book called the *60-Minute Chef*, 60 minutes from the time you enter your home until the dinner is on the table, that was it. It was a rotation. It got to seven and went back to one. (laughs) And Jane, my daughter, when she is in her high school years, she becomes increasingly aware of the enormous difference between Daddy's cooking and Mommy's cooking, and she decides that not only should Daddy be the weekend and company cook but he should be the everyday cook. This was to me like Tom Sawyer getting the fence painted. I haven't cooked a meal, we have been living in Washington, D.C., since 1980, I have not cooked a meal in all of those years. When Marty died, my daughter Jane felt responsibility for having fazed me out of the kitchen, so she comes once a month, cooks up a storm, makes individual dinners for me which we put in the freezer, and then we do something nice in the evening. So, when Marty died, the wife of Justice Alito decided that the tribute that would be just right for him was a cookbook, and it is called *Supreme Chef*, that is Marty. Each section is introduced by the spouse of another Justice in seniority order, so it starts with Maureen Scalia, and it is one of the best-selling books in the Supreme Court gift shop.

I think I knew then what has been reaffirmed over and over again. The Supreme Court is what lawyers call [a] "hot bench." That is, every Justice has done his or her homework, is armed to the teeth for oral argument, uses their power effectively. That is not true of all appellate benches, and I remember one argument in a Federal Circuit Court, I will not say which number.

My students came with me to this argument, and I thought our reply brief was devastating. I start arguing it, and I sense early on that the panel, far from reading my reply brief, had not even read the opening brief. So I had to go back to being a kindergarten teacher and lead them in the direction I wanted them to go. But that can be very disillusioning to an advocate, if you are dealing with a cold bench. . . .

I got a clerkship with a District Judge, . . . called every judge in the Eastern Southern district, every judge in the Second Circuit, finally came to one Judge Edmund, who was a Columbia college graduate, and a Columbia Law School graduate, and always took his clerks from Columbia. . . .

One lesson is that on questions on statutory interpretation, as distinguished from constitutional interpretation, statutory interpretation does not have the last word. So I thought my colleagues had erred. . . . My dissent on that case was, the ball is now in Congress's court, to correct the error in[to] which my colleagues have fallen. There was a ground swell to pass that Lilly Ledbetter Fair Pay Act. Again, in the Act, large majorities, Republicans, Democrats—[the] Lilly Ledbetter Fair Pay Act was the first piece of legislation that President Obama signed when he took office. And really, [the] story was a story familiar to every woman of my generation, and of hers. She was an area manager at a Goodyear Tire, it was a job dominated by men. She came on board in the seventies. She didn't want to be viewed as a troublemaker. She didn't want to rock the boat. . . . One day someone put a paper in her mailbox. It was a series of numbers, she recognized what those numbers meant. They were the pay of every other area manager, and she saw the young man she had trained to do the job was getting more than she was earning. She said, I have had it, I will sue. She began a Title VII lawsuit, succeeded in District Court. It was a jury case, she got a good verdict. By the time it got to the Supreme Court, . . . Lilly you sued too late. Title VII says you must file a complaint within 180 days of the discriminatory incident. And here you are coming along a dozen years later, you are way, way out of time. In my dissent I explained, she doesn't want to rock the boat. Besides, if she had said early on, they're paying me less because I'm woman, they would say almost certainly it has nothing to do with really being a woman, she just doesn't do the job as good as a man. But, what, she's been working there year after year, and getting good performance ratings—that offense that she doesn't do the job as well as a man is no longer available to them. She has a winnable case, but the Court says she sued too late. My dissent, was the sole simplicity, I said the discrimination that she encountered is repeated, every month, because this is reflected in every paycheck she receives. So as long as she sues within 180 days of a paycheck, her suit is timely. And that is exactly what they amended Title VII to say, what I thought . . . all along.

You're hoping over time, the Court will see it the way you do, that's where we're arriving. Most immediately I'm trying to get my dissent circulated. That hope is often disappointed, but, there is always a chance. . . .

United States against Virginia . . . [says] the state of Virginia cannot leave an educational opportunity available to one sex only. The faculty saw that this was an opportunity to upgrade their applicant pool. Many people said to me, What woman would want to go, to subject herself to that rigorous and brutal program? . . . I said, Well, I wouldn't. If you are a man, you probably wouldn't either. But there are some women who do want that experience, and are well equipped to pursue it. Soon I went back, now it's . . . the 20th anniversary, . . . the 21st, and everyone was so proud. . . . These women wanted to be engineers, it was a great. . . .

I've told law students on more than one occasion, watch what we do. Law students like to have a secure handhold, so there is rational basis, intermediate, and so on. And then Sandra wrote an opinion that said . . . a number of statutes are being held invalid under the rational basis, so the bottom is moving up, the top is moving down. And I think Justice Marshall had it right when he said there are not these three tiers, there is a sliding scale, it depends upon the strength of the government's interest. And the importance of the right that the person is asserting. The words are, shall any state deny any person the equal protection of the law? . . . Except that the 14th amendment was meant to deal with the burning issue of the day, slavery, and in the second section of the 14th amendment, for the first time, the word male appears in the text of the Constitution. Before the 15th amendment there was an effort to stop the southern states from barring African Americans from voting, and the mechanism was, if you keep people from the polls then you will lose. To the extent that you are not allowing men to vote, your representation in Congress will shrink, in proportion to the people that you have kept from voting. It didn't work, so they then passed the 15th amendment. By the way, since we've started talking about the 19th amendment, the 19th amendment follows the wording of the 15th amendment. The 15th amendment was honored in the breach, so [for] many years one of the concerns, one of the concerns on the part of some of the southern politicians was, does that mean that we will have African American women voting? That was a serious concern. As it turned out, the barriers to minority voters continued, and it affected women as well as men. So initially, the 19th amendment gave white women the right to vote, and it took a measure like the Voting Rights Act to break that.

I'm pleased that one of my former law clerks is spending a good deal of her time getting 18-year-olds to register to vote, especially minority women. Going with them to the registration place, taking them there. But I think that young people are going to make a difference, and what our government does now is going to be affecting their lives, so they should care deeply about exercising the right to vote.

And there should be great efforts to see that, when they try to vote, they are registered properly. . . .

First on the subject of the 19th amendment, there is a very good exhibition, at the Archives, and when do we visit? It was last week? And the story is told, it is accessible as could be. There are some things that are very funny, like the letter from the woman in Iowa, she wanted to lead the troops, be a soldier, when we do this, that, and the other thing, but they shouldn't vote.

There [are] such inconsistent arguments. One was, they're just going to do what their husbands tell them to do, so it won't make a difference. The other was, this is going to cause dissension in the home. . . . There a couple of cartoons of men taking care of screaming babies so that their wives can go and vote. But it took, with 1848, it's now seven years later, we have to be patient. What was it . . . . [Susan B.] Anthony said, failure is impossible. She never got to see the 19th amendment, but she knew it would happen. I recommend that exhibition, and in my long life, I've seen such positive change. Yes, there are things that make us all worry, like a dysfunctional Congress, if the parties so sharply divide. But think of how it was, not all that long ago in 1993, when I was nominated and confirmed 96 to 3, no questions asked about the ten years I spent, most of my time as cofounder of the ACLU women's rights project. And one of the four general counsels to the union, Justice Scalia, he had written a lot as a law professor, so he was a known quantity, the vote for him was unanimous. Justice Breyer, who followed me by a year. In the nineties, it hasn't been that way, for the last set of nominations. But I am hopeful that there will be leaders on both sides of the aisle who will say, it's time to get together, and work for the good of the country. And that is my hope. I would be content if I could see it happen in my lifetime.

Print Citations

CMS: Bader Ginsburg, Ruth. "On the Centennial of Women's Right to Vote." Speech on C-Span, Washington, DC, February 10, 2020. In *The Reference Shelf: Representative American Speeches, 2019-2020,* edited by Annette Calzone, 173-177. Amenia, NY: Grey House Publishing, 2020.

MLA: Bader Ginsburg, R. "On the Centennial of Women's Right to Vote." C-Span, 10 February 2020, Washington, DC. Speech. *The Reference Shelf: Representative American Speeches, 2019-2020,* edited by Annette Calzone, Grey House Publishing, 2020, pp. 173-177.

APA: Bader Ginsburg, R. (2020, February 10). Speech on the centennial of women's right to vote. C-Span, Washington, DC. In Annette Calzone (Ed.), *The reference shelf: Representative American speeches, 2019-2020* (pp. 173-177). Amenia, NY: Grey House Publishing.

Harvey Weinstein Trial Verdict

By Cyrus Vance III

Manhattan District Attorney Cyrus Vance held a press conference in February discussing the verdict in the trial of Harvey. Vance praised the courage of the witnesses who came forward to testify against Weinstein, and reflected on the game-changing nature of the verdict, stating that it changed the landscape for survivors of sexual assault in America.

DA Cyrus Vance: Okay, good. Good morning, welcome. Thank you for being here. Dawn Dunning Miriam Haley, Jessica Mann, Annabella Sciorra, Tarale Wulff, Lauren Young, Megan Hast, Joan Illuzzi-Orbon. Eight women who have changed the course of history in the fight against sexual violence. These are eight women, who pulled our justice system into the 21st century by declaring that rape is rape and sexual assault is sexual assault, no matter what. Rape is rape, whether it's committed by a stranger in a dark alley or by an intimate partner in a working relationship. It's rape whether it's committed by an indigent person or a man of immense power, prestige, and privilege. Rape is rape whether the survivor reports within an hour, within a year, or perhaps never. It's rape despite the complicated dynamics of power and consent after an assault. It's rape even if there is no physical evidence and even if it happened a long time ago.

This is the new landscape for survivors of sexual assault in America, I believe. And this is a new day. It's a new day because Harvey Weinstein has finally been held accountable for crimes he committed. The women who came forward courageously and at great risk made that happen. Weinstein is a vicious, serial sexual predator who used his power to threaten, rape, assault, trick, humiliate, and silence his victims. He has been found guilty of criminal sexual act in the first degree and will face on that count a state prison sentence of no less than five years and up to 25 years. To the jurors, I want to thank the jurors for their service and careful attention. Their verdict turned the page in our justice system on men like Harvey Weinstein. I want to say thank you to the assistant district attorneys, paralegals, and analysts who worked on this case. Including Maxine Rosenthal, Kevin Wilson, Shannon Goldberg, Carey Dunne, John Irwin, Alyssa Marino, Andy Clark, Danny Mahalia Cruz, Stephanie Latell, and Emily Hogan.

And especially to Harriet Galvin, Megan Hast, and Joan Illuzi-Orbon. Who conducted a terribly difficult and meticulous investigation. And performed masterly a trial under the brightest of spotlights. And finally to the survivors of Harvey

---

Delivered on February 24, 2020, in New York, NY.

Weinstein. I owe and we all owe an immense debt to you who had the courage beyond measure to speak your story to the world, to this courtroom, at great personal risk and in great personal pain. To those of us who were privileged to be in the courtroom when they testified, you know what I mean. These survivors weren't just brave, they were heroic.

Words can't describe adequately the sacrifices the survivors made to pursue justice. Weinstein with his manipulation, his resources, his attorneys, his publicists and his spies did everything he could to silence the survivors. But they refused to be silent. They spoke from their hearts and they were heard. They were heard by Weinstein's other survivors and by sexual predators all over the world. They sacrificed their privacy and self protection, knowing better than anyone the extent of Weinstein's power, manipulation, retribution and abuse. To them I would say, "You broke silence to hold him accountable." And believe me when I say that because you have done so, a generation of sexual assault survivors and all of us heard your every word. Thank you. I'll take a couple of questions.

Speaker 5: Sir, are you fully satisfied with this verdict or do you feel in some way you came up short? You just mentioned it could be as little as five years.

DA Cyrus Vance: Well, I'm certainly not dissatisfied by the verdict. I think this was a very difficult case, a very challenging case. And a case that really moved our understanding of what sexual assault is, where it can occur. Shattered myths that I think have been part of the criminal justice system for a long time. So I believe a B felony conviction with a maximum of up to 25 years, it is not the top counts in the indictment, but by no means am I disappointed with the jury's unanimous statement that Harvey Weinstein is guilty of sexual assault and rape. Any other questions?

Speaker 6: Some of the women like Annabella Sciorra and Jessica Mann, it appears the jury repudiated their testimony. Do you have any concerns that women are going to have to endure such terrible cross examination that they endured at the hands of Weinstein's lawyers?

DA Cyrus Vance: Well, I think with regard to Jessica Mann, Harvey Weinstein was convicted for rape in the third degree.

Speaker 6: Right.

DA Cyrus Vance: Ms. Sciorra took great risks and was in substantial pain testifying about that happened to her many years ago. I can't look behind the jury's verdict or how they arrived at that. We have to respect that process. But by no means is it a statement against Ms. Sciorra or against anything that she said in court. Jurors find a way through to a solution that they believe adequately brings them all together with the unanimous verdict. In terms of the cross-examination, I think we saw cross-examination, the kinds that we've seen for years and years and years. I hope that with this verdict it will become more obvious that those kinds of attacks on the survivors and victims when they're on the stand, making it seem like it's all their fault, will be realized as legal attacks that just simply are no longer going to work in this day and age. And it's time that lawyers stop using them and continuing the myths that I think the jury verdict must've today.

Dean: DA Vance, what's your message to women about coming forward? Because some have questioned why did it take the women so long to come forward? What's your message to women who may be attacked? Whether it's today to last year, what's you message to them?

DA Cyrus Vance: Well first of all, I would say that, Dean . . . It was Dean right? With this verdict, I hope that survivors will see that in this justice system, prosecutors, judges, and juries will believe them. Even when the facts are not simple and even when the dynamics of the relationships between the survivors and the abuser are complicated. So I think, Dean, the message is, "This is a big day. This is a new day." And I hope women will understand the significance of the jury verdict today. In terms of the time it takes to report a sexual assault, Dean, we cannot put ourselves in the shoes of a victim of sexual assault to understand what is going through his or her mind. You heard on the witness stand the reasons why a number of these women, survivors, did not come forward with. They weren't deathly afraid of Harvey Weinstein for one thing. And that he would ruin their career.

So there's all sorts of dynamics that make survivors of sexual assault not comfortable to come forward. However, those stories are now part of what we all now understand better after this trial, that survivors have to go through. So Dean, I thin, my hope is with this verdict, survivors of sexual assault, whether it's of Mr. Weinstein or whether it's someone else, will come forward. And our office and others like our office will, I hope, be there to listen to them and to help them move forward.

Print Citations

CMS: Vance III, Cyrus. "Harvey Weinstein Trial Verdict." Speech in New York, NY, February 24, 2020. In *The Reference Shelf: Representative American Speeches, 2019-2020,* edited by Annette Calzone, 178-180. Amenia, NY: Grey House Publishing, 2020.

MLA: Vance III, Cyrus. "Harvey Weinstein Trial Verdict." 24 February 2020, New York, NY. Speech. *The Reference Shelf: Representative American Speeches, 2019-2020,* edited by Annette Calzone, Grey House Publishing, 2020, pp. 178-180.

APA: Vance III, C. (2020, February 24). Speech on Harvey Weinstein trial verdict. New York, NY. In Annette Calzone (Ed.), *The reference shelf: Representative American speeches, 2019-2020* (pp. 178-180). Amenia, NY: Grey House Publishing.

NASA and SpaceX: Dragon Space Launch Press Conference

By SpaceX Crew

Members of the SpaceX crew and NASA officials held a press conference in May about the launch of the first American human space flight from the Kennedy Space Center in nine years. Topics discussed ranged from the prospects for commercial spaceflight to the ability of space to unify people around the world to what astronauts eat for breakfast. The need for cooperation to maintain both Russian and American astronauts on board the International Space Station was stressed.

Bettina Inclán: Hello. I'm Bettina Inclán with NASA's Office of Communications, and thank you for joining us today as we have one day to launch of the historic NASA SpaceX Demo 2 Mission. We move this press conference indoors, originally planned for the countdown clock, due to weather. But we have good news. The weather has improved, and right now we have 60% chance of favorable weather for launch. But today, we'll hear lots about the launch by our great guests today. We have Bob Cabana, Center Director for Kennedy Space Center. Jim Bridenstine, the NASA Administrator. We have commercial crew astronauts Nicole Mann and Kjell Lindgren, and NASA Deputy Administrator, Jim Morhard. We'll be hearing more from them in a minute, but first let's talk to Bob Cabana.

Bob Cabana: Thanks, Bettina. Well, good morning, and welcome to the Kennedy space center. I don't have to tell you all how exciting it is to have the first flight of humans to space from the Kennedy Space Center in nine years. And what a historic pad to be doing it from. We went to the moon from pad 39A, and 82 of our 135 shuttle missions launched off that pad, including three of my flights, and now rather than rushing away in the salt air through our partnership with SpaceX, that pad is being used once again. And it's now for our commercial crew program, as well as other missions for SpaceX, and I think that's absolutely outstanding. Truly an historic time from a historic pad. We're really pleased to have our NASA administrator Jim Bridenstine with us this morning. As a member of Congress, Jim was a huge advocate and proponent for aviation and space flight as a member of the Armed Services Committee, and also the Science, Space, and Technology Committee, and now he's sharing that passion with all of us as he leads NASA into a new era of space exploration. Jim?

Press conference on May 27, 2020, at Kennedy Space Center, Merritt Island, FL.

Jim Bridenstine: Well, thank you Bob. It's great to be here at the Kennedy Space Center. We are, once again, launching American astronauts on American rockets from American soil. And this is a big moment in time. It's been nine years since we've had this opportunity. And Bob Cabana, we want to thank you for all the great work you've done getting us up to this point, getting the Kennedy space center ready. Everything is looking good. As of right now, we are go for launch. As Bettina said, the weather is about 60% favorable for launch tomorrow, which is good news compared to where we were yesterday. We were at 40%. So the trend is in the right direction, and we are very, very excited. So I think I'd like to start by saying, again, this room is empty. We would love to have this room full. We would love to have it filled with reporters. We'd love to have it filled with space enthusiasts, and unfortunately, we're in the middle of the Coronavirus pandemic. Our country has been through a lot.

But this is a unique moment where all of America can take a moment and look at our country do something stunning again. And that is launch American astronauts on American rockets from American soil. And we're going to go to the International Space Station. And what we do there, of course, is we're transforming how we do space flight in general. The commercial crew program is in fact about commercializing low earth orbit. We've got resupply, now we're going to have crew, soon we're going to have commercial space stations, and this is a unique opportunity to bring all of America together in one moment in time, and say, "Look at how bright the future is." That's what this launch is all about. And yes, in the midst of the Coronavirus pandemic, we've taken extraordinary measures to keep our people safe, and we are one day away from launch. So this is an exciting day. Thank you, Bettina. And I'll turn it back to you.

Bettina Inclán: Yeah. Next we'll hear from Deputy Administrator Morhard.

Jim Morhard: Oh, I just echo what Jim and Bob have said. This is a historic milestone. And the reality is that in the past, NASA developed, designed, and built and then operated spacecraft and rockets. This is the first time that a commercial company is building and going to operate this spacecraft and capsule. And we're really looking to be a customer to SpaceX and to other companies in the future. And that's what we're trying to do is to create and expand . . . really expand the economy in low earth orbit. That's really what this is about tomorrow.

Bettina Inclán: Thank you. And our commercial crew astronauts, let's start with Nicole.

Nicole Mann: Thank you so much. It is incredibly exciting to be here. People always ask, "What's it like to be in the Astronaut Office and train with folks that are flying on so many different spacecraft?" We have Soyuz, SpaceX, Starliner, and then we're already starting to lay the foundation for Orion. So, it's just an incredible time to be training with all these different opportunities in front of us, and we are so proud and happy for Doug [Hurley] and Bob [Behnken]. It feels kind of like one of your close family members having a great lifetime achievement, and really that's what it is. So on a personal level, I think I could speak for the Astronaut Office, and that's how we all feel. So proud for everything that they've accomplished with the NASA and Space X team to get ready for this launch.

And it's so important because it's not just about one launch. I mean, this is Launch America. It's not launch NASA. It is Launch America, and it's huge. My son is eight years old, and so he's never seen Americans launch from the United States ever. It's kind of foreign to him. And as I was getting ready to come on this trip yesterday, he asked me, "Hey, mom, are we going to the moon? Is this our first flight to the moon?" And I said, "Well, son, I mean, not technically, but it is the first big step on our roadmap to the moon for the . . . mission, and eventually to Mars. And he, as a young boy, sees that. And so I know there's a lot of kids out there that will be watching the launch tomorrow. And it's just an exciting team for all of NASA, SpaceX, and a proud moment for all of America.

Bettina Inclán: Great. Kjell?

Kjell Lindgren: Yeah. I echo Nicole sentiments exactly. What a privilege to be here today, to be a part of this team. Commercial and government entities working together, SpaceX and NASA, to pull something off like this. And what a privilege to be here just a day away from launch. We are so incredibly excited to be a part of this. I had the opportunity to launch with our international partners to International Space Station back in 2015, and that's at the core of what we're doing here today is to continue that incredible legacy of work that we've done on the International Space Station. We have had humans living and working on that orbital outpost for almost 20 years, conducting science and research to extend our presence in the solar system, and to improve life back here on earth. And this launch represents an extension of that capability, and having the ability to launch Americans from American soil on a US spacecraft is absolutely amazing.

I think about my launch and the family and the few family and guests that I was able to have out there to watch that. And I think about now, so many Americans in the future being able to congregate down here and watch this incredible vehicle take off. For people that live here in Florida, just to go out on their porches or to look up from a parking lot and to see this vehicle claw its way into space. To watch Americans flying into low earth orbit and to the International Space Station, and the absolute power of that to inspire our future generation of explorers and leaders. It is truly a privilege to be a part of this, to be able to witness this historic moment, and to see where this journey ultimately takes us. . . .

Speaker 1: When will Europeans or Canadians or Russians fly on Crew Dragon for the first time, do you expect?

Jim Bridenstine: That's undetermined at this point. I can tell you, Crew One we will have Japan with us, our first international partner launching on a Falcon rocket with a Crew Dragon. So we're excited about that, but as far as other international partners in the future, that has not yet been determined. . . .

Bettina Inclán: Thank you. Our next question comes from Marine Carrin of *The Atlantic*.

Marine Carrin: Hi everyone. Thanks for your time and best of luck tomorrow. A followup to the question that was just asked now. I'm wondering if NASA personnel are allowed to intervene and take over from Space X at any point during the mission, if NASA feels that it is necessary?

Jim Bridenstine: The answer to that question is yes. We, of course, are the customer here, and so we do, but look, our goal is to have Space X be able to do missions one day without NASA. We want them to go get customers that are not us. And so we want to make sure that they're making decisions. But if we see something that we disagree with, certainly we have the right to intervene. I don't that being necessary at this point, but yes, we can intervene if necessary. . . .

Bettina Inclán: Thank you. Our next question comes from Keith Cowling.

Keith Cowling: Hi, I have a question as a member of the Apollo generation. I know Jim Morhart will remember that when we were kids, we wanted to know everything that astronauts did, and NASA went out of their way to tell us everything, including what they ate. Yesterday, Marine asked a pretty straightforward, honest question, "What are they going to have for breakfast?" And the answer was, "I don't know, but we'll get back to you."

And then, Joey Rulette did some checking and found out that the astronaut breakfast menus are not subject to disclosure. Is that really the answer? I mean, how do you explain to a sixth grader in the Artemis generation that we can't tell you what the astronauts are eating? I mean, shouldn't there be a little more transparency in some of this?

Bob Cabana: Can I take that one Bettina? Well, I don't think, as far as transparency goes, I can tell you what it's like in the past and astronauts get anything they want for breakfast. You got your choice, whether it's breakfast, lunch, or dinner, it's made to order. And I can go from my personal experience on my first flight. I'd heard that some folks get space sick, and I certainly didn't want to get sick. I don't get air sick, and so I had a toasted English muffin and a cup of coffee because I'm addicted to caffeine.

I was going easy, but one of my crew mates had steak and eggs and hash browns and he's pouring the hot sauce on and he didn't get sick, but so they may not have even decided what they want for breakfast yet tomorrow. So it's kind of hard to release what you don't know, but I'm sure they'll make a decision and they'll get anything they want. . . .

Bettina Inclán: Great. All right, we'll go to the next question. It's Jackie Goddard with *The Times* of London.

Jackie Goddard: Hello. Yes, thank you. My question is from Mr. Bridenstine. Both astronauts are dads, and I wondered what you would say or what you have said that you can share to their two little boys about what their dads are doing and the significance of it. Thank you.

Jim Bridenstine: So I had a hard time hearing it. It was a question about the children of the astronauts?

Jackie Goddard: Yeah. I said both astronauts are fathers. So I wondered what you would say or what you have said that you can share with us to their two little boys about what their dads are doing and the significance of it.

Jim Bridenstine: Absolutely. So I would start by saying, and they know this, their dads are heroes, American heroes, they're laying the foundation for a new era in human space flight. It's an era in human space flight where more space is going to be available to more people than ever before.

We envision a future where low Earth orbit is entirely commercialized, where NASA is one customer of many customers, where we have numerous providers that are competing on cost and innovation and safety, that they're driving down cost, they're increasing access. And we are proving out a business model, a public/private partnership business model that ultimately will enable us to go to the moon this time sustainably.

In other words, we're going to go to the moon to stay. We love Apollo. The Apollo era was fantastic. The problem is that it ended, and now we've got the Artemis program, which is our sustainable return to the moon named after Artemis is the twin sister of Apollo in Greek mythology, and she was the goddess of the moon. And this time, when we go to the moon, we get to go with all of America, a very diverse, highly-qualified astronaut core that includes women.

And what Bob and Doug are doing is they are the final step in proving the success of a public/private partnership business model that drives down costs and is going to enable us to go, not just to the moon, but to go sustainably, with reusable landers, to the surface of the moon, and all of this ultimately is for a purpose, and that is to get to Mars.

So when those little boys are 40 years old, and we have a permanent presence on the moon, and we have astronauts on Mars, they're going to know that their dads played a critical role in enabling, not just this country, but the world as we lead international partners, to humanity going further into the solar system than ever before. Beyond that, I would remind the children that their dads are both military aviators that have served their country boldly. Yesterday was Memorial Day. We had an opportunity to reflect on the people who've serve this country, and of course, these two gentlemen have done that as well. So they're heroes in so many different ways. But as I said, when they arrived here at Kennedy, I'm 44 years old, I'm about to turn 45, and when I grow up I want to be like Bob and Doug. . . .

I'm a big believer in the commercialization of space. We need it to be successful. It's how we're going to get to the moon and onto Mars. If we keep using American taxpayer dollars to develop capabilities in low earth orbit, we'll never get to the moon and onto Mars. That's what this program is all about. It's about commercialization where we are ready to commercialize and then using NASA money to do the things that commercial industry is not yet ready for with a purpose and that is to eventually commercialize those capabilities as well.

Moderator: I'll go to our next question, that way we can get as many as possible. Marcia Smith from *SpacePolicyOnline*.

Marcia Smith: Thanks so much. This is for Jim Bridenstine. Could you expand a little bit more on the discussions with the Russians about flying on the commercial cruise ships? Dmitry Rogozin had a bunch of comments yesterday. He talked about being enthusiastic about having an alternative to Soyuz, but then he said he was confused about NASA's plans for Gateway. Could you just fill us in on where the negotiations stand about us flying on Soyuz and Russia was flying on Commercial Crew. Is that at all tied in with the discussions on Gateway or are they on parallel paths? Or are you trying to get a whole big package of future US-Russian space co-operation? Could you just expand on that a bit?

Jim Bridenstine: Yeah, absolutely. When we think about the Commercial Crew Program, remember the goal here is to have . . . the International Space Station, half of it is Russia and the other half is American. Of course on the American segment, we've got a lot of international partners. When we think about the International Space Station, if we are going to maintain a compliment of both Russian and American astronauts on board, then we need to be willing to launch Russian cosmonauts on Commercial Crew. They need to be willing to launch American astronauts on the Soyuz.

In my last conversations with Dmitry Rogozin, I think we were both in strong agreement that that was necessary for both nations as we move forward. That's kind of the low earth orbit, International Space Station, Commercial Crew, and the Soyuz program. I think we're in agreement in how we need to go forward there.

Now, it is true that when we talk about the Gateway, that's a separate kind of level of discussion for what the future looks like. Yes, we have made proposals to Russia as far as we've asked them how would they like to participate in the Gateway? We've offered suggestions. Right now we're in a holding pattern waiting to hear back. But the partnership has been strong. This partnership goes back to 1975, the year of my birth with the Apollo-Soyuz program. Then of course the Shuttle-Mir program. Now of course the International Space Station program. This has been, I think, a bright, shiny object that demonstrates that space can unite people. It's really above terrestrial geopolitics, literally above terrestrial geopolitics. I think it's a relationship that we are interested in maintaining and of course we'll continue to work with them. . . .

Moderator: Thank you. Our last question will come from Ken Chang of the New York Times.

Ken Chang: Hi, thank you very much for taking my question. This is for Mr. Bridenstine. A few days ago, you tweeted noting President Trump's leadership for getting to this moment. Is there a reason that a former NASA astronaut pointed out that Commercial Crew started in 2010 under President Obama and of course, Commercial Cargo goes back to George W. Bush. I was wondering if you could just talk about credit we're giving to this milestone for your predecessors and for previous presidents?

Jim Bridenstine: Absolutely. So, this is a program that demonstrates the success when you have continuity of purpose going from one administration to the next. If we go back all the way to Commercial Crew, that started under President George W. Bush, or no, Commercial Resupply. And then Commercial Crew under President

Obama, and Charlie Bolden did absolutely magnificent work as the NASA Administrator at a time when this particular program, and Bob, you remember this, it didn't have a lot of support in Congress.

And Charlie Bolden, who is a NASA astronaut and an American hero, he's an F-18 pilot. I got to put the F-18 pilot plug in there, but Charlie Bolden did just yeoman's work in order to get this program off the ground, to get it going. And here we are, all these years later having this success. I will reiterate that the Human Spaceflight Program under President Trump has really blossomed. Our budgets now are as high as they've ever been in nominal dollars, they're the highest ever. In real dollars, they're still very high. Not maybe as high as Apollo, but that was a little bit of an anomaly in the history of NASA's budget.

But it's also true that it's being backed up. The rhetoric isn't just there, it's being backed up with the budgets, and it's bi-partisan. I did an event with Speaker Pelosi out at the Ames Research Center. Goodness, that would have been August, last August. And it was Women's Equality Day and I thought it was important and we reached out to her and asked her if we could do Women's Equality Day. She was going to do it in San Francisco. We asked her to do it at Ames and in a press conference after the event, we talked about Artemis, the importance of going to the moon with all of America, now going with women. And we did it on Women's Equality Day, and in the press conference afterwards she said, "We're all counting on you to get not just the next man, but the first woman to the moon." And she said, "I'm so glad that you called the program Artemis."

Look, this space program that we have in this country unites people, period. It always has. We look at the most divisive times in American history, we think about the Vietnam War, the 1960s, not just the war, but the protests. We think about the civil rights abuses and the civil rights protests, the very divisive, challenging times. And here we are, in all these years later in the midst of the coronavirus pandemic and we have this moment in time where we can unite people again. And that's really what this launch is going to do. It's not just going to unite Republicans and Democrats. It's going to unite the world. The whole world is going to be watching this particular launch and all of our international partners are very interested. In fact, they participated in the Flightnet Readiness Review, because their astronauts are one day going to fly on this rocket and they're already big operators of the International Space Station, where this crew Dragon will dock. So this mission is I think a very uniting mission.

Space exploration in general unites Republicans and Democrats, it unites people across geopolitical boundaries, and that's really what's unique about NASA and what's unique about space. But look, I will not hesitate to tell you that President Trump has been a massive space advocate. He promised to launch American astronauts on American rockets. He promised to create a moon program and he's done both of those and he's backed it up with his budget requests, not just with the words.

Print Citations

CMS: SpaceX Crew. "NASA and SpaceX: Dragon Space Launce Press Conference." Press conference at the Kennedy Space Center, Merritt Island, FL, May 27, 2020. In *The Reference Shelf: Representative American Speeches, 2019-2020,* edited by Annette Calzone, 181-188. Amenia, NY: Grey House Publishing, 2020.

MLA: SpaceX Crew. "NASA and SpaceX: Dragon Space Launce Press Conference." Kennedy Space Center, 27 May 2020, Merritt Island, FL. Press conference. *The Reference Shelf: Representative American Speeches, 2019-2020,* edited by Annette Calzone, Grey House Publishing, 2020, pp. 181-188.

APA: SpaceX Crew. (2020, May 27). Press conference on NASA and SpaceX: Dragon space launch. Kennedy Space Center, Merritt Island, FL. In Annette Calzone (Ed.), *The reference shelf: Representative American speeches, 2019-2020* (pp. 181-188). Amenia, NY: Grey House Publishing.

Memorial Service for John Lewis

By Mitch McConnell and Nancy Pelosi

Members of Congress set aside their differences to honor fellow U.S. Representative John Lewis, who passed away in July. Lewis was a key figure of the early Civil Rights Movement, and served in Congress from 1987 until his death in 2020. Lewis's recorded words urged the American people to: "Never become bitter. Never become hostile. Never hate. Live in peace. We're one, one people and one love."

Speaker 1: Good afternoon. It is an official, personal, and very sad honor to welcome my colleague, John Lewis, back to the Capitol, to welcome his family and his many friends, to acknowledge his sacred life. Please stay standing for the invocation by Reverend Dr. Grainger Browning, Jr., Ebenezer AME Church.

Grainger Browning, Jr.: Let us bow our heads in a word of prayer.

Eternal God, our father, I come before you today in the name of Jesus, thanking you for the many different faiths and beliefs and religions that make up your beloved community that come to celebrate the life and the legacy of John Lewis. We come today thanking you for the faith foundations that his mother and father established in Troy, Alabama. We thank you for his leadership of Snick in the March on Washington. We thank you for how he was bloodied for us, bruised for us. He marched for us, sat in for us and was willing to give up his life that we might have life, liberty, and the pursuit of happiness. And on today as his colleagues and friends and especially family members come, as he lays in state in this hallowed rotunda, we come on this day, recommitting ourselves to march as he marched to ballot boxes and to, this year, for mailboxes and for voting rights and for civil rights and for human rights.

And we'll keep doing that until that day justice rolls down like mighty waters and righteousness like a mighty stream. And finally, on July 17th, we want to say thank you that he crossed another bridge, not the Edmund Pettus Bridge that we pray that one day will be named the John Lewis Memorial Bridge, but the bridge from earth to glory. And when it got there, Elijah Cummings and the congressional cloud of witnesses welcomed him home as they marched down that street paved of gold. We want to say thank you from Emmett Till to George Floyd, said, "Thank you for allowing our deaths not to be in vain."

And when he got to the lily white throne, we want to say thank you. We heard you say, "Well done, my good and faithful servant. You have done the good fight and

---

Delivered on July 27, 2020, at the U.S. Capitol, Washington, DC.

you have kept your eyes on the prize. And now enter into the joy of the Lord." And after you said that, Gabriel told the angels to lift every voice and sing. And we heard Dr. King in the background saying, "Free at last. Free at last. The consciousness of Congress is free at last." In Jesus' name we pray. Amen.

Speaker 2: The honorable Mitch McConnell, Majority Leader of the United States Senate.

Mitch McConnell: Please be seated.

In his memoirs, John Lewis described a childhood home that was quite different from the place he lies today. That farmhouse in Pike County, Alabama had no running water or electricity. It stood on the first land his father's family had ever owned in a part of the country where segregation had led to almost total isolation along racial lines. It would have been hard to conceive back then that the young child tending his family's chickens would, by age 23, be leading the movement to redeem American society. That he'd be addressing a hundreds of thousands of civil rights marchers from the steps of the Lincoln Memorial. I was lucky enough to be there that day. I marveled at the massive crowds. The sight gave me hope for our country. That was John's doing. Even on that day as his voice echoed across the mall, I wonder how many dared imagine that young man would come to walk the halls of the Congress.

America's original sin of slavery was allowed to fester for far too long. It left a long wake of pain, violence, and brokenness that has taken great efforts from great heroes to address. John's friend, Dr. Martin Luther King, Jr. famously said, " The arc of the moral universe is law, but it bends toward justice." But that is never automotive. History only bent toward what's right because people like John paid the price to help bend it. He paid that price at every Nashville lunch counter, where his leadership made segregation impossible to ignore. He paid it in every jail cell where he waited out hatred and depression. He paid that price in harassment and beatings from a bus station in South Carolina to the Edmund Pettus Bridge.

John Lewis lived and worked with urgency because the task was urgent. But even though the world around him gave him every cause for bitterness, he stubbornly treated everyone with respect and love, all so that, as his friend Dr. King once put it, we could build a community at peace with itself. Today we pray and trust that this peace maker himself now rests in peace. All of John's colleagues stand with his son, John Miles, their family, and the entire country in thanking God that he gave our nation just hero it needed so badly. May all of us that he will leave behind under this dome pray for a fraction of John's strength to keep bending that arc on toward justice.

Speaker 2: Ladies and gentlemen, the honorable Nancy Pelosi, Speaker of the United States House Of Representatives.

Nancy Pelosi: To the family of John Lewis, welcome to the rotunda. Under the dome of the US Capitol, we have bid farewell to some of the greatest Americans in our history. It is fitting that John Lewis joins this pantheon of patriots resting upon the same catafalque of President Abraham Lincoln. John revered President

Lincoln. His identification with Lincoln was clear 57 years ago at the shadow of the Lincoln Memorial, where John declared our minds, souls and hearts can not rest until freedom and justice exist for all people. Words that ring true today. Mr. Leader, I too was there that day, my student years.

Between then and now John Lewis became a titan of the Civil Rights Movement and then the conscience of the Congress. Here in Congress, John was revered and beloved on both sides of the aisle, on both sides of the Capitol. We knew that he always worked on the side of the angels, and now we know that he is with them. And we are comforted to know that he is with his beloved Lillian. And may it be a comfort to John's son, John Miles, and the entire Lewis family, Michael Collins, the entire staff that so many mourn their loss and are praying for them at this sad time. God truly blessed America with the life and leadership of John Lewis. We thank you for sharing him with us. May he rest in peace.

John Lewis often spoke of a beloved community, a vision that he shared with the Reverend Dr. Martin Luther King, Jr, of a community connected and uplifted by faith, hope, and charity. And indeed John had deep faith, believing that every person has a spark of divinity making them worthy of respect. And he had faith in the charity of others, which is what gave him so much hope. And as he wrote in his book, "Release the need to hate, to harbor division, and the enticement of revenge. Release all bitterness. Hold only love, only peace in your heart, knowing the battle for good to overcome evil is already won." John, the optimist. Through it all, John was a person of greatness and he also was a person of great humility, always giving credit to others in the movement.

John committed his life to advancing justice and understood that build a better future, we had to acknowledge the past. Exactly one year ago, it was a privilege to be with John and members of the Congressional Black Caucus, Madam Chair, Karen Bass, on a pilgrimage to Ghana to observe 400 years since the arrival of the first slaves from Africa. Some of the descendants of those slaves would build this Capitol, where John lies in state on the Lincoln catafalque.

I wish you could have seen the response that John received when he was introduced to the Ghana Parliament. My colleagues are shaking their heads. It was overwhelming. But I wish you could have seen him at the door of no return, which enslaved people were sent through on to the death ships to cross the Atlantic. I wish you could have seen what it meant to him. He knew that the door of no return was a central part of American history, just as is the Edmund Pettus Bridge, the March on Washington, the Selma March to Montgomery are. When John made his speech 57 years ago, he was the youngest speaker at the March on Washington program. How fitting it is that in the final days of his life, he summoned the strength to acknowledge the young people peacefully protesting, and in the same spirit of that march, taking up the unfinished work of racial justice, helping complete the journey begun more than 55 years ago.

We have all seen the photographs of John being brutally beaten in Selma, which painted an iconic picture of injustice. What a beautiful contrast to see John and the Mayor of Washington who's with us today at the Black Lives Matter Plaza, standing in solidarity with the protestors, an iconic picture of justice that will endure and will inspire a nation for years to come.

John firmly focused on the future, on how to inspire the next generation to join the fight for justice, and his quote, "To find a way to get in the way." As one of the youngest leaders of the Freedom Rides, March on Washington as I said, and March to Montgomery, he understood the power of young people to change the future. When asked what someone can do who was 19 or 20 years old, the age that he was when he set out to desegregate Nashville, Lewis replied, "A young person should be speaking out for what is fair, what is just, what is right. Speak out for those who have been left out and left behind. That is how the movement goes forward," John said. Imagine the great joy he had traveling the country to share that message of action with young people. No need to imagine. It is my personal privilege right now for me to yield to our beloved colleague, the distinguished gentleman from Georgia, Congressman John Lewis.

John Lewis [recording]: I grew up in rural Alabama, 50 miles from Montgomery, outside of a little place called Troy. My father was a sharecropper, a tenant farmer. But back in 1944 when I was only four years old, my father had saved $300. And with the $300, he bought 110 acres of land. My family is still on that land today. How many of you remember when you were four? What happened to the rest of us?

It was many, many years ago when we would visit the little town of Troy, visit Montgomery, visit Tuskegee, visit Birmingham. I saw those signs that said white men, colored men, white women, colored women, white waiting, colored waiting. I would come home and ask my mother, my father, my grandparents, my great grandparents, why. They would say, "That's the way it is. Don't get in the way. Don't get in trouble."

But one day in 1955, 15 years old in the 10th grade, I heard about Rosa Parks. I heard the words of Martin Luther King, Jr. on our radio. 1957, I met Rosa Parks at the age of 17. In 1958 at the age of 18, I met Martin Luther King, Jr. And these two individuals inspired me to get in the way, to get in trouble.

So I come here to say to you this morning on this beautiful campus, with your great education, you must find a way to get in the way. You must find a way to get in trouble, good trouble, necessary trouble. Use your education. You have wonderful teachers, wonderful professors, researchers. Use what you have. Use your learning. Use your tools to help make our country and make our world a better place where no one would be left out or left behind. You can do it and you must do it. It is your time. In a few short days, we will commemorate what we call the Mississippi Summer Project where more than 1000 students from all over America, many from abroad-

From all over America, many from abroad, made a trip to Mississippi to encourage people to register to vote. And that summer night of June 21st, 1964, three young man that I knew, two whites and one African American: Micky Schwerner, Andy Goodman and James Chaney went out to investigate the burning of an African American church that was used for voter registration workshop. These three young men detained by the sheriff, taken to jail, taken out of jail, turned over to the Klan, where they were beaten, shot and killed.

And I tell students today, these three young men didn't die in Vietnam. They didn't die in the Middle East or Eastern Europe. They didn't die in Africa or Central or South America. They died right here in our own country, trying to help all of our citizens become participants in a democratic process.

As young people, you must understand that there are forces that want to take us back to another period, but you must say that we're not going back. We made too much progress and we're going forward. There may be some setbacks, some delays, some disappointment, but you must never ever give up or give in. You must keep the faith and keep your eyes on the prize. That is your calling. That is your mission. That is your moral obligation. That is your mandate. Get out there and do it. Get in the way.

In the final analysis, we all must learn to live together as brothers and sisters. We all live in the same house. And it doesn't matter whether we all black or white, Latino, Asian American, or Native American. It doesn't matter whether you're straight or gay. We are one people. We are one family. We all live in the same house.

Be bold. Be courageous, stand up. Speak up. Speak out and find a way to create the beloved community, the beloved world, a world of peace, a world that will recognize the dignity of all human kind. Never become bitter. Never become hostile. Never hate. Live in peace. We're one, one people and one love. Thank you very much. . . .

Speaker 5: Ladies and gentlemen, please rise for the benediction . . . the Honorable James. E. Clyburn of the United States House of Representatives.

James. E. Clyburn: God, grant me the serenity to accept the things I cannot change, courage to change the things I can, and the wisdom to know the difference, living one day at a time, accepting hardships as a pathway to peace, taking, as he did, the sinful world as it is, not as I would have it, trusting that he will make all things right if I surrender to his will, that I may be reasonably happy in this life and supremely happy with him forever in the next. Amen.

Print Citations

CMS: McConnell, Mitch, and Nancy Pelosi. "Memorial Service for John Lewis." Speeches at John Lewis Memorial Service, U.S. Capitol, Washington, DC, June 27, 2020. In *The Reference Shelf: Representative American Speeches, 2019-2020,* edited by Annette Calzone, 189-194. Amenia, NY: Grey House Publishing, 2020.

MLA: McConnell, Mitch, and Nancy Pelosi. "Memorial Service for John Lewis." John Lewis Memorial Service, U.S. Capitol, 27 June 2020, Washington, DC. Speeches. *The Reference Shelf: Representative American Speeches, 2019-2020,* edited by Annette Calzone, Grey House Publishing, 2020, pp. 189-194.

APA: McConnell, M., & Pelosi, N. (2020, June 27). Speeches at memorial service for John Lewis. John Lewis Memorial Service, U.S. Capitol, Washington, DC. In Annette

Calzone (Ed.), *The reference shelf: Representative American speeches, 2019-2020* (pp. 189-194). Amenia, NY: Grey House Publishing.

Abraham Accords Signing Ceremony

By Donald Trump

Israeli Prime Minister Benjamin Netanyahu, Minister of Foreign Affairs for Bahrain Abdullatif bin Rashid Al Zayani, Minister of Foreign Affairs for the United Arab Emirates Abdullah bin Zayed Al Nahyan, and U.S. President Donald Trump participated in a signing ceremony for the Abraham Accords in September 2020. The agreement normalized informal but longstanding foreign relations between Israel and the UAE, which became the first Persian Gulf country and the third Arab country, after Egypt in 1979 and Jordan in 1994, to formally normalize its relationship with Israel.

President Donald Trump: Thank you very much. Please. Thank you. The First Lady and I are honored to welcome to the White House Prime Minister Netanyahu of Israel, and Mrs. Netanyahu. Thank you so much. Thank you, Sara. And Foreign Minister Abdullah bin Zayed, United Arab Emirates, UAE. Thank you very much.

And Foreign Minister Abdullatif Al Zayani of Bahrain. Thank you. Thank you very much. We're here this afternoon to change the course of history. After decades of division and conflict, we mark the dawn of a new Middle East. Thanks to the great courage of the leaders of these three countries, we take a major stride toward a future in which people of all faiths and backgrounds live together in peace and prosperity. In a few moments, these visionary leaders will sign the first two peace deals between Israel and the Arab state in more than a quarter century. In Israel's entire history, there have previously been only two such agreements; now we have achieved two in a single month, and there are more to follow.

Israel, the United Arab Emirates and Bahrain will establish embassies, exchange ambassadors, and begin to cooperate and work together so strongly, to cooperate as partners across the broad range of sectors from tourism to trade and healthcare to security; they're going to work together. They are friends.

The Abraham Accords also open the door for Muslims around the world to visit the historic sites in Israel and to peacefully pray at Al-Aqsa Mosque in Jerusalem, the third holiest site in Islam.

Together, these agreements will serve as the foundation for a comprehensive piece across the entire region, something which nobody thought was possible, certainly not in this day and age, maybe in many decades from now, but one founded on shared interests, mutual respect and friendship, to our honored guests from

Signing ceremony on September 15, 2020, at the White House, Washington, DC.

Israel, the United Arab Emirates and Bahrain. Congratulations on this outstanding achievement. Congratulations. Fantastic.

I also want to thank Vice President Mike Pence. Thank you, Mike. Great job. Secretary of State Mike Pompeo. Mike, thank you very much. National Security Advisor Robert O'Brien. Robert, thank you. Mr. Jared Kushner. Jared, thank you very much. Ambassador Brian Hook. Thank you very much, Brian. Thank you. Thank you. And Avi Berkowitz. Avi, thank you very much. I also want to give a very special thanks, he's been an incredible ambassador to Israel, David Friedman. That's a very great group of people, great group of patriots. They wanted this to happen so badly, they worked so hard, and again, nobody thought it could happen and they thought it could happen; they never even doubted it. So I want to thank you all very much. Thank you. For generations, the people of the Middle East have been held back by old conflicts, hostilities, lies treachery; so many things held them back. Actually, lies that the Jews and Arabs were enemies and that Al Aqsa Mosque was under attack. Constantly, they would say it was under attack. These lies passed down from generation to generation fueled a vicious cycle of terror and violence that spread across the region and all over the world. These agreements prove that the nations of the region are breaking free from the failed approaches of the past. Today's signing sets history on a new course, and there will be other countries very, very soon that will follow these great leaders.

The people of the Middle East will no longer allow hatred of Israel to be fomented as an excuse for radicalism or extremism. So important. And they'll no longer allow the great destiny of their region to be denied. On my first foreign trip as president, I had the honor of addressing the leaders of more than 54 Arab and Muslim nations in Saudi Arabia. My message that day was very simple. I urged the nations of the Middle East to set aside their differences, unite against the common enemy of civilization, and work together toward the noble aims of security and prosperity. I offered America's friendship, I offered America's help, but I said clearly that the nations of the regions had to decide what kind of a future they wanted for their children and for their families and for their nation itself. No one could make that choice for them. They had to do that themselves.

Today, the world sees that they're choosing cooperation over conflict, friendship over enmity, prosperity over poverty, and hope over despair. They are choosing a future in which Arabs and Israelis, Muslims, Jews, and Christians can live together, pray together and dream together, side by side in harmony, community and peace. Once again, let me congratulate the people of Israel, the people of the United Arab Emirates and the people of the kingdom of Bahrain. God bless you all. This is an incredible day for the world. This is a really wonderful and beautiful occasion.

I want to thank all of the members of Congress for being here, senators, Congressmen, Congresswoman. We just appreciate it so much. Everybody wanted to be here. It's a very important day for the world. It's a very important day for peace. Before the parties sign the Accords, I'd like to ask Prime Minister Netanyahu to say a few words, followed by the foreign minister of the United Arab Emirates and the foreign minister of Bahrain. Thank you very much. It's a great honor. Thank you.

Prime Minister Benjamin Netanyahu: Our dear friend, President Trump, First Lady Melania Trump, thank you for hosting me, my wife, Sara, and our entire delegation on this historic day. I want to recognize Vice President Pence, Secretary Pompeo, National Security Advisor O'Brien, and other Cabinet members, Jared Kushner, Avi Berkowitz, Ambassador Friedman, and other members of the President's able peace team, Senators, members of Congress, Israeli Ambassador Ron Dermer, his Emirate and Bahraini counterparts, as well as all the dignitaries gathered here on this sunny day. I want to also express my gratitude for all the Israelis who've worked for years, sometimes in less sunny . . . to bring this date. And I thank each and every one of you. Thank you.

Ladies and gentlemen, Mr. President, this day is a pivot of history. It heralds a new dawn of peace. For thousands of years, the Jewish people have prayed for peace. For decades, the Jewish state has prayed for peace. And this is why, today, we're filled with such profound gratitude. I am grateful to you, President Trump, for your decisive leadership. You have unequivocally stood by Israel's side. You have boldly confronted the tyrants of Tehran. You've proposed a realistic vision for peace between Israel and the Palestinians, and you have successfully brokered the historic peace that we are signing today, a peace that has broad support in Israel, in America, in the Middle East, indeed in the entire world. I am grateful to Crown Prince Mohammed bin Zayed of the United Arab Emirates, and to you, Foreign Minister Abdullah bin Zayed.

I thank you both for your wise leadership and for working with the United States in Israel to expand the circle of peace. I am grateful. I'm grateful to King Hamad of Bahrain, and to you foreign minister Abdullatif al-Zayani for joining us. Joining us in bringing hope to all the children of Abraham.

To all of Israel's friends in the Middle East, those who are with us today, and those who will join us tomorrow. I say, peace onto the, Shalom. And you have heard from the president, that he is already lining up more and more countries. This is unimaginable a few years ago, but with resolve, determination, a fresh look at the way peace is done, this is being achieved. Thank you, Mr. President. Ladies and gentlemen, the people of Israel, well know the price of war. I know the price of war. I was wounded in battle, a fellow soldier, a very close friend of mine, died in my arms. My brother Yoni lost his life while leading his soldiers, to rescue hostages held by terrorists at Entebbe. My parents' grief over the loss of Yoni, was unrelieved until their dying day. And over the years, when I've come to console the families of Israel's fallen soldiers and victims of terror, I've seen that same grief countless times, and this is why I am so deeply moved to be here today. For those who bear the wounds of war, cherish the blessings of peace. And the blessings of the peace we make today, will be enormous. First, because this peace, will eventually expand to include other Arab States. And ultimately, it can end the Arab Israeli conflict once and for all.

Second, because the great economic benefits of our partnership will be felt throughout our region and they will reach every one of our citizens. And third, because this is not only a peace between leaders, it's a peace between peoples, Israelis, Emirates, and Bahrainis are already embracing one another. We are eager to invest in a future of partnership, prosperity and peace. We've already begun to cooperate on combating Corona, and I'm sure that together we can find solutions to many of the problems that afflict our region and beyond. So, despite the many challenges and hardships that we all face, despite all that, let us pause for a moment to appreciate this remarkable day. Let us rise above any political divide. Let us put all cynicism aside, let us feel on this day, the pulse of history. For long after the pandemic has gone, the peace we make today will endure. Ladies and gentlemen, I have devoted my life to securing Israel's place among the nations, to ensure the future of the one and only Jewish state. To accomplish that goal, I work to make Israel strong, very strong. For history has taught us, that strength brings security, strength brings allies, and ultimately, and this is something president Trump has said again and again, ultimately strength brings peace.

King David expressed this basic truth thousands of years ago in our eternal capital Jerusalem. His prayer immortalized in the book of Psalms in the Bible, echoes from our glorious past and guides us towards a brilliant future. May God give strength to his people. May God bless his people with peace.

Mr. President, distinguished guests, this week is Rosh Hashanah, the Jewish new year, and what a blessing we bring to this new year. A blessing of friendship, a blessing of hope, a blessing of peace. Thank you.

Speaker 2: Ladies and gentlemen, his Highness, the minister of foreign affairs and international cooperation of the United Arab Emirates.

Abdullah bin Zayed Al Nahyan: Mr. President, Mr. Prime Minister, and my friends . . . distinguished guests, let me start by conveying the best regards of the UAE people and the leadership. And especially to you Mr. President and everyone gathered here today. I'll continue my speech in Arabic and I'm sure there will be translation to that.

Translator: I stand here today to extend a hand of peace and receive a hand of peace. In our faith, we say, "Oh God, you are peace and from you comes peace." The search for peace is an innate principle. Yet principles are effectively realized when they are transformed into action. Today, we are already witnessing a change in the heart of the Middle East, a change that will send hope around the world.

This initiative would not have been possible without the efforts of his Excellency, President Donald Trump and his team who worked hard and sincerely for us all to reach here. Most notably my counterpart, secretary of state, Mike Pompeo, and Jared Kushner, senior advisor to the President of the United States, and all those who are genuine about the principle of peace in the United States, who have strived to realize this measure achievement. Thank you. Your Excellency Prime Minister Benjamin Netanyahu, prime minister of the state of Israel, thank you for choosing peace and for halting the annexation of Palestinian Territories. A decision that reinforces our shared will to achieve a better future for generations to come.

Ladies and gentlemen, we are witnessing today a new trend that will create a better path for the Middle East. This peace accord, which is a historic achievement for the United States of America, the state of Israel and the United Arab Emirates will continue to have a positive impact, as we believe that its reverberations will be reflected on the entire region. Every option other than peace, would signify destruction, poverty, and human suffering. This new vision, which is beginning to take shape as we meet today for the future of the region full of youthful energy, is not a slogan that we raise for political gain. As everyone looks forward to creating a more stable, prosperous and secure future.

At a time when science is prevailing, the region's youth are looking forward to taking part in this great humanitarian movement. We are pleased that the United Arab Emirates will be part of the momentum towards stability and the growth of human potential in a new, civilized approach that opens wide the doors of opportunity for those who look forward towards peace, prosperity and the future. Our societies today possess the foundation of modern human development, such as infrastructure, a solid economy and scientific achievements that will enable them to advance the future of the Middle East. The United Arab Emirates believes that the role of the United States in the Middle East is positive, and this belief is evidenced by the accord that we are signing today at the White House for which you have taken the lead and will remain a beacon in human history for all peace-loving people around the world. And as for us in the United Arab Emirates, this accord will enable us to continue to stand by the Palestinian people and realize their hopes for an independent state within a stable and prosperous region. This accord builds upon previous peace agreements signed by Arab nations with the State of Israel. The aim of all these treaties is to work towards stability and sustainable development.

In this difficult year, when the world is suffering from the repercussions of the COVID-19 pandemic, my country, the United Arab Emirates, has reinforced its humanitarian commitments established by our nation's founding father, Sheikh Zayed, who taught us that standing with others, regardless of their religious or ethnic affiliation, is a humanitarian duty and a firm principle.

During this difficult time, the United Arab Emirates, my country, was able to launch a probe to Mars. The Hope Probe indeed represents hope that our region is capable of advancement and progress, if governments and people embrace science. After the United Arab Emirates sent astronaut, Hazzaa al-Mansoori, last year as the first Arab astronaut to reach the International Space Station, and launched a peaceful nuclear power plant, this accord opened up prospects for a comprehensive peace in the region.

Thank you, Mr. President.

Ladies and gentlemen, peace requires courage, and shaping the future requires knowledge. The advancement of nations requires sincerity and persistence. We have come today to tell the world that this is our approach, and that peace is our guiding principle. Those who begin things in the right way will reap achievements, with the grace of God. Thank you.

Donald Trump: Thank you very much.

Abdullah bin Zayed Al Nahyan: With grace of God, sir.

Donald Trump: Thank you very much. I appreciate . . .

Abdullah bin Zayed Al Nahyan: Thank you.

Donald Trump: Great job.

Announcer: Ladies and gentlemen, the minister of the foreign affairs of the Kingdom of Bahrain.

Abdullatif bin Rashid Al Zayani: Mr. President, the First Lady, Prime Minister, Your Highness, ladies and gentlemen, good afternoon.

For too long, the Middle East has been set back by conflict and mistrust, causing untold destruction and thwarting the potential of generations of our best and brightest young people. Now, I'm convinced we have the opportunity to change that. Today's declaration was made possible by the vision, courage and commitment of His Majesty King Hamad bin Isa Al Khalifa, who, supported by the people of Bahrain, has protected, institutionalized and enhanced Bahrain's centuries-old spirit of coexistence and harmony, and has the wisdom to recognize that genuine cooperation is the most effective means to achieve peace and to safeguard legitimate rights. Thank you, Your Majesty, for this vision of peace for the region based on trust, respect and understanding between all faiths, races and nations. To our brothers in the United Arab Emirates, I congratulate you on your own momentous peace accord being signed today with Israel. His Highness Sheikh Mohammed bin Zayed, has shown great leadership and foresight to make peace possible and secure a brighter future for our region.

For the state of Israel and Prime Minister Netanyahu, we welcome and appreciate these steps from you and your government, recognizing that enduring peace and security is only possible through a genuine engagement that protects the rights and interests of countries and peoples in the region.

In particular, I want to express my deep appreciation to President Donald Trump and his administration. Mr. President, your statesmanship and tireless efforts have brought us here today and made peace a reality. And to Secretary Pompeo, Senior Advisor Jared Kushner and Special Representative Avi Berkowitz and others, many others, who have carried out their mandates with dedication and skill.

Ladies and gentlemen, today's agreement is an important first step. And it is now incumbent on us to work urgently and actively to bring about the lasting peace and security our peoples deserve. A just, comprehensive and enduring two-state solution to the Palestinian-Israeli conflict will be the foundation, the bedrock of such peace. We have shown today that such a path is possible, even realistic. What was only dreamed of a few years ago is now achievable. And we can see before us a golden opportunity for peace, security and prosperity for our region. Let us, together and with our international partners, waste no time in seizing it. Thank you.

Donald Trump: Great job. That's a great job.

Abdullatif bin Rashid Al Zayani: Thank you, thank you.

Donald Trump: Beautiful.

Abdullatif bin Rashid Al Zayani: Thank you.

Donald Trump: Fellas, come on over here.

Speaker 3: The President of the United States, the Prime Minister of the State of

Israel, and His Highness, the Minister of Foreign Affairs and International Cooperation of the United Arab Emirates will sign a treaty of peace, diplomatic relations and full normalization. They will each sign three copies, one in English, Hebrew, and Arabic. We kindly ask that all guests remain seated for the signing of the documents.

Sheikh Abdullah bin Zayed Al Nahyan: Where my name is to go?

Hi, Prime Minister, can you be helpful here and tell me where my name?

Benjamin Netanyahu: Right here.

Sheikh Abdullah bin Zayed Al Nahyan: Okay.

Benjamin Netanyahu: You do the same for me in Arabic.

Sheikh Abdullah bin Zayed Al Nahyan: I will.

Benjamin Netanyahu: So which one is mine?

Minister of Foreign Affairs, Kingdom of Bahrain: Right here.

Benjamin Netanyahu: Right here.

Sheikh Abdullah bin Zayed Al Nahyan: That'll be the easiest.

Donald Trump: It's easiest.

Sheikh Abdullah bin Zayed Al Nahyan: Yes. . . . I just wanted to say, Prime Minister, thank you.

Donald Trump: So glad . . .

Benjamin Netanyahu: Thank you.

Minister of Foreign Affairs, Kingdom of Bahrain: Congratulations. Congratulations, sir. Congratulations.

Speaker 4: Thank you, sir.

Speaker 3: The President of the United States, the Prime Minister of the State of Israel, and the Minister of the Foreign Affairs of the Kingdom of Bahrain will now sign the Declaration of Peace. They will each sign three copies, one in English, Hebrew, and Arabic. We kindly ask that all guests remain seated for the signing of the documents. . . .

Speaker 3: The President of the United States, the Prime Minister of the State of Israel, His Highness, the Minister of Foreign Affairs and International Cooperation of the United Arab Emirates, and the Minister of the Foreign Affairs of the Kingdom of Bahrain will now sign the Abraham Accords. They will each sign four copies, one in English, one in Hebrew and two in Arabic.

Abdullah bin Zayed Al Nahyan: This is easiest. You can decide. . . .

Speaker 4: Now they're all done.

Benjamin Netanyahu: Okay, we're good. That's great.

Donald Trump: Thank you.

Print Citations

CMS: Trump, Donald. "Abraham Accords Signing Ceremony." Signing ceremony at the White House, Washington, DC, September 15, 2020. In *The Reference Shelf: Representative American Speeches, 2019-2020,* edited by Annette Calzone, 195-202. Amenia, NY: Grey House Publishing, 2020.

MLA: Trump, Donald. "Abraham Accords Signing Ceremony." The White House, 15 September 2020, Washington, DC. Signing ceremony. *The Reference Shelf: Representative American Speeches, 2019-2020,* edited by Annette Calzone, Grey House Publishing, 2020, pp. 195-202.

APA: Trump, D. (2020, September 15). Signing ceremony for the Abraham Accords. The White House, Washington, DC. In Annette Calzone (Ed.), *The reference shelf: Representative American speeches, 2019-2020* (pp. 195-202). Amenia, NY: Grey House Publishing.

Memorial Speech for Ruth Bader Ginsburg

By John Roberts

Chief Justice of the United States John Roberts remembered Supreme Court Justice Ruth Bader Ginsburg, who passed away in September of 2020. Roberts lauded her unaffected and precise opinions, and noted that these would steer the Court for decades. He spoke of her achievement in being one of the few women in law school at the time she attended, as well as her friendship with Justice Antonin Scalia, who often held opposing views. Roberts stated, "When she spoke, people listened."

Thank you, Rabbi Holtzblatt, for those compelling words. Jane, Jim, the entire Ginsburg family, on behalf of all the justices, the spouses of the justices and the entire Supreme Court family, I offer our heartfelt condolences on the loss of Ruth Bader Ginsburg. That loss is widely shared, but we know that it falls most heavily on the family. Justice Ginsburg's life was one of the many versions of the American dream. Her father was an immigrant from Odessa, her mother was born four months after her family arrived from Poland. Her mother later worked as a bookkeeper in Brooklyn. Ruth used to ask, "What is the difference between a bookkeeper in Brooklyn and a Supreme Court Justice?" Her answer, one generation. It has been said that Ruth wanted to be an opera virtuoso, but became a rock star instead. But she chose the law. Subjected to discrimination in law school and the job market because she was a woman, Ruth would grow to become the leading advocate, fighting such discrimination in court.

She was not an opera star, but she found her stage right behind me in our courtroom. There, she won famous victories that helped move our nation closer to equal justice under law to the extent that women are now a majority in law schools, not simply a handful. Later, she became a star on the bench where she sat for 27 years. Her 483 majority concurring and descending opinions will steer the Court for decades. They are written with the unaffected grace of precision. Her voice in court and in our conference room was soft, but when she spoke, people listened. Among the words that best describe Ruth, tough, brave, a fighter, a winner, but also thoughtful, careful, compassionate, honest. When it came to opera, insightful, passionate. When it came to sports, clueless. Justice Ginsburg had many virtues of her own, but she also unavoidably promoted one particular one, humility in others.

For example, on more than a few occasions, someone would approach or call me and describe some upcoming occasion or event that was important to them, and I knew what was coming, could I come and speak? But no. Instead, could I pass along

Delivered on September 23, 2020, at the U.S. Capitol, Washington, DC.

an invitation to Justice Ginsburg and put in a good word? Many of you have seen the famous picture of Justice Scalia and Justice Ginsburg riding atop an elephant in India. It captured so much of Ruth. There she was doing something totally unexpected just as she had in law school, where she was not only one of the few women, but a new mother to boot. And in the photograph, she is riding with a dear friend, a friend with totally divergent views. There is no indication in the photo that either was poised to push the other off. For many years, of course, Ruth battled serious illness.

She met each of those challenges with a combination of candid assessment and fierce determination. In doing so, she encouraged others who have their own battles with illness, including employees here in the Court. And she emerged victorious time and again against all odds. But, finally the odds went out and now Ruth has left us. I mentioned at the outset that Ruth's passing weighed most heavily on her family and that is true. But the Court was her family too. This building was her home to. Of course, she will live on in what she did to improve the law and the lives of all of us. And yet still, Ruth is gone and we grieve. Let us have a moment of silence for reflection.

(Silence).

May she rest in peace.

Print Citations

CMS: Roberts, John. "Memorial Speech for Ruth Bader Ginsburg." Speech at the U.S. Capitol, Washington, DC, September 23, 2020. In *The Reference Shelf: Representative American Speeches, 2019-2020,* edited by Annette Calzone, 203-204. Amenia, NY: Grey House Publishing, 2020.

MLA: Roberts, John. "Memorial Speech for Ruth Bader Ginsburg." U.S. Capitol, 23 September 2020, Washington, DC. Speech. *The Reference Shelf: Representative American Speeches, 2019-2020,* edited by Annette Calzone, Grey House Publishing, 2020, pp. 203-204.

APA: Roberts, J. (2020, September 23). Speech at the memorial of Ruth Bader Ginsburg. U.S. Capitol, Washington, DC. In Annette Calzone (Ed.), *The reference shelf: Representative American speeches, 2019-2020* (pp. 203-204). Amenia, NY: Grey House Publishing.

USSC Nomination Acceptance Address

By Amy Coney Barrett

Amy Coney Barrett promised to be mindful of those who served on the Supreme Court before her, including Ruth Bader Ginsburg, as she accepted the nomination for Justice of the United States Supreme Court. Barrett acknowledged that her approach to interpreting the law is to apply the law as written, a philosophy she shares with Antonin Scalia, whom she clerked for. Barrett also reflected on the importance of mutual respect, pledging to respect even those whose views are diametrically opposed to hers.

I clerked for Justice Scalia more than 20 years ago, but the lessons I learned still resonate. His judicial philosophy is mine too: A judge must apply the law as written. Judges are not policymakers, and they must be resolute in setting aside any policy views they might hold.

Thank you very much, Mr. President. I am deeply honored by the confidence that you have placed in me. And I am so grateful to you and the First Lady, to the Vice President and the Second Lady, and to so many others here for your kindness on this rather overwhelming occasion.

I fully understand that this is a momentous decision for a President. And if the Senate does me the honor of confirming me, I pledge to discharge the responsibilities of this job to the very best of my ability. I love the United States, and I love the United States Constitution. I am truly—I am truly humbled by the prospect of serving on the Supreme Court. Should I be confirmed, I will be mindful of who came before me. The flag of the United States is still flying at half-staff in memory of Justice Ruth Bader Ginsburg to mark the end of a great American life. Justice Ginsburg began her career at a time when women were not welcome in the legal profession. But she not only broke glass ceilings, she smashed them. For that, she has won the admiration of women across the country and, indeed, all over the world.

She was a woman of enormous talent and consequence, and her life of public service serves as an example to us all. Particularly poignant to me was her long and deep friendship with Justice Antonin Scalia, my own mentor.

Justices Scalia and Ginsburg disagreed fiercely in print, without rancor in person. Their ability to maintain a warm and rich friendship, despite their differences, even inspired an opera. These two great Americans demonstrated that arguments, even about matters of great consequence, need not destroy affection. In both my personal and professional relationships, I strive to meet that standard.

Delivered on September 26, 2020, at the Rose Garden, White House, Washington, DC.

I was lucky enough to clerk for Justice Scalia, and given his incalculable influence on my life, I am very moved to have members of the Scalia family here today, including his dear wife, Maureen.

I clerked for Justice Scalia more than 20 years ago, but the lessons I learned still resonate. His judicial philosophy is mine too: A judge must apply the law as written. Judges are not policymakers, and they must be resolute in setting aside any policy views they might hold.

The President has asked me to become the ninth justice, and as it happens, I'm used to being in a group of nine: my family. Our family includes me, my husband Jesse, Emma, Vivian, Tess, John Peter, Liam, Juliet, and Benjamin. Vivian and John Peter, as the President said, were born in Haiti and they came to us, five years apart, when they were very young. And the most revealing fact about Benjamin, our youngest, is that his brothers and sisters unreservedly identify him as their favorite sibling.

Our children obviously make our life very full. While I am a judge, I'm better known back home as a room parent, a carpool driver, and birthday party planner. When schools went remote last spring, I tried on another hat. Jesse and I became co-principals of the "Barrett E-learning Academy." And, yes, the list of enrolled students was a very long one. Our children are my greatest joy, even though they deprive me of any reasonable amount of sleep.

I couldn't manage this very full life without the unwavering support of my husband, Jesse. At the start of our marriage, I imagined that we would run our household as partners. As it has turned out, Jesse does far more than his share of the work. To my chagrin, I learned at dinner recently that my children consider him to be the better cook. For 21 years, Jesse has asked me, every single morning, what he can do for me that day. And though I almost always say "nothing," he still finds ways to take things off my plate. And that's not because he has a lot of free time—he has a busy law practice. It's because he is a superb and generous husband, and I am very fortunate.

Jesse and I—Jesse and I have a life full of relationships, not only with our children, but with siblings, friends, and fearless babysitters, one of whom is with us today. I am particularly grateful to my parents, Mike and Linda Coney. I spent the bulk of—I have spent the bulk of my adulthood as a Midwesterner, but I grew up in their New Orleans home. And as my brother and sisters can also attest, Mom and Dad's generosity extends not only to us, but to more people than any of us could count. They are an inspiration.

It is important at a moment like this to acknowledge family and friends. But this evening, I also want to acknowledge you, my fellow Americans. The President has nominated me to serve on the United States Supreme Court, and that institution belongs to all of us.

If confirmed, I would not assume that role for the sake of those in my own circle, and certainly not for my own sake. I would assume this role to serve you. I would discharge the judicial oath, which requires me to administer justice without respect to persons, do equal right to the poor and rich, and faithfully and impartially discharge my duties under the United States Constitution.

I have no illusions that the road ahead of me will be easy, either for the short term or the long haul. I never imagined that I would find myself in this position, but now that I am, I assure you that I will meet the challenge with both humility and courage.

Members of the United States Senate, I look forward to working with you during the confirmation process, and I will do my very best to demonstrate that I am worthy of your support.

Thank you.

Print Citations

CMS: Coney Barrett, Amy. "USSC Nomination Acceptance Address." Speech at the Rose Garden, White House, Washington, DC, September 26, 2020. In *The Reference Shelf: Representative American Speeches, 2019-2020,* edited by Annette Calzone, 205-207. Amenia, NY: Grey House Publishing, 2020.

MLA: Coney Barrett, Amy. "USSC Nomination Acceptance Address." Rose Garden, White house, 26 September 2020, Washington, DC. Speech. *The Reference Shelf: Representative American Speeches, 2019-2020,* edited by Annette Calzone, Grey House Publishing, 2020, pp. 205-207.

APA: Coney Barrett, A. (2020, September 26). USSC nomination acceptance address. Rose Garden, White House, Washington, DC. In Annette Calzone (Ed.), *The reference shelf: Representative American speeches, 2019-2020* (pp. 205-207). Amenia, NY: Grey House Publishing.

Index